KINGS
OF THE
HILL

KINGS OF THE HILL

An Irreverent Look at the Men on the Mound

NOLAN RYAN

with Mickey Herskowitz

HarperCollins*Publishers*

HarperCollins books may be purchased for educational, business, or sales promotional use. For information, please call or write: Special Markets Department, HarperCollins Publishers, Inc., 10 East 53rd Street, New York, NY 10022. Telephone: (212) 207-7528; Fax: (212) 207-7222.

FIRST EDITION

Designed by Ruth Kolbert

Library of Congress Cataloging-in-Publication Data
Ryan, Nolan, 1947–
    Kings of the hill: an irreverent look at the men on the mound / Nolan Ryan, Mickey Herskowitz.
        p.   cm.
    Includes index.
    ISBN 0-06-018330-6
    1. Pitchers (Baseball)—United States—Biography.
I. Herskowitz, Mickey.   II. Title.
GV865.A1R93   1992
796.357'092'2—dc20
[B]   91-50444

92 93 94 95 96 AC/RRD 10 9 8 7 6 5 4 3 2 1

To Ruth, Reid, Wendy, and Reese,
the one team that never tried to trade me
or let me play out my option—
no matter how much they may have wanted

CONTENTS

ACKNOWLEDGMENTS

The sporting thing would be to start by thanking all the hitters who swing at bad pitches and provide employment for a lot of pitchers.

You can stretch the team concept kind of thin, but thanks are owed to a whole roster of people, beginning with Ivy McLemore, now the sports editor of the *Houston Post* and a former baseball writer. Ivy was invaluable in helping out with the many interviews and transcripts, with an assist from Kevin Newberry. Rusty San Juan and Vince Tortorice, Jr., rummaged for photographs, and Jim Walden helped with the fact checking.

Kim Spilman, as always, kept the office running and messages channeled while all around her the book was growing.

Appreciation is due to two respected agents, Bill Adler for developing the idea and Matt Merola for encouraging it. We benefited from the support of our editor, Jim Hornfischer, who kept us on course with his patience and enthusiasm.

John Blake and Larry Kelly of the Texas Rangers, Bob Rosen of the Elias Sports Bureau, and Brent Lockhart and Cheryl Corbitt of The Summit Group were all generous in providing information or sharing research and photographs, The versatile Ruth Ryan and a good friend, Don Sanders, offered ideas and suggestions.

Thanks are also due to the research staff at *Sports Illustrated* and to Mike Olson of the Toshiba Computer Systems division for their help and services.

Many pitchers, past and present, created the material that appears here. To all of them, for all the good times, I am ever grateful.

—Nolan Ryan

PREFACE

When Nolan Ryan was in high school, he would get up at one o'clock in the morning to bundle up copies of the *Houston Post*, and then go around tossing them on most of the doorsteps in Alvin, Texas, his hometown. In a nice co-incidence—nice for me, anyway—I was breaking in as a sportswriter for the same newspaper. It is not often in this business, or any other, that you get to watch a legend grow up before your very eyes.

I was the baseball writer for the *Post* when Nolan signed out of high school with the New York Mets. In a bit of whimsy, the paper gave itself a promotional plug by claiming that Ryan had developed his legendary arm by throwing our newspapers on all those inky dark mornings.

Nolan didn't get the joke, still doesn't. Years later, in his autobiography, he took pains to point out that he made the throw backhanded, with his left arm, while steering his '52

Chevy with his right. So the story, which had been repeated, as stories are, couldn't be true. To be fair, however, he added that he thought rolling up all those papers helped strengthen his fingers and wrists.

This was vintage Nolan Ryan, not finding much that is frivolous in how he developed his pitching style yet giving what credit he can. We accept it cheerfully.

Now we flash forward to the first day of May 1991, when Nolan delivered a performance so compelling that it seemed to distill his entire career.

He pitched his record seventh no-hitter over the Toronto Blue Jays, a 3-0 victory, in front of a crowd that kept growing in Arlington Stadium, even as cable television flashed the game across the land.

His son Reid, a freshman at Texas, dropped a report on a Louis L'Amour book to watch his father pitch the last two innings. At Shea Stadium, the San Diego Padres and the New York Mets put their postgame buffets on hold and crowded around the TV sets in the clubhouses.

And at the ballpark in Kansas City, while the Royals were playing the Tigers, they picked up Ryan's no-hitter in progress on the Diamond Vision screen in center field. Let the strangeness of this setting sink in: the fans in Kansas City were ignoring a game they had paid to see, taking place on the field in front of them, to watch the telecast of a game being played a thousand miles away.

Meanwhile, in Arlington, a scene both dramatic and eerily symbolic was unfolding. From the press box, from the sixth inning on, you could see the headlights of cars backed up for miles, threading their way to the ballpark. Anyone who saw *Field of Dreams* would have recognized the scene. Fans were desperate to buy a ticket to a game that was nearly over, hoping to grab at least a concluding glimpse of Ryan pitching one more hitless gem.

Nolan's final out was Roberto Alomar. When Ryan pitched his first no-hitter for the California Angels eighteen years earlier, his second baseman was Sandy Alomar, Roberto's father. "I've known that kid since he was a toddler," said Ryan. "He wanted to be a pitcher." But Nolan gave him no mercy. He struck him out, his sixteenth strikeout of the game, and his seventh no-hitter was his.

At that instant, in Kansas City, the fans gave a standing ovation to the television screen, which showed a close-up of a smiling Ryan, his right arm punching the air as his teammates swarmed to the mound. They hoisted him onto their shoulders and carried him off the field.

In Austin, Reid Ryan crushed a Coke can and jumped up and down. In Arlington, Nolan's wife, Ruth, left her seat in the stands to wait for her husband outside the clubhouse. She had flown in from Alvin on a neighbor's plane only minutes before game time.

Nolan Ryan has inspired the kind of awe you usually have to be dead to receive. Opposing batters speak of him the way minstrels spoke about ancient kings.

"There's always one guy that defies the odds," said Joe Carter of Toronto. "He's the guy."

You study Lynn Nolan Ryan's eyes. They are brown and soft and there is no meanness in them. Calf eyes, one might say, a description not unsuitable for Ryan, the Texas cattleman. Try to imagine the hours those eyes have spent staring into the discolored leather of a catcher's mitt.

If the eyes show no fatigue, you wonder about the arm. In a career that began a quarter of a century ago, he has worked 5,000 innings, averaging a strikeout per inning. This is power. This is consistency. This is the essence of the game: the will of the solitary man to take on the many.

Ryan discovered the meaning of life in Arlington—the ballpark, of course, not the national cemetery. "The secret," he said, "is knowing that there is no secret." There is just raw talent refined by hard work and humility.

Even after his seventh no-hitter, with the reporters jockeying for position around his locker and still lobbing questions at him, he politely excused himself and walked over to the stationary bike. He did his 45 minutes, already preparing for his next start.

Nolan called this no-hitter his most meaningful, partly because "It was more of a reflection of me as a complete pitcher," and partly because it happened in Arlington, in front of the Rangers fans, "who have been so good to me."

This is one of the keys to Ryan's long and spectacular career. This is how he could join a new club in 1989, adjust to new teammates and new surroundings, and finish the season with sixteen wins and a major league–leading 301 strikeouts, all at the age of forty-three.

Every nine or ten years he changes leagues so that a new generation of hitters will have surfaced, all potential jelly for his toast. It worked that way in 1971, when he fled from New York and landed in California, and in 1979, when he left the Angels for Houston. Then, one more time, he shed his skin and reappeared as a Texas Ranger. In Houston, the fans have mixed feelings about Nolan. Some miss him every day of their lives, and some just miss him every fifth day.

Throughout this process, Nolan was putting to rest once and for all the charge that has dogged and aggravated him most of his career: that he was little more than a .500 pitcher.

No one will threaten the record that Ryan established in 1985, most strikeouts in a career. He has carried that record to another dimension. At the end of the 1991 season, he was beyond 5,500 and still counting.

In a poetic sense he might have stopped at 5,000, which has such a nice, round, rich, historic ring to it. But he won't stop. He can't. His arm won't let him. It has taken over his soul. Pete Rose called it the greatest arm in the history of baseball. People talk about that arm as though it were a creature with a liver and a kidney inside it.

Not all of this attachment has to do with his skill at delivering a baseball. It has to do with the fact that this is one of the best human beings ever to play ball. Of course, the job is temporary, and better than most of the players of his time he has understood this.

Are other examples in order?

He pitched his sixth no-hitter in Oakland, against the power-hitting Athletics in June 1990, and he did it despite a stress fracture in his lower back. His son Reese, then fourteen, was on the trip and in the dugout, working as a ballboy. He patted Nolan on the leg and rubbed his back. After eight innings, he assured his father, "We only need three more."

Rangers manager Bobby Valentine, who had played center field in Ryan's first no-hitter, said, "It was a Norman Rockwell scene."

A month later, Ryan won his 300th game as the TV networks and reporters from the major newspapers and magazines poured into Milwaukee to cover this latest milestone. Nolan beat the Brewers 11-3, and he did it the old-fashioned way, throwing mostly fastballs.

Four years after his fortieth birthday, he still threw a fastball clocked at ninety-six miles an hour. When most fastball pitchers are forty, they are throwing knucklers if they are not playing first base in a softball league.

Is there any need to note that he is the oldest ever to throw a no-hitter and that he did so in three different decades? He is a no-hit pitcher who too often labored for no-hit teams. The pitchers on the 1919 Chicago Black Sox got better run support from players who were trying to dump games.

A lot of athletes seize on a modest amount of success to flaunt their importance. Not Ryan. With remarkable patience, he mapped his campaign over the years. He was his own coach, his own trainer, his own chaperone. He built his monument one brick at a time. No one has ever heard of Nolan Ryan knocking a manager or a teammate.

He has pitched in four cities under ten managers and thrown no-hitters to seven different catchers without becoming confused as a person. Now he is the only player in the majors who is a member of the FDIC, having purchased the Danbury State Bank, ten miles from Alvin.

I covered his first start and his first win for the Mets, both occurring in the Astrodome before his family and friends. I have written about him off and on for twenty-five years, a fringe benefit of my profession but not one that entitles me to claim any special intimacy. Nolan is most at ease with his neighbors, who have known him all his life, and his teammates, with whom he has shared the day-to-day grind. This is part of his character. You do not become his friend by lining up and taking a number.

Yet writing about him has been a source of unending satisfaction. He has made our job easier because time hasn't changed him for the worse, not as a person and not as a pitcher. He never saw himself as a matinee idol or a showman. He is what he seems. If you search for more you may miss the very center of him.

I once asked Ruth Ryan, school beauty, state tennis champion, and onetime Alvin hula hoop champion, if Nolan had ever blown a gasket, really lost his temper. She started to think about it. When I left, after an hour or so, she was still thinking about it.

After pitching his only National League no-hitter for Houston over the Los Angeles Dodgers, his fifth, in October 1981, Nolan autographed one of the no-hit baseballs for a friend, Don Sanders, a stockbroker and shareholder in the Astros. "I'm glad you were able to see this game," Nolan wrote. Underneath that line, in parentheses, appeared the word "(over)." On the other side of the ball he added, proudly: "I can hit, too."

Only Nolan would be so considerate as to alert the reader of a baseball that the message was continued on the other side.

The reference to Ryan's hitting was not simply a joke. Nolan did not want to be branded as a one-dimensional fellow, able only to pitch. The first game he ever pitched in a Houston uniform, in April 1980, is remembered not because he pitched well—he lasted six innings and had one of his famous no-decisions—but because he batted well. In fact, he hit the first home run of his big league career, a three-run blast off an unfortunate fellow named Don Sutton. He would not hit another, and his return to the American League, with its designated hitter, assured that he had run out of chances.

Writers must exercise particular care when it comes to Nolan Ryan, because they tend to lose their critical faculties. I remember when the Astros commissioned the artist LeRoy Neiman to paint Nolan's portrait. The finished work showed Nolan halfway into his delivery, with the flag visible behind him in center field.

"That was how I saw him," said Neiman. "I had at my disposal a pitcher of such idealism that it was impossible to present him as anything other than the All-American baseball player."

You can evoke all the rhythm and flavor and texture of the sport with one freeze-frame of Ryan blowing a strike past a big hitter. It is John Unitas, unflinching in the pocket, pumping his fake, winging one fifty yards. It is Babe Ruth taking those pigeon steps around the bases.

When Ryan pitched his seventh no-hitter, Molly Ivins, a political columnist for the *Dallas Times-Herald*, wrote: "Throwin' the hell out of the ball at his age is fair defiance of decay, if not death."

In more than one hundred years, only five pitchers in their careers held more than two teams hitless. The others were Koufax with four, and Bob Feller, Cy Young, and Larry Corcoran with three each. Young retired in 1908. You may not remember Corcoran. His big year was 1880, when he started 60 games, completed 57, and won 43. Nice numbers. This is the company Ryan keeps. In 1983 *Time* magazine named a dozen active players as cinch Hall of Famers: Johnny Bench, Reggie Jackson, Rod Carew, Pete Rose, Joe Morgan, Carl Yastrzemski, Steve Carlton, Tom Seaver, Gaylord Perry, Jim Palmer, Ferguson Jenkins, and Ryan. Nine already have been inducted. One has been to prison, suspended from the game. One is still pitching. He does so with a reputation still spotless, without a jealous or envious bone in his body. Nor has he sacrificed his sense of humor.

A few years ago, the popular Astros outfielder José Cruz, at forty Nolan's fellow antiquarian, was honored in a distinctive way. Jim Ewell, Houston's longtime trainer, wrote a song about him called "Chéo," which was Cruz's nickname, a Spanish variation on José. The song was sung to the melody from the calypso tune "Day-O," whose familiar refrain is, "Daylight come and I wanna go home . . ."

Ewell actually got to sing a verse on network television, during a pregame show, a performance that did not exactly make the world forget Harry Belafonte. Still, the beat was catchy (once, after a big game late in the season, Cruz's teammates even serenaded him with it in the clubhouse).

"But it got me in trouble with Nolan," revealed Ewell. "He came in one day and said, 'Doc, I don't care what my two boys pick up hanging around here, but when my little girl wakes up in the morning singing the Chéo song, that's it. I can't take it any more. Your songwriting career has to go.' "

Every man has his breaking point, and that was as close as Nolan Ryan, the well-known family man, ever came.

—Mickey Herskowitz
Arlington, Texas
December 1991

INTRODUCTION

Baseball, I am told, is a writer's game. There are writers who write gracefully and with affection about baseball's timelessness and unique day-to-day rhythm. Writing about it is one thing, but I can tell you, playing the game can be a brute.

We pitchers are at the center of the contest, and we come in all shapes and sizes, tempers and ages. A Joe Nuxhall pitched his first big league inning at fourteen, during the war, and then went back to high school for a couple of years. A Satchel Paige broke in as a rookie at forty-two after decades of legendary deeds in the Negro Leagues. When Bill Veeck signed Satchel for the Indians during the 1948 season, *The Sporting News* carried an editorial branding the move a publicity stunt, and saying it was demeaning to the game.

"I demeaned the game pretty good that year," Satchel once said. "I was six and one."

For every Leroy Paige who comes along once in a lifetime, there are dozens who have a single game or a single season that they never come close to matching again. Bo Belinsky pitches a no-hitter his rookie year, becomes an instant celebrity, and never again lives up to it. Mark Fidrych captivates everyone with his pure talent and enthusiasm, and then gets cut down by an injury after one starry summer. Some players become so popular you need only mention a first name, like Fernando. He came out of a village in Mexico where many of the homes had dirt floors, but Valenzuela, the pudgy left-hander with the moon face and the baffling screwball, walked off with the 1980s. Then there are the Gaylord Perrys and the Phil Niekros—and I can't leave myself out—who threaten to go on forever, forcing baseball to get a court order to make us retire.

I want the reader to discover that world, because it has been my world for a quarter century. Pitching is a little like being married; you love it, fear it, and are often puzzled by it. But pitchers care about their craft and each other in a way that makes them interesting.

I'm not sure mystique is the word for what I have described, but it is here, in these pages, in the records and stories of the pitchers of my time. Some of them have been larger than life in talent, some in ego or color or thirst. I didn't have any mathematical formula to apply in deciding who landed on the pages. Some were teammates, others close and good rivals.

I am partial to those who have hung around for twenty years or so, the better to get to know them. But one or two who are in the book won fame by having their careers cut short, or by having no career at all.

I tried to narrow the field to those who were active in the years I have been on the scene, from 1966 to the present, fudging the time frame in a few special cases. The goal was to offer a cross-section of the pitchers of my era, how I saw them and how they saw themselves. There is no point in listing, or making excuses for, the pitchers who were omitted or given less attention than their records seem to deserve. I have seen a couple hundred come and go.

There was a certain amount of curiosity among people in baseball when they heard I had signed with the Texas Rangers in 1989. This reaction was related to how I would get along with Tom House, the team's innovative pitching coach.

Over the years, my coaches were men like Tom Morgan, a onetime pitcher with the Yankees, or former catchers like Rube Walker or Les Moss, who might have been twice my age. House is my contemporary. Our forty-fifth birthdays are three months apart, his in April of 1992, mine in January.

One of Tom's ideas, and he has several, is that pitchers ought to throw a football between starts. That concept was on my mind the first day we met, and I asked if it would be a problem for him if I didn't jump right in. He said I should do whatever made me comfortable.

But I watched, and then I tried it and quickly saw that the exercise worked. I didn't join in to give Tom support, but in a way I was pleased because the traditional thinkers were constantly trying to tear him down. I had to laugh to myself a few times that first year, when I would run into some old pro and he would start right off: "Well, I guess they got *you* throwing the football, too."

He thought he was being sarcastic, until I answered, "Yep, I sure am."

Then he wouldn't know what to say. Here I was, with twenty-odd years in the game, and the old pro figured, "Surely Ryan wouldn't be throwing that stupid football."

If someone asked why, I gave a simple answer: My attitude is that I'm always open to new theories, new methods. I am willing to try them and if they work I incorporate them into my program. So now I throw a football between starts more than I throw a baseball. Tom's theory is that you can't throw a spiral unless you have the proper mechanics. It just can't be done. And the mechanics are the same for pitching a baseball or passing a football. I found that my arm loosened up faster, so even on the nights I start I throw the football for about five minutes before I take my regular warm-ups.

I've gotten so I can throw a nice tight spiral. But this isn't my version of the fantasy league. I don't try to imagine myself in the pocket, dropping back and setting up. Then I would have to imagine one of those 6'-8", 320-pound defensive linemen coming at me.

Tom House and his story are part of what I take from the game. In a collection of this kind, people are not going to fit neatly into every category, and some will be absent altogether. I'm pleased to have a chance to write about him here because he overcame his history. He was a pitcher with a label.

During his pitching career, he was his own worst enemy. He was a product of Southern Cal, went through the drug culture and the age of rebellion, and was tagged as an irritant by the defenders of baseball tradition. Tom had to deal with that label coming back into the majors as a coach, armed with his computer and with new information and technology that goes against the grain.

But the point is, I'm heading into my twenty-fifth season and I have learned from him. A pitcher must never lose his capacity to be surprised. You just go on, knowing that something different lies ahead.

It may be a Scar Wars controversy about pitchers defacing the ball. Or it may be a new pitch, like the split-finger fastball, that sends the hitters scurrying to find a cure. Or it may be a Mark Fidrych or a Fernando Valenzuela or a Doc Gooden tearing up the league.

Comparisons are often made between pitchers and the quarterbacks, who are the glamour guys of their sports. But a baseball team has ten or eleven pitchers on its staff, so there are more personalities, more tinkering with the craft, more ways to go wrong.

In these pages I have tried to break down the types of pitchers I have known into categories. This is arbitrary, of course, and elastic, and for the most part tongue in cheek. So

I have a chapter on left-handers, not all of whom are crazy. There is a chapter called "The Intimidators," who are called many other things by the batters. There are chapters on flakes, and the deep thinkers, and the marathon men—all fairly self-explanatory. Even an indifferent fan will recognize that "The Ace Hardware Men" deals with the workshop school of pitching and the charges of scuffing the ball or putting everything on it except chocolate syrup. It is about cheating—with an asterisk. In this chapter we also examine the art of corking a bat. Turnabout is fair play.

There is a chapter on the duel between the batter and the pitcher, with special attention to the battles between Pete Rose and myself, fair and lively battles, the memories of which are unspoiled by the troubles that later engulfed him.

In "The Young and the Restless," I describe some of the careers that were ruined or shortened by bad luck or awful judgment. I have found that pitchers are easy prey to the too-much-too-soon syndrome, because their job, more than any other on the diamond, goes from exhilarating highs to excruciating lows. Sometimes this happens from one pitch to the next. It isn't all stress-related, of course. Every team will have a few party animals. In another era they were called night walkers. They can be good for a club—if they can handle the hours, have their fun, and still pitch.

I think more allowances are made for temperament—or even a little daffiness—in a pitcher than in a quarterback. It isn't just that football is so physical or demands more discipline, although clearly it does. But the nature of baseball encourages horseplay. You don't get penalized for delaying the game or for pumping your fist after a strikeout.

In the early 1980s, the Cincinnati Reds had a left-handed relief pitcher named Brad Lesley who was nicknamed "The Animal." He was 6'-6", 220, and when he struck out a hitter he celebrated by beating his chest like a gorilla. It was so weird it was funny, and I don't recall the hitters on my team, the Astros, getting upset.

But in the final game of a season, against the Reds, I

struck out Dewayne Walker in the first inning, turned to their dugout and imitated Lesley. I thumped my chest and flapped my arms and grinned like a fool. In both dugouts, guys were doubled over laughing. I don't know why I did it. I just did. That's another thing I love about pitching. You don't always need a reason for giving in to your impulses.

A big part of pitching is internal, mental. The fact is, I know most of my peers only as competitors. I am rarely on the field during the fine twilight hours, when opposing players get to banter, because my workout routine keeps me inside. Although I pitched against him off and on for nearly twenty years, I didn't know Ferguson Jenkins until he became a minor league pitching coach with the Texas Rangers. Then we spent time together in spring training and in the clubhouse. I count myself fortunate to have met him then, rather than not at all.

I have faced Steve Carlton, Burt Hooten, and Fernando Valenzuela fairly often. Yet Tom Seaver, when he was with Cincinnati, and I were in the same division for six years and never pitched against each other.

Teams try so hard to stick with their rotations today that you no longer see the special effort to arrange a pitching showcase, the matchups of Bob Feller against Hal Newhouser, or Vic Raschi against Mel Parnell. In the 1940s and 1950s, clubs would pitch their ace a day later or a day earlier to go against the other club's ace and build up the gate.

Comb these pages as you will, there are no diagrams here to tell you how to throw a better curve. What I hope you find is an insight into how pitchers think.

You will see that, like an old man whittling wood, pitchers keep shaving their thoughts until their philosophy is as smooth and fine as they can shape it. Lew Burdette of the Braves put it simply: "I exploit the greed of all hitters."

There is this advice from Satchel Paige: "Just take the ball and throw it where you want to. Throw strikes. Home plate don't move."

You get the idea. "A pitcher needs two pitches," said

Warren Spahn. "The one they're looking for and one to cross 'em up. Hitting is timing. Pitching is upsetting timing."

Before Steve Stone's career was cut short, he had reduced the task of the man on the mound to an internal duel: "Pitching is really just a struggle between the pitcher and his stuff. If my curveball is breaking and I'm throwing it where I want, then the batter is irrelevant."

There is a feeling you get when you settle into a groove, when the ball goes right where you want it to, that is close to the euphoria that distance runners describe. I used to experience it a lot more often than I do now, but it is a grand feeling, just short of believing you have supernatural powers. Yet that can be a problem, too. You worry about finding something in your life that can replace it when it's gone.

Although surrounded by his teammates, a pitcher is a lonely soul whose paranoia is not hard to understand. One night, Bob Uecker, then catching for the Braves, went to the mound to talk to Lew Burdette with two runners on base and no one out. When he got to within a few feet of the mound, Lew yelled out: "What the hell do you want?"

Uecker said, "Nothing. I just came out to give you a breather."

Lew backed away from him. "Don't be coming out here," he said. "I don't want you out here. They"—and he waved his gloved hand at the crowd—"they think you're giving me advice. And the only thing you know about pitching is that you can't hit it."

Uecker said nothing, returned to his position behind the plate, and told the batter what pitch was coming next.

—Nolan Ryan

Kings
OF THE
Hill

The
Naked
and
the Dead

When I walked into my first major league clubhouse in early September 1966, the scene actually startled
me. I was nineteen, with high school and a year of minor
league ball behind me, and I had never seen players smoking
cigars.

That was about all they were doing, that and playing
cards and answering their fan mail by sailing letters into the
nearest trash can. These were the New York Mets, the last of
the lovable, comical, pie-in-the-face Mets, and—I say this
with no disrespect—the strangest collection of athletes you
can imagine. It was as if someone had taken a truck to a
union hall and picked up a load of day workers.

Don't get me wrong. Several of them had been solid big
leaguers, even famous. But now they were punching the
clock, finishing out careers that had once flourished somewhere else. The others in the room were raw kids like me, up

from one of the farm clubs to see if we might make the big jump the next spring: a preview of coming attractions.

Many of the names were familiar. Dick Stuart had started the season at first base; in Philadelphia he had been known as "Dr. Strangelove." Ron Hunt would set the National League record for getting hit by a pitched ball. Ken Boyer, 35, an All-Star third baseman in his prime with the Cardinals, would lead the team in runs batted in with 61. Age and injuries had undone Roy McMillan, the slick-fielding former Redleg, and at shortstop Eddie Bressoud, a fringe player, was trying to hold off a rookie named Bud Harrelson.

The pitching staff included Dallas Green, Bob Friend, Dick Selma, Jack Fisher, and Jack Hamilton, who boasted that his best pitch was the spitter. In June, the Mets picked up Bob Shaw from the Giants. A tough competitor, he won eleven games for them. Out of that group you might have developed a really fine rotation five years earlier.

The manager was a squat ex-catcher, Wes Westrum, in his first full season as the successor to the legendary Casey Stengel. Westrum had none of Casey's color or his gift for strangling the language, but he had an interesting habit. No matter how fast the writers, and some of the players, got to the clubhouse, Wes would be in his office without a stitch of clothing. He must have started unbuttoning his shirt in the seventh inning, untying his laces in the eighth, unbuckling his pants in the ninth. By the time he got to his door I guess everything just fell off.

The writers would walk in and Wes would be sitting behind his desk, an open can of beer in his hand, a plate of cold cuts in front of him, naked. Totally naked. I'm not sure what the symbolism was. He had been a lifetime .217 hitter for the New York Giants, the regular catcher under Leo Durocher, a guy who had to sweat for every hit.

The Mets turned to him after Stengel broke his hip near the end of the 1965 season and the doctors told Casey to retire at seventy-five. The club had finished last every year, and while not even Stengel could keep the fans from noticing, he entertained and distracted them. Westrum was a man trapped in a bad job by good timing. After one loss, he told the press, "I never got a break in my life." He seemed to mean it.

And yet something strange was happening, I mean, stranger than usual. No one knew it at the time, but the Mets had turned a corner. They were bringing along some promising young players, Ron Swoboda, Cleon Jones, Harrelson, and pitchers named Tug McGraw, Jerry Koosman, and Jim McAndrew. A quirk in the free agent draft had won them the best college prospect in America, Tom Seaver, out of Southern Cal. Their first bonus baby, Ed Kranepool, was already a veteran.

They used six catchers, including Choo Choo Coleman. The job was won by Jerry Grote, a rookie they acquired out of the Houston farm system. Of all the receivers I have known, arm, glove, handling the pitcher, Grote was the best.

The Mets lost less than 100 games for the first time in their history and finished ninth, ahead of the Chicago Cubs, managed by Durocher. Houston, our expansion rivals, squeezed ahead of us for eighth.

I had been promised a start on the last day of the season, October 2, at Shea Stadium. But with so much at stake they went with one of the veterans. As it was, I made two appearances that month. I pitched two innings of relief against Atlanta and allowed two runs, including a homer by Joe Torre. I lasted one inning in my debut as a starter against Houston, my hometown. Westrum lifted me for a pinch hitter after I gave up three runs.

My line for 1966 was one loss, five hits, five runs, six strikeouts, three walks, and an earned run average of 15.00. My biggest regret was that I hadn't been around for the previous season. It was not only the last hurrah for Stengel. Yogi Berra was activated from the coaching staff for a few days, singled twice in nine at bats, and retired again. I wonder how many people realize Yogi actually played for the Mets?

And 1965 was also the final season for Warren Spahn,

the winningest left-hander of all time, who had signed with the Mets as both a pitcher and a pitching coach after a bitter exit from the Braves. He had won 20 games or more in thirteen different years, more times than anyone else. He was forty-four years old that summer and trying to regain his touch in New York. His career with the Braves ended after a 6-and-13 year and his refusal to go to the bullpen. Many older pitchers did in those days, of course. A starter switched to relief, hoping to milk another season or more out of what was left in his arm.

But not Spahn, fiercely proud and tireless. He always pitched batting practice two days before his starts. Today no one on the regular staff throws batting practice. In a sense, he was my first pitching coach, but I never talked to him that season. I went directly to the Mets farm club in Marion, Virginia, where I led the Appalachian League, a rookie league, in hit batsmen. Later, Spahn was the minor league coach for the California Angels, and our paths crossed more often.

I heard a lot about him that summer of 1965. There was some grumbling in the organization that Spahn had cheated himself, and the Mets, by trying to do two jobs. He wasn't helping the other Met pitchers and the staff fell apart early.

This is one of the stories they tell: Spahn was obsessed with the idea of proving that he could pitch nine innings. Starting against Claude Osteen, nineteen years his junior, in the Dodgers' home opener, he nursed a 3-0 lead into the ninth. Then the Dodgers scored twice and had the tying and winning runs at first and third with none out.

Stengel went to the mound and asked Spahn, the pitching coach, who he wanted from the bullpen. The pitching coach made it clear he wanted to stay with the starter, and Casey nodded and walked back to the dugout.

Strikeout. Ground ball. Strikeout. When Spahn climbed onto the team bus that night, they applauded him.

I believe pitchers are more interesting than other players because they have more obsessions. Of course, I have no research to back that opinion, just 25 years of personal observation.

But Spahn was a prime example. He was playing amateur ball in Buffalo at the age of nine. He signed with the Boston Braves at eighteen, before bonuses were given, spent three years in the minors and three more in the army. He became the only big leaguer ever to win a battlefield commission for bravery in action.

He was twenty-five when he reached the big leagues to stay, and it looked as though they might need another war to make him quit. He wouldn't admit what others could see. The batters began knocking him out in the seventh, then in the fifth, then in the second. He won four games with the Mets, and three more with the Giants, for a total of 363. He lost sixteen. The next year he said, "I can still pitch," but no one offered him a contract, not even to pitch relief.

He considered himself immune to time. He never doubted he could win again, if only he could straighten out his mechanics. But no longer did his breaking pitches dip and wobble like a tired moth. They came to the batter straight and flat, and all the knowledge in that stubborn head of his couldn't save him. Pitching for a tenth-place team didn't help, either.

Even today a young pitcher can look at films of Spahn and marvel at the perfect form. From ground level he seemed to be turning over, in a rhythm similar to an old riverboat wheel, with no more strain on the arm itself than on the spoke of a wheel.

I liked what Spahn said when reporters asked him how badly he had wanted his 300th win. "I wanted this one," he agreed. "I wanted the last one, and I want the next one."

I am not prepared to say that the pitchers whose careers were ending in the 1960s, as mine began, had more heart or perseverance than those of the 1990s. But what wonders they were: Spahn, Robin Roberts, Whitey Ford, Early Wynn, Johnny Podres, Don Drysdale. Sandy Koufax, who retired in

1966, was a special case, gone way before his time because of a troubled elbow.

Of course, the kid pitchers on the Mets like me were fascinated by Spahn. What drove him? Why would a guy be hanging on at forty-four? The only answer was pride. The pride of Robin Roberts sent him back to the minors, to Reading, Pennsylvania, where the church bells played Hoagy Carmichael's "Stardust" at five o'clock each night. He wanted to stay in shape in case another big league called and gave him the chance to win 300 games. The call never came, but he made it to the Hall of Fame with 286 victories.

Pitchers of more recent vintage qualify in the pride and obsession categories. Gaylord Perry, Steve Carlton, Don Sutton, and Phil Niekro went on and on. Jim Palmer tried a comeback after six years away from the mound, with his likeness already on display in the Hall of Fame.

And I anticipate your next objection. Yes, here I am, still hanging on at forty-five, a year older than Spahnnie when the calendar police kicked in his door. And I admit it, I feel a little defensive when I hear one of my teammates say, as Mike Scott once did, "You won't see me hanging around when I get to be forty." Believe me, this isn't anything I planned.

Yet I don't feel obsessed and I don't know of any mystic force that propels me. I will concede that the money is wildly higher than in the era of Spahn, who never earned a salary of more than $100,000 in his career. But what keeps me going is this: I still have a respectable fastball. I'm still getting hitters out. When I can't, I'm gone. It's that simple. They won't have to come for me in the second inning. I'll be back home in Alvin, or at the ranch.

In every clubhouse I have ever seen, there is a kind of weather all its own. In the minor league parks I had recently played in, you usually had a nail to hang your clothes on. The training room was barely large enough for a table and a tub. There were usually showerheads but no hot water. It was like the public showers at the beach, where you stood there on one leg, just long enough to wash the sand off your feet and get your hair wet.

The Mets clubhouse was modern and roomy, with a training room the size of a maternity ward. The older players were not unfriendly, but the weather was subject to sudden change.

Warren Spahn wasn't there the day I walked into the clubhouse, where I saw a lot of guys of uncertain age doing almost nothing. They went out to the field and took batting practice as though there wasn't anything better to do. What I saw, or didn't see, made a lasting impression on me. When I'm asked about my longevity in baseball, I can't offer any fancy theory about genetics. I only know that I made it a point to understand my body and how to condition it. The seeds were planted that day.

It was disillusioning to have been in Class A ball, where so many kids were dying to get to the big leagues, and then discover that the players already there seemed bored with it. I started the season in Greenville, at the bottom of their farm system. We were mainly teenagers, a year or two out of high school, a few with some college experience, but not much. As I moved up the chain, I found more players with four or five years in the minors. But they still had that hunger, that attitude: if it isn't the big leagues, it isn't living. Once I get there, I'm never going back.

The truth is, I looked around the clubhouse in Shea Stadium—through nineteen-year-old eyes—and I saw people whose records I admired, Hamilton and McMillan and Chuck Hiller and the rest. They were thirty to thirty-five years old and they had that kicked-around look. I thought to myself, "Gawd, I don't want to be like that in ten or twelve years." I promised myself that however long I was going to be there, I would make the most of it. I grew up in a family with a strong work ethic and I knew I could build on that.

I don't preach about physical fitness or anything else. I don't go around singing the praises of high-fiber muffins. But I know what has worked for me. When you try to be honest about records, a certain amount of it comes off as aw-shucks, digging at the dirt with your toe. But my recent records—the 300 wins, the 5,000th strikeout—were the product of time travel. They were attainable if I lasted long enough. The seventh no-hitter, on the other hand, defied time. I guess I'll just take credit for that one.

It hasn't been easy putting together a complete season since I turned forty. I don't remember the last time I got through a day without feeling some discomfort. I consider that part of the cost of doing business. I make a distinction between that feeling and actual pain, a sharp, throbbing toothache kind of sensation. Most of what I encounter is that creakiness, not being able to sit or stand or lie flat without being aware of a pressure point. This comes from overuse.

I view myself like a car that has over a hundred thousand miles on the speedometer. The car wasn't designed to go that far. Now things constantly pop up that need attention—the alternator, the water pump. I have a mindset that says those things are going to happen and I have to deal with them. This is the price you pay to stay on the road.

In the 1991 season alone, I have missed starts, or left games early, because of shoulder, elbow, heel, and back problems. I answer questions about my trapezius muscles as if this were a really normal and interesting topic of conversation. So I shudder when writers and fans suggest that a player has qualified for "immortality." Knowing just how mortal I am has enabled me to keep pitching.

Less so today than in the 1960s, but too many athletes still smoke, still chew, still eat and drink their hearts out at the late-night buffet table provided in the clubhouse after every game. Then they go home to bed, and they might as well have put a load of cement in their stomachs.

I feel peer pressure just like anyone else. But the key is sticking to a routine. If it becomes optional, it becomes useless. After my seventh no-hitter, I didn't chug champagne and I didn't make a run for Taco Bell. I rode a stationary bike for 30 minutes, using a computerized program that simulates pedaling up a hill.

When my body says enough, my head usually answers, "That's it." I pitch sore but not hurt. You learn that a pulled hamstring or a tight calf muscle isn't something you can pitch your way through; you have to listen to your body.

As Woody Allen once said, the mind is filled with delusions. The body never lies.

None of this was yet clear to me back in 1966. I didn't have a goal or a plan, and neither did the Mets, or so it seemed. The club slipped back into last place in 1967, and Westrum was fired. I missed most of the season because of an arm injury and my army reserve obligations. I gave serious thought to forgetting about baseball.

Two developments kept me from quitting. In June I married my high school sweetheart, Ruth Holdorf, which cured much of the homesickness. And Tom Seaver, 22 but poised beyond his years, joined the Mets and was voted rookie of the year. He was 16-and-13 for a team that won only 61 games.

You could see the pitching staff taking shape, and behind every arm was a story. Jerry Koosman was on active duty with the army at Fort Bliss, Texas, when the Mets first spotted him in 1965 pitching for the base team. His catcher was the son of an usher at Shea Stadium. The Mets sent Red Murff, who had signed me out of high school, to scout Koosman on the recommendation of the usher, acting at the behest of his son.

In 1968, Koosman would surpass even Seaver's rookie year, winning nineteen games and pitching seven shutouts. He barely lost out in the rookie of the year balloting to Cincinnati's Johnny Bench. Seaver was showing the consistency that would stamp his whole career, again winning sixteen games against twelve losses. I was still bouncing around, not yet a fixture in the starting rotation. I finished 6-and-9, striking out 133 batters in 134 innings.

The new manager was the one-time Brooklyn Dodger first baseman Gil Hodges, a soft-spoken but intimidating figure. Hodges made the commitment to stick with youth, and now the outfield was set with Cleon Jones, Tommy Agee, and Swoboda, with Art Shamsky off the bench.

And then suddenly it was 1969, the year the Mets truly became amazing. I felt lucky to be there, lucky to be a part of the Miracle of Flushing Meadow. I still do.

It happened in a way that defied logic. The Mets had finished last or next to last every year of their existence. The club was baseball's answer to Pinky Lee, the comic whose act consisted mainly of taking a cream pie in the face.

Seaver blossomed into a dominating pitcher that year, with a 25-and-7 record, and he simply willed the Mets into taking themselves seriously. Koosman won seventeen games and Gary Gentry added thirteen. Tug McGraw saved twelve and won nine out of the bullpen. Hodges hadn't quite decided where I fit in, but I was 6-and-3 as a spot starter and reliever.

We came from nine and a half games behind the Cubs in August and won the pennant in a closing rush. The Mets were the lullaby of Broadway, and the World Series would match the team that came from nowhere against a great Baltimore team, the pride of the American League.

None of it seemed real. A reserve outfielder named Rod Gaspar joined the club late in the season, and after we beat Atlanta in the playoffs he was quoted in the papers as saying, "Bring on the Orioles." A few days before the series opened, Frank Robinson was on the "Tonight" show, and when Johnny Carson repeated the quote to him, he said, "Who is Rod Gaspar?"

The truth is, we really didn't know what we were doing there. Most people thought it was a joke, and we kept thinking we would wake up and find out they were right. We had a meeting the day before the opener to go over the hitters. The Orioles had Frank Robinson, Brooks Robinson, Boog Powell, Don Buford. Our scouts kept saying, "Don't throw this and don't throw that." It went on that way with each hitter. Finally, Jerry Koosman said, "Well, what the hell do we throw these guys?" We never did get an answer.

A few minutes before the first game in Baltimore, I was sunning myself in the visitors' bullpen when some of the boys noticed a stir in the bleachers. A group of Mets wives were parading through the stands, carrying a huge bedsheet emblazoned with the stirring words, "Go, Mets, Go!"

The fans were throwing hot dogs and popcorn boxes and pouring beer on them. I said, "Man, I'm glad I told Ruth not to leave her seat." Then somebody said, "You better take another look, Nolan. She's right in the middle of them."

I said, "Gimme those binoculars." Sure enough, there she was. I had a fit. I don't remember all that I said to her, but I let her know how I felt. In the late 1980s, during a pennant race in Houston, I told the story over dinner with friends. Ruth smiled sheepishly and said, "I was young and impulsive then. I wouldn't do it now."

I nodded and said, "I'm older and less emotional now. It wouldn't bother me if you did."

I wish I could say I learned something profound about myself during that season, or about pitching. I did confirm something Yogi Berra was supposed to have said: "You can observe a lot just from watching." It was already obvious to me that if I was going to improve—and survive—I had to figure out for myself what it took to win. I spent a lot of time watching Seaver and Koosman. They had two assets I lacked. They threw strikes and pitched with confidence. Both would come to me in time.

Mostly, I wish I had enjoyed the miracle more and worried less about the things I couldn't control. There is nothing in sports—no records, no trophies, no amount of money—that can equal the ecstasy of being in a championship clubhouse. I honestly don't know which comes first, the winning or the caring about each other. But there is a rapture and a closeness that you know might not come your way again. I spent the rest of my career trying to rediscover it.

You tend to romanticize the kind of season the Mets had,

as young and unsophisticated as most of us were. Hodges was the perfect manager for that club, patient and slow to boil, but not to be trifled with. Once, he banned cowboy hats on road trips and Ron Swoboda asked casually if the rule was his or if it had come down from the front office.

Right away, you could see the veins pop out in Hodges's neck. They looked like fire hoses. The next thing you knew, he was right in Swoboda's face, letting him know who made the rules. You didn't want to rile him if you could avoid it.

The pitching staff could dazzle you, but we had only one genuine .300 hitter in Cleon Jones. In a sense, our third baseman, Ed Charles, best reflected the spirit of the Mets. He wrote poetry in his spare time. His nickname was The Glider. Once he hit a home run, ducked into the dugout, and yelled, "You never throw a slider to The Glider."

All during the World Series, we were laughing and having a grand time, and the Orioles were getting tighter and tighter. Not at first, of course. Tom Seaver started the opener and gave up a home run to the first batter he faced, Don Buford, as the Orioles went on to win. Most people thought it was over right then. But after that game everything just turned to magic. We got great pitching. Al Weis hit a homer and Donn Clendenon delivered some clutch hits. Ron Swoboda made two spectacular catches. The Mets came back to stun the Orioles by winning four games in a row and closing out the series. I picked up a save in the third game, in relief of Gentry.

Long after the last out had been recorded in game five and the Mets were officially champions of the planet Earth, our fans were still celebrating, racing across Shea Stadium, some colliding like asteroids on those computer games that kids play in shopping arcades.

Most of the players were at a party the owners gave in the stadium club, and we looked out the windows and watched the fans. They were digging chunks of turf out of the field, stealing the bases, gouging dirt out of the pitcher's mound, just going crazy. It was a once-in-a-lifetime feeling.

NOLAN RYAN'S
TOP TEN NAMES BORN TO PITCH

1. Jay Hook

2. John Strike

3. Early Wynn

4. Mike Palm

5. Chief Bender

6. Darcy Fast

7. Rollie Fingers

8. Bill Hands

9. Bob Walk

10. Eric Plunk

Some of My Best Friends Are Left-Handed

I don't want to overstate this and make it sound as if I'm describing my first Tahitian sunset, but big league baseball became real to me the summer before my senior year in high school, the day I saw Sandy Koufax pitch for the Dodgers against the Houston Colt .45s.

The .45s were named after the gun that won the West, but when the home team moved indoors it picked a name, the Astros, that was more in tune with the space age.

Until then, I knew about major league ball only in my imagination and from watching the Game of the Week on television—with Dizzy Dean doing the color. Now and then I picked up a Cardinals game on radio out of St. Louis.

I wasn't the kind of kid who went overboard on heroes or role models, if we even used that term in the 1960s. I didn't plaster my walls with pictures of ball players, and when my friends and I collected any cards we used them as flaps in our bicycle spokes. (My sons just groan when they hear that.)

My early favorites were Mickey Mantle, Yogi Berra, and Whitey Ford because you saw so much of the Yankees on TV. Later, I was a fan of Henry Aaron, a quiet, understated man who hit home runs with the snap of his wrists.

A distinction may be helpful here. There are power pitchers and finesse pitchers; there are starters and relievers. But in terms of a natural separation there are right-handers and left-handers. Left-handers grow up in a world not designed for them. If you eat next to one, he bumps into your elbow. They have to write across their bodies, like a kid in school trying to keep you from copying off a test. Maybe this makes them more guarded, more self-centered. Aside from the obvious inconveniences, left-handed pitchers have additional stresses. To begin with, they choose from a smaller selection of gloves.

With runners on base, they have their backs to third base, where the action is critical. This alone can make you a wreck. But despite their insecurities, lefties are always in demand. Every club needs a reliable left-handed starter and one or two in the bullpen, and teams are always willing to recycle a Willie Hernandez or a Dan Schatzeder or a Juan Agosto.

According to Steve Howe, who got another chance with the Yankees after he had served six suspensions, there is essentially one test for a southpaw: "Can you breathe? If you can, they'll give you a shot."

The demand for lefties has grown as the game has become more specialized. Managers are slaves to the theory that lefties are more effective against left-handed hitters. "It has gotten to the point," says Stu Miller, the Pirates pitching coach, "that teams will take a mediocre lefty over a quality right-hander. I think that's stupid."

I don't know of any survey that proves left-handers are stranger characters than right-handers, but still, going through life with your back to third base can do something to you.

There are classic lefties and there are eccentric lefties. You almost never find one who is both.

And then there is Sandy Koufax. When I first saw him, it was like watching a line of poetry come to life. He gave meaning to every baseball cliché I had ever heard: the stylish, graceful left-hander, the blinding fastball, the wicked curve, and, not right away, the uncanny control. He had something else: an aura that suggested invincibility.

So that day I hung on every pitch Koufax threw. No pitcher in my time, maybe in anyone's time, ever made hitters look as awful as he did. Against his fastball or his curve, they looked helpless and clumsy. If you think of pitching as an art form, if you study the different practitioners, you see that Sandy was the classic model.

He seemed slight next to Drysdale but was actually 6-2 and 210, with long fingers and powerful back muscles.

He was the one pitcher I always wanted to know better; to sit with and talk to for hours about baseball, about pitching, to ask the hows and whys. But my rookie year was his last with the Dodgers and the chance to visit with Koufax never came, not for more than a minute or two.

The next best thing was talking about him with Don Drysdale, when Don was a broadcaster during the years I pitched for the Angels. Koufax was a mystery man who let few people really get close to him. I wonder if he ever understood what a genius the other pitchers in baseball considered him.

He had a shyness so basic that when he didn't want to be disturbed, he would sometimes hide his telephone in the oven. The management of the Dodgers used to complain that when they needed to reach Sandy, they frequently had to send him a telegram.

He never appeared comfortable in the limelight, being idolized, having people expect so much of you. Pitching in New York or Los Angeles magnifies the problem. When the fame machine starts humming, and people build you up, shower you with awards, there is a need to step back and say, Wait a minute. Give me a chance to be human.

It is one thing to be idolized by Little Leaguers. To them a major league player represents the pinnacle, the dream. But when adults treat you with awe, there is a pressure to keep your dignity. Nor do you want to overreact simply because others treat you like public property.

In Arlington, Ruth and I were having lunch one day when a fan hobbled over to our table on crutches. He had his leg in a cast and, with both hands, he lifted his leg and put it on the table, the bottom of his bare foot almost touching our plates. He handed me a fountain pen and I signed the cast. The encounter was so casual and unexpected, as he hobbled off, I looked at Ruth and just laughed out loud.

It took me a long time to be comfortable with people. I still try to avoid mob scenes, nor do I enjoy having people look at me as if I were not from this planet. If my presence is a distraction, I can't enjoy a football or basketball game, or dinner in a restaurant. It isn't adulation that I mind, it's what I call the Lite Beer mentality. You don't like to put on a mask, but you don't want strangers putting their arms around you, either.

Koufax bucked the system, struggling to protect his privacy, then and later. If you charted his life after baseball, you would find that Sandy looked for homes in such places as Vermont, North Carolina, and San Luis Obispo. His home now is in Vero Beach, Florida. During the summer he has traveled to New Zealand, still seeking out remote places.

More than a few of his teammates questioned how important the game was to Sandy. He grew up in a home in Brooklyn where baseball was never discussed. His father was a lawyer, his mother an accountant. He went to the University of Cincinnati on a basketball scholarship, planning a career as an architect.

Just the sort of background you would expect of the fellow who became the best pitcher in creation. He had finished his freshman year when he signed with the Brooklyn

Dodgers for a bonus $14,000. The Dodgers figured he might develop into a gate attraction; he was both a home boy and Jewish. I don't think he sold many tickets. He won nine and lost ten his first three seasons, and then the Dodgers left Brooklyn.

Drysdale remembers Sandy changing almost overnight from ordinary to almost unbeatable. His hair had started graying early, and it was like a signal to get busy. He told Drysdale, "Maybe the problem was that I never had a burning ambition to be a baseball player. If I had, I might have realized sooner how much work was involved."

Over a period of five seasons, Koufax won 102 games, lost only 38, and pitched four no-hitters. He led the league in earned run average four times. But the numbers told only half the story. Few pitchers ever meant as much to a club. Few have meant as much to baseball.

He made the Dodgers defense stronger. On the nights when he struck out, say, twelve batters, the fielders were then responsible for only fifteen outs. In each of his last two seasons, he had 27 complete games. He kept the starting rotation in order and the bullpen rested. You can't put a value on what it meant to the relief pitchers to have an almost guaranteed night off, nights when no one had to warm up.

He accomplished what he did in spite of a series of injuries that took big bites out of his seasons: a back ailment, a dead finger, and, finally, a condition in his elbow called traumatic arthritis. After a game, the trainer would haul out the ice bucket and slip on a rubber sleeve that stretched from his shoulder to his fingers. Then Koufax would soak the arm in the pail. He kept his arm submerged for maybe an hour, but he knew that when he woke up the next day the elbow would be so swollen it looked like a knee.

You couldn't convince opposing teams that he had a problem. He won 26 games in 1965, and Drysdale won 23 as the Dodgers went to the World Series against the Twins. There Walter Alston made one of the more interesting decisions a manager ever had to face.

He decided to start Koufax on two days' rest in the seventh game, even though Drysdale, his beast of burden, was due in rotation. Alston tried to be diplomatic when he explained the move. He said it would allow him to have Drysdale, who could warm up quickly, in the bullpen.

Don accepted the news with grace, but the reasoning was really more subtle. They were playing in Minnesota, where the ballpark was the size of an orchestra pit. Drysdale was more likely to give up a home run ball.

At the start, Sandy's curve was hanging and he walked two batters. Drysdale trotted down to the bullpen to loosen up. I can only imagine what went through the minds of the Minnesota players. There on the mound was Sandy Koufax, and waiting to come in, if needed, was Don Drysdale. Which do you prefer, the blade or the rope?

Koufax worked his way out of the inning and went on to shut out the Twins on three hits, 2-0, as the Dodgers won the championship. He kept shaking off John Roseboro's sign for the curveball until the catcher quit calling for it. He relied almost the entire game on his fastball.

His control was so fine that when Bob Allison came to the plate in the ninth as the tying run, Koufax decided, "I wasn't going to give him a pitch that caught more than an inch of the plate."

A pitcher who thinks that way, and then does it, isn't going to lose. Allison struck out.

A chill went through the National League that day. "My God," said Chub Feeney, then the president of the San Francisco Giants. "Now that they know he can pitch on two days' rest, what hope do any of us have?"

That winter, Koufax and Drysdale sent shock tremors throughout baseball by asking for $1 million between them for three years of labor. They staged a joint holdout and wound up settling for much less. But it is pretty clear, in light of the salaries that are paid today, that their tactic changed the way superstars were paid, and may have hastened the arrival of the players' union.

It made interesting reading that off-season. Walter O'Malley, the owner of the Dodgers, vowed that he would never give in, but he did, finally settling with them shortly before the season was to open. It was traditional in Los Angeles to have a preseason game between the Dodgers and a team composed of Hollywood celebrities. Drysdale and Koufax claimed that they were sitting on movie offers and could afford to pass up the season. O'Malley may or may not have believed them, but for a time there it appeared that the Hollywood All-Stars were going to have a heckuva pitching staff.

The numbers that were kicked around had Sandy signing for $140,000 and Don a little less. This was a turning point for the players; six-figure salaries were still rare around the league.

At the end of the 1966 season, having won 27 games and his third Cy Young award, Koufax retired at the age of thirty. Fans around the country were stunned, but no more so than the Dodgers front office.

Some speculated that Sandy felt the arthritis in his elbow would keep him from functioning as he wanted, and his pride would not allow him to lower his standards. Sandy himself said later that pain, not pride, was the factor. "I second-guessed myself for years," he said. "I have wondered what would have happened if I had tried to keep going. But the problem I faced was simple. I had to decide whether more pitching would leave me with a permanent injury." The medical opinion was that it would.

For years the Dodgers kept a light in the window, hoping that with time Koufax would miss the excitement and decide to test his elbow and return. The call never came.

In 1965, while I was reporting to my first minor league, a rookie left-hander named Steve Carlton was joining the Cardinals for spring training in St. Petersburg.

He pitched in a preseason game, and later in the clubhouse he rushed up to his catcher, Tim McCarver, and said earnestly, "Hey, you've got to call more breaking pitches when we're behind in the count."

By then McCarver was moving into his sixth season, having established himself in the 1964 World Series as a coming star. He backed up the startled pitcher against a wall and screamed at him, "You sonofabitch! You got a lot of guts telling me that. What credentials do you have?"

McCarver apologized the next day, Carlton did not. That, as Tim described it, was the beginning of a long and beautiful friendship, tight enough that the Phillies would bring him out of one retirement just to catch Carlton.

If you need to pick out any record or distinction that explains the kind of career Steve Carlton had, this one will do: his nickname. His teammates called him "Lefty," and that is as fine a compliment as a southpaw pitcher can earn, when you consider those who went before him: Warren Spahn in his era, Sandy Koufax in his.

Our histories are entwined in this respect: we dueled through the 1983 season in pursuit of Walter Johnson's strikeout record of 3,508. I got there first, but there was a period in midsummer when the lead switched depending on which one of us pitched that day. Then I went on the disabled list, and Carlton pulled away. As strictly a power pitcher, my career didn't figure to last as long as his. I predicted that Lefty would own the record when he retired.

It didn't quite work out that way, reminding me again that it is foolhardy to try to outguess what the baseball fates will decree. Injuries began to nag Carlton and he lost a little speed off his slider.

Carlton's greatness could be judged not by what he said but by what he did. For eight years he didn't say anything, not to the press. But he would rank high on virtually any classification you can invent. He had one of the superior fastballs. He intimidated hitters. He qualified as a workhorse. He was a prototype left-hander, with a liquid delivery and one of the best pickoff moves in the game. He was too serious to be labeled a character, but he might be fairly described as quirky.

Compared to the average player, he was a recluse, the Howard Hughes of baseball. But there was nothing average about him. He was a left-handed hitter's nightmare. "Like drinking coffee through a fork," said Willie Stargell.

No pitcher can be great without a great pitch, and the slider was Carlton's. It confused the hitters because it acted like a fastball until the last instant. He probably got more checked swing strikes than any pitcher I ever saw. He threw what we call a "tight" slider, one that spun tightly like a gyroscope. And because he threw so hard, it would break and drop.

"Carlton does not pitch to the hitter," said Tim Mc-Carver, "he pitches through him. The batter hardly exists for Steve. He's playing an elevated game of catch."

One of his trademarks was the quick tempo he always established. He was all business, to the point where he went to the mound with cotton plugs in his ears. He was tough on broadcasters, though. While an announcer tried to complete a 60-second commerical, Lefty might have two outs on the scoreboard and a fly ball in the air.

I respected Carlton and liked what I saw of him, but can't claim that we knew each other as friends. There was no small talk in him, no time for the sociable asides—"how's your family," that sort of thing. He never wanted to stop pitching, and he did not go easily into that long, dark night of retirement. But he probably cared less for records than anyone who played the game.

The day after he broke Robin Roberts's record for most career strikeouts by a Philadelphia pitcher, he had to call the club's publicity office. "What was that record I broke?" he asked. "Some lady wants me to write it on a ball."

When Carlton decided to stop giving interviews or even to talk with the media, a lot of players waited to see if he could get away with it. No one was really sure what his motivation was. But he wasn't angry about anything, didn't feel abused or burned, wasn't making a moral statement. He just decided that he could better use that time and energy by putting it into his pitching, and he did. Got away with it, too.

No player was more stubborn, or more committed to his ideas. His vow of silence lasted roughly from 1978 until 1987, after he had been released by the Phillies and picked up by San Francisco. Releasing Carlton was an embarrassment for Bill Giles, the owner, who hoped Lefty could be persuaded to retire.

He believed he could still win, and he did add eleven victories—and twenty-one losses—as he drifted to the Giants, the White Sox, the Indians, and the Twins, where he delivered his last pitch in 1988. In the end he had 329 wins, with six seasons of winning 20 or more. He was the only man to win four Cy Young awards.

He appeared at a press conference when he joined the Giants. Many a writer revived the line once applied to a temperamental actor who finally mellowed: "He learned to say hello when it was time to say goodbye." He had been with the Phillies for fourteen years, silent for the last eight, and the assembled reporters had to struggle to think of things to ask.

He had contacts with four other teams, he said, but he chose the Giants because of Roger Craig, the manager, who was a former pitcher, and because of the charms of San Francisco: "Napa Valley's close. I'm sort of a wine buff."

I respect him for accepting the consequences of the trade-off he made. He wanted to be left alone to concentrate on his work, and he knew that over time he might be viewed, not only by the press but by the fans, as cold and arrogant. But the players knew that Carlton, when he talked, had a dry wit. He looked around Montreal's Olympic Stadium on a day when the weather was 39 degrees and observed: "This place would make a good wine cellar."

He wanted to keep pitching, he said, because he knew his arm was sound. The problem had been with his mechanics. But he was 1-and-3 in six games with the Giants and they let him go.

When a longtime rival retires, one who has been a superb competitor, you do feel that a little of yourself goes with him. No matter how cynical or jaded or distant you may be, it is a tough and sometimes touchy moment for anyone when a great player hangs up his glove. You feel something for him, and perhaps you feel more than you should, as if you had had a small window to view the parade and now it is gone.

I was in the visitors' dugout in the final week of the 1980 season when the Dodgers realized they had custody of someone special. A year later, his first full season in the National League, Fernando Valenzuela helped knock the Astros out of the playoffs. He was named rookie of the year, won the Cy Young Award, and beat the Yankees in the game that turned around the 1981 World Series.

At his best, I regarded Valenzuela as the most effective pitcher of the 1980s, one who could dominate the hitters even without an overpowering fastball. When I pitched against him, the games were usually tight and low-scoring. My only question was about his age. When I first saw him, the Dodgers said he was twenty, born in November 1960, and it must have been true because they sent a scout to his hometown in Mexico to bring back his birth certificate.

But he had an old arm, had pitched a lot of innings. I wasn't surprised when the wear and tear began to show. He missed the last two months of the 1988 season and never regained his form. The ligaments and tendons were so badly stretched that he could scratch his back without bending his left elbow.

Since he was twelve, he had been pitching in pickup games in Mexico, where both sides put up their pesos and bet on the outcome. That meant the games were serious.

He was the last of twelve children, a seventh son, and he lived in a small village whose name no one could pronounce. He grew up in a four-room house shared by seventeen relatives, and he slept in a room with his six brothers.

I'll never forget the first time I saw him. He was 5-11 and

the Dodgers listed his weight as 180 pounds, although he looked heavier. He looked like the Pillsbury doughboy. He spoke no English and didn't drive a car, and fame made no impression on him, possibly because he didn't know it was out there.

In no time at all, it seemed, he was their most popular and colorful player. A newspaper held a contest to give him a nickname, and from over 3,000 entries a panel selected "El Toro." The losing suggestions included The Big Enchilada, El Pauncho, and Tortilla Fats.

But he wasn't fat and he didn't have a beer belly. He was just barrel-chested and thick-waisted, with a round, happy face. For a time he appeared to be indestructible. He didn't miss a start in his first six seasons, even though he threw the most damaging of all pitches, the screwball. Fernando had great control, and if he had thrown hard too he might never have had to learn another pitch.

In my career there have been three pitchers who relied on a true screwball, Tug McGraw, Mike Marshall, and Fernando. If you wonder why there were so few, the answer is that in terms of anatomy it is almost impossible to throw a screwball. Valenzuela had both the anatomy and the disposition, and his scroogie—as pitchers call it—was the best since Carl Hubbell developed it in 1925.

By definition, a screwball is a reverse curve, so that when a left-hander delivers it the ball breaks away from a right-handed hitter. No matter how often they see it, hitters have trouble believing a breaking ball from a southpaw will behave that way.

The trick is to throw it over the top with exactly the same motion you use on the fastball. What a hitter looks at is your hand, and what crosses him up is the last surge of the pitcher's arm and wrist.

The screwball is thrown with great arm extension, and it comes out of the back of your hand with a wrist snap. In effect, you are going against the grain. It helps to be really loose in all the joints, but nature never intended for a man to turn his hand over in such a way. Valenzuela threw it 50 percent of the time in a typical game, mixing it in with fastballs and curves.

Fernando had an edge because his motion was so effortless. In spite of his portly shape, he did everything smoothly. He had the best pickoff move in the league; he picked off Tim Raines five times in one season. He nearly always got the sacrifice bunt down. Few pitchers were his equal as a fielder.

Hubbell always said that it wasn't the way a screwball broke that bothered the good hitters. It was the change of speed compared to the fastball. I knew that Fernando was having problems early in 1989, when Kevin Mitchell of the Giants beat him with a three-run homer.

After he had been told that Valenzuela said the homer was off his fastball, Mitchell was quoted in the next day's papers, *"That* was his *fastball*? I didn't know I hit his fastball."

A hitter could hardly insult a pitcher more deeply, especially when there is no needling intended. To anyone who asked, Fernando said that he only needed time to regain his arm strength. Meanwhile, the Dodgers were struggling to stay out of last place.

Sparky Anderson once said that if you get off to a slow start but know you have a good team, there is no point in worrying. And if you have a bad team, there is even less reason to worry. The Dodgers were good again in 1990, finishing second to the Reds, and they had a decision to make on the pitcher who had filled their stadium and the stadiums in a lot of other places.

I was in Florida with the Rangers when the Dodgers gave Valenzuela his unconditional release in the spring of 1991. No hill in Mexico had been as green as Fernando when he charmed all of baseball as a rookie ten years earlier. The 1980s had been his decade. You couldn't help but feel sorry to see it end.

Jerry Reuss pitched for eight teams, and he may have been the most underrated left-hander ever to last 21 seasons and win 220 games. He was 6-5 and 200, threw smoke, and made every clubhouse he walked into a livelier place, including some that were not his own.

Reuss was one of those pitchers that contending teams always felt might put them over the top, and the judgment in his case wasn't wrong. Blond and blue-eyed, with the Nordic look of a ski instructor, Jerry had a devilish mind.

When he was pitching well with the Dodgers, his name kept coming up in trade rumors involving the Yankees. After his team finished a game against the Cubs in Wrigley Field, he picked up an equipment bag, stuffed it with towels, and caught a taxi to Comiskey Park, where the Yankees were playing the White Sox.

There he talked his way into the Yankee clubhouse and barged into manager Lou Piniella's office.

"Pleased to meet you," Reuss told Piniella. "I pitched Friday so I'll do whatever you want, start or relieve."

A startled Piniella said, "What the hell are you talking about?"

Casually, Reuss said, "Didn't George call?" referring, of course, to Steinbrenner. "We just made the deal."

After Piniella closed the door to talk to his new pitcher, coaches Joe Altobelli and Gene Michael leaned around the corner to eavesdrop, and Dale Berra, Yogi's son, nervously inquired who had been traded for Reuss.

It was, of course, another Reuss practical joke. He pitched two days later for the Dodgers. The gag did have a kind of sequel. In 1988 he wound up in Comiskey Park, pitching for the White Sox. He finished with a 13-9 record.

But Jerry always made it clear that his best days were spent in Los Angeles. Wistfully, he said, "Watching Linda Ronstadt in shorts and a Dodger jacket sing the National Anthem made me realize what playing in the big leagues was all about."

I could probably write off to coincidence the fact that so many Dodger pitchers are in this chapter and throughout this book.

But if one organization has consistently turned out fine pitching, all during my career, it has been Los Angeles.

It is partly their tradition, and partly their mystique, which is what you develop when you combine talent with an attitude that you know something nobody else knows.

More than any club since the postwar Yankees, the Dodgers have all but automated the idea of good pitching. There is a uniformity all through their minor league system, in the way they teach and in the way they scout.

I have my own notions about why they succeed, why they always have a great one, sometimes two, a Koufax and Drysdale, a Sutton, Valenzuela, or Hershiser. All were home-grown, meaning they try to keep what they harvest. One thing the Dodgers do better than most other clubs: they don't try to change the mechanics of a young prospect who already has at least one very effective pitch.

Another factor that I think helps is that many of the managers and coaches in their organization are former pitchers. All my life, I have been told that the best candidate for a managing job is a player, usually an infielder, of average talent who had to really study the game.

There is a logic to this argument, but it doesn't exactly square with the timeless belief that pitching is at least 75 percent of the game. I don't think I can devote a chapter to left-handers and their essential characteristics without acknowledging Tommy Lasorda and his success as manager of the Dodgers.

Lasorda had one real shot at pitching in the majors, in 1955 when the Dodgers were still in Brooklyn. The manager was Walter Alston, the man he would succeed 22 years later. As Tommy tells the story, Alston suspended Don Newcombe for refusing to throw batting practice, and Lasorda the rookie was given his first start, against the Cardinals.

He walked the first two batters, and one moved to third on a wild pitch. Working on the next hitter, Stan Musial, he threw another wild one and the runner on third tried to score. "No way is he gonna score without cutting me in half," said Lasorda. "He hits me like a truck. Pretty rugged country ball player named Wally Moon.

"The run scores. I strike out Musial. I strike out Rip Repulski. I get out of the inning and in the dugout they notice my uniform is getting red around one knee. I'm thinking, I gotta make this club. Getting hurt is a mark against you, almost as bad as losing. They got a doctor near the dugout. He looks at the knee and says, 'Son, if you try to pitch on that knee you may never pitch again. You've been spiked so badly, every tendon and ligament is exposed.'

"Well, the hell with that. I gotta pitch. I gotta make the club. Next inning, I start toward the mound but two other players who heard the doctor grab me by the throat and hold me back. By the throat! That's how I got taken out. The date was May 5, 1955.

"Then the front office sends me to the minors. Before I leave, I go in to appeal to Buzzie Bavasi, the general manager, and he says: 'Put yourself in my chair; who would you send out?' I tell him, hell, there's a kid left-hander on this club who can't even throw a goddamned strike. Bavasi says, 'Maybe, but the kid left-hander was paid a bonus to sign and the rule is that a bonus baby has to stick with the big club for two years or else you lose him.' "

I have heard the punch line at a sports banquet and it always gets a roar from the crowd. The bonus baby who couldn't throw a strike was Sandy Koufax. "It hurt ten times worse than the spiking, being shipped out," said Lasorda. "But I always said, it took the greatest left-hander in history to get me off the Dodgers."

NOLAN RYAN'S
TEN GREATEST
SOUTHPAWS

(THAT I SAW PITCH)

1. Sandy Koufax

2. Warren Spahn

3. Steve Carlton

4. Fernando Valenzuela

5. Tommy John

6. Sparky Lyle

7. Tug McGraw

8. Ron Guidry

9. Mickey Lolich

10. Jerry Koosman

The
Thinking
Men

There is a game that stands out in my mind as one of the most amazing I have ever seen. In 1980, Kenny Forsch of Houston, a tough, solid right-hander, shut out the Cincinnati Reds on 11 hits! I can honestly say I have never seen anybody else give up hits in double figures and hold the other team scoreless.

He walked a couple of batters, too. There were maybe three double plays behind him, but the main thing was that Ken made the pitch when he needed it to get the ground ball that set up the double play. He got the strikeout when he needed one and the pop fly to keep a runner on third from scoring.

I mean, that whole game was a true marvel to me.

I have to contrast that performance by Ken Forsch with one another teammate of mine pitched ten years later. In 1990, Kevin Brown threw a nine-inning, four-hit shutout for the Texas Rangers against the Minnesota Twins and needed only eighty pitches. That was unheard of, and he did it on natural ability. He had so much movement on his sinker that the hitters were swinging at anything they could reach.

Let me assure you, there is a huge difference between a four-hit shutout on eighty pitches and a Kenny Forsch getting one while allowing eleven hits. Kevin Brown achieved his on pure natural ability. Forsch earned his on guile and willpower.

Now, I give them both credit. They still had to throw strikes. But as a fan of other pitchers, I would rather watch the kind of game Forsch pitched. He couldn't relax or let up; all his senses were heightened. Elsewhere in these pages I have mentioned another pitcher I admire whose name may not be familiar to most fans, Vern Ruhle. I would watch Vern set up a hitter and then throw a leisurely 83-mile-an-hour fastball right past his hands. That's hard to do.

This is what I mean by the phrase "The Thinking Men." You don't need a Ph.D. to be a Thinking Man. Nor is it true that the thinking pitchers are always the ones who get by with finesse, or craftiness, or an unorthodox pitch. That isn't how I classify them. Rather, they *know* how to win without their best stuff, or when their big pitch takes a night off.

Of course, you can have a great fastball and still qualify, as Tom Seaver has shown. I think he was born knowing how to pitch. Ron Fairly tells a story about returning to his old school, the University of Southern California, and facing Seaver in the annual alumni game. Ron was already established himself as an outfielder and first baseman with the Dodgers, but he didn't want to look bad against this young varsity pitcher.

Fairly looked at one pitch and out of the side of his mouth said to the catcher, "Prominent alumni." That was a code word for "Help!" The kid catcher called out to the mound, "Fastball." Fairly timed his swing and drove the ball 400 feet for a home run.

That was very nearly a major league farm club that Coach Rod Dedeaux operated at USC. It is probably safe to assume that when they met in the big leagues Tom never again gave Fairly a break. Once Tom left the campus, his mission in life was to make hitters as miserable as possible.

Speaking as a semiprominent alumnus of the New York Mets, I can say without hesitation that no one did more to change the image of that franchise than Tom Seaver. He came to them as a young talent, educated, with class and pride. He was rookie of the year in 1967 and a sixteen-game winner in each of his first two seasons as the club began to shake off its identity as lovable losers. Seaver never bought the idea that losing could be cute or funny. Along with Gil Hodges, he changed the way the players thought.

Anyone who joined the Mets in the mid-1960s knew the team's legacy. How Casey Stengel had coined the phrase "the Amazing Mets" and given it wide circulation even before the club had signed its first losing player. When Casey realized, in 1962, that he would be managing the worst team ever assembled on a major league field, he saw, or pretended to see, that the future was going to be splendid. "I'll tell you about youth," he said. "Look how big it is. They break a record every day."

Seaver and, to a lesser degree, the rest of us were what Casey had in mind. He was so good, so confident, so removed from whatever the Mets had been before, he became the symbol of the new breed, the better times looming.

He had that good year of experience behind him when I moved up to the Mets to stay. I thought Tom was everything a pitcher needed to be. He was brainy, polished, self-motivated, durable, consistent, a student of the game and of people. Johnny Bench paid him the ultimate compliment: "He was a pitcher who thought like a catcher. I never knew a pitcher with such a knowledge of pitching. He could outthink the hitters. That's the difference that makes the great ones great."

There have been a rare few pitchers who were able to get

the absolute most from their skills because they had baseball smarts. They were crafty and analytical and aware at all times of their limits. Baseball smart isn't quite the same as being intelligent in the worldly sense. But Tom was both.

Seaver was what people in sports used to call a golden boy, a phrase identified with the 1950s and earlier, more innocent times. I think of an athlete who has it all, the look, the talent, the timing, a smooth ride to the top. There may have been some jealousy of Tom among the older Mets, but I don't remember any. It helped that he was a decent person who took himself less seriously than others did.

I am not sure how to describe our friendship. It wasn't city slicker and country cousin, although that impression might not have been far off the mark. He was open and articulate, while I was wary and unpolished. Tom had a sophisticated side, but he didn't go out of his way to impress people. On the road he stayed in his room. Even after a day game, he would get into his pajamas early, read a book, and work on a few crossword puzzles.

In those years, I roomed with Jerry Grote and Tom with Bud Harrelson. We were growing up together, Seaver with a head start. Our idea of a night on the town was dinner and then talking baseball for hours.

Tom did have one weakness. He liked to go to Trader Vic's and order those tropical drinks with a paper umbrella in them. He would have a couple and start to get silly. Grote used to threaten that he was going to write a book about him and title it *All-American Boy, My Ass.*

I have said often that I adjusted poorly to New York; my progress as a pitcher was ragged, money was a struggle, and the charms of the city eluded us. Still, it was the city of Babe Ruth, Jack Dempsey, and Joe DiMaggio. And 1969 turned out to be a Cinderella year, with Tom Seaver and Joe Namath leading their teams to improbable world championships.

I wish I had taken the time to appreciate New York more. It was fun being young there when Tom Seaver and Joe Namath were young.

There isn't much that really needs to be added here to the saga of the 1969 Mets, who won 11 games in a row in June and 38 of our last 49 games to go roaring past the Cubs to win the pennant.

"Everybody on the team might pick a different game," said Seaver. "But I came to the realization that we could win it all after a game against the Dodgers at Shea Stadium. We were in a scoreless game going into the fifteenth inning. Then Garrett hit a ball up the middle with a man on second. There was going to be a close play at the plate. Willie Davis came charging in and the ball went under his glove. The winning run scored. There was real electricity. I remember going into the clubhouse and making eye contact with Grote. It was like an electrical charge."

In mid-July, Seaver had come within two outs of pitching a perfect game, in a 4-0 shutout over Chicago. A rookie outfielder named Jimmy Qualls looped a clean single to left with one away in the ninth, and he was the only Cub to reach base. That victory was important because it showed the Cubs how good the Met pitching really was. If they entertained no doubts before, they did now.

Seaver, Koosman, and Gentry were the Big Three. My army reserve duties made it hard for me to stay in the rotation; I continued to have a problem with blood blisters on the middle finger of my pitching hand. With the inactivity and uncertainty, I was wilder than ever. There were too many days when I had no clue where the ball was going.

I suppose a part of me enjoys baseball most when I'm not involved in it, when I'm in the dugout and can concentrate on a pitcher whose work I admire. I wasn't nearly as involved in the team's plans as I would have liked, so there was plenty of time to admire Seaver. I watched the way he set up a hitter, the attention he gave to his mechanics. His form was flawless, almost on a par with Koufax. He was goal-oriented; I had never thought much about goals.

I think Tom believed in me when a lot of people were unsure. We felt comfortable enough in our friendship to joke around. There was a period when I pitched behind him and we were winning, and my spirits were up. Then Seaver had to come out of a game, trailing 14–7, and I walked up the runway with him. "You wimp," I said, "you couldn't even hold a seven-run lead."

The next day, I got shelled after blowing a big lead. I'm not sure, but when Seaver tells the story it's eight runs. This time he followed me up the runway, shouting, "You big lug, you can't hold a lead no matter how big it is."

Seaver was one of the first to understand that the '69 Mets were not a fluke and to explain it to a skeptical press: "This was a clear case," he said, "of a team being underrated. I grew up in California studying the Dodgers. I saw how far pitching takes you. We had good pitching in New York and other young people who could play. We were coming up steadily and we got there that year. We were going to compete for a long time to come."

Not many pitchers ever had a year to compare with what Seaver did in 1969—he won his last ten games to finish 25-and-7 and earn the first of his three Cy Young awards. Consistency? In the next four seasons he won 18, 20, 21, and 19 games.

Tom was two years my senior, meaning that in the baseball universe we followed as kids the great players spent their careers with one team, or so it seemed: Feller, DiMaggio, Williams, Musial, Mantle, Kaline. That it failed to work out that way for me wasn't surprising. In Seaver's case it was. He had been the franchise.

By 1977, the people who had nurtured the franchise through the hard and kooky times, notably Stengel and George Weiss and Bing Devine, were gone. When the front office and Seaver couldn't agree on his value, they sent him to Cincinnati as punishment. The move left Tom disenchanted and the fans furious.

In an indirect way, I was a minor factor in the outcome. I had found myself in California, had started my run of no-hitters and big strikeout seasons, and won 62 games in my first three seasons. In 1977, the Angels gave me a new, $100,000 contract.

That may or may not have been more than Tom was making, but whatever the case the Mets did something totally classless. They used it as ammunition in the public relations war that so often accompanies a salary dispute.

They wanted to take a tough stand with Seaver to set the example for future negotiations. It was apparent to anyone familiar with front office intrigue that the club planted information with Dick Young, the veteran sports columnist for the *Daily News*. Young speculated that Tom wanted a new contract because his wife, Nancy, was jealous of the money the Ryans were making in California. Tom understood where that came from, and the meanness of it. He went to the general manager, Joe McDonald, and asked to be traded.

The deal with the Reds was made in one phone call, and when Tom met the press in front of his locker the next day he couldn't hold back the tears.

I hated to see him leave the Mets, but there is something inherently wrong with a team trying to sabotage one of its players, one of its leaders. They were trying to bring him down a notch in the way the public viewed him, and, under the circumstances, he couldn't stay. I was two thousand miles away and didn't enjoy being used to undercut a friend, either.

But winding up on the Big Red Machine with Bench, Pete Rose, Joe Morgan, and Tony Perez wasn't exactly like getting sent to Siberia. The Machine was beginning to develop rattles, and Sparky Anderson was fired in the winter of 1978. But Tom had solid years there, winning fourteen games and losing two in the strike-shortened 1981 season.

And he had Johnny Bench, the best catcher of his generation, as a batterymate for five and a half years. Bench offered an insight into how Seaver thought: "Tom wasn't the kind of pitcher who would knock your hat off. He had control and when the count was three-and-one, he'd just rear back and throw as hard as he could. I appreciated the fact that he challenged you, that he was willing to go one-on-one with you. You knew the fastball was coming, and you still couldn't hit it."

Bench liked to recall their first meeting at a charity golf tournament years before Seaver came to Cincinnati. Bench had some chewing tobacco and Tom walked over and asked if he could borrow a plug. They sat down and talked and the impression Bench had of Seaver as a cosmopolitan New Yorker was dispelled. "You never know somebody," said John, "until you've had a chew with him."

I don't chew, but I think I know what he meant.

With the Mets under new management in 1983, they brought Seaver back and righted an old wrong. And then a year later, in what the club described as an administrative error, he was left unprotected and the Chicago White Sox claimed him. There was an interesting scene when the owner and general manager of the White Sox personally knocked on his hotel room door to tell him the news. Seaver listened, looked at them, and then asked to see their identification.

In Chicago, he pitched to another great catcher, Carlton Fisk, winning his 300th game in early August 1985. He beat the Yankees, 4-1, at Yankee Stadium, just across town from where it all began. He was forty years old, no longer the overpowering pitcher of his youth, but wiser and no less intense.

I thought back to our first full season together in 1968. That either of us would last long enough to win 300 games was not even a speck on our radar screens. Even then, as Tom put down the Yankees, mine was five years into the future.

Later, when we had a chance to visit, he reconstructed the final moments. The Yankees put two on with two out in the ninth; a hit and a fly ball had carried to the wall. Don Baylor, a pinch hitter, represented the tying run.

The White Sox held a conference at the mound and Dave Duncan, the pitching coach, said, "It's up to you." Seaver turned to Fisk and said, "What do you think?"

"You've got good stuff," Fisk reassured him. "You can get him."

Seaver nodded and said, "Let's go."

On the first pitch—in my mind I can see the top-to-bottom motion—Baylor lifted a high fly to left and it was over. "If you can't get up for the one out that will get you to 300," said Seaver, "then you ain't ever gonna get up."

His career had taken him to the Mets twice, to the Reds, and to the White Sox. It would end in Boston, in 1986, with a Red Sox team that lost the World Series in seven games—to the New York Mets. A knee injury had made him ineligible for postseason play, so he was merely an injured presence in the Boston clubhouse, on the scene but not part of it. For a player of his pride, that had to be intolerable. I could picture Tom Seaver as a manager, a broadcaster, or a senator, anything but a spectator.

The Mets tried to talk him out of retirement in midseason 1987, when their pitching staff came up short. He started working out, curious to see if there were any pitches left in an arm that had won 311 big league games.

But he concluded the tank was empty. He did not come back for the best of reasons: He didn't want to embarrass himself. The joy of pitching and winning was what kept Seaver going. To his credit, no amount of money could persuade him to fake it.

Don Sutton was hardly ever what he appeared to be, and that applied as much to his pitching record as the labels that have been pinned on him. He was my teammate for nearly two seasons in Houston—it seems longer—and I would be hard-pressed to think of anyone who could take over a clubhouse so effortlessly. It was fun to listen to Sutton, although sometimes one person could not do it alone.

I don't think you can give Sutton enough credit for what he achieved, and how. He may have been the best finesse pitcher I ever saw, the pitcher least likely to give a hitter anything decent to chase. He gave them crumbs. I rank Sutton with Pete Rose as a player who took less than exceptional physical ability and wasted nothing. Everything went into the blender. Sutton succeeded with the cerebral approach, determination, and cunning.

He could beat you with four different pitches, but he didn't have a great anything. Don had another edge: He could read himself so well that it was almost like being your own therapist. He might con an opponent or even a teammate, but he never deceived himself. And he had answers.

He refused to be typecast, even in Los Angeles, where typecasting is an art form. As his managers were quick to discover, Don Sutton was never one of those trained pigs who would roll around in the slop for you (as we say on the farm).

He was glib, quick, California smooth. There was no straw in his hair. In fact, when he joined the Astros in 1981 as a free agent, from the Dodgers, his hair had been permed. He had all these tight golden-brown curls, with a little gray creeping up the sides. He did it because he had figured out how many minutes he would save by not having to comb or brush or style his hair every morning.

And yet he was a sharecropper's son, born in Alabama and schooled in Florida, a throwback to the kind of kid who learned to pitch by pegging rocks at a circle drawn on the side of a barn. His background was not much different from my own. On nights when I was in my room in Alvin listening to the Houston games on radio, Don would be picking them up over WWL in New Orleans. His family had a farm near Pensacola then, and he would tune in the games, he said, while he sorted soybeans on the back of a flatbed truck.

There are some contradictions about Sutton. He was always one of the first players the press sought out, and his instincts in this area were sharp. But while he seemed to know exactly what he wanted to say, and said it well, he could be dangerously undiplomatic.

When Walter Alston retired after his long run as the

manager of the Dodgers, Sutton was asked if there was anyone he wanted to see get the job. There was. Jeff Torborg. Instead the position went to Tommy Lasorda, and Don had a fairly vivid reminder of why the secret ballot is so popular.

His encounters with Lasorda were few, but tended to be loud and colorful, and I never grew tired of hearing his accounts of them. "With Tommy," he said, "the volume of your argument got louder and louder, until it's like two people trying to see who can outyell the other without listening. Once, Tommy took me out of a game in Pittsburgh when I had a 1-0 lead in the fifth inning. So I go into the clubhouse and I'm throwing things around, and somebody overhears me say in the anger of the moment, 'If I were one of Lasorda's bobos this would never have happened to me.' It was something I said to the trash can while I flung a uniform at it. (If that trash can could only talk.) We laughed about it later.

"I had a little trouble changing myself to fit Tommy's personality. It took me a while, but the last two or three years I played in Los Angeles, we had a tremendous respect for each other."

I think it would be hard to dislike someone with as much personality as Don Sutton, but evidently some tried. I don't think it was true, as stories over the years suggested, that the fans of Los Angeles had a love-hate relationship with him. The fans did love Don, it was simply that they loved him less than Sandy Koufax or Don Drysdale, whose records he broke.

The fans had no reason to reject him, but they rarely took his side when he tested the authority of his managers, or made noises about being traded, or wrestled on the clubhouse floor in 1978 with the popular Steve Garvey.

Whatever actually happened between Sutton and Garvey, and no one I talked with was ever certain, no accommodations were made. They remained civil and cool long after they had gone their separate ways.

Don hinted, but never went into details, that their differences existed before they clashed over a story that, ironically, featured neither of them. Sutton was asked for a quote by a Los Angeles writer for a story about Reggie Smith. He said something to the effect that Reggie wasn't caught up in the Madison Avenue image like some people on the team.

At the time, Garvey and his first wife, Cindy, were appearing prominently on television commercials and newspaper ads. One word led to another, as words often do, and the next thing anyone knew the pitcher and the first baseman were rolling around on the clubhouse carpet. The clubhouse happened to be in Shea Stadium, and New York is one of the very worst places to be if you're trying to keep a low profile.

Sutton refused to comment on the incident, which was a little out of character. Meanwhile, public interest mounted and the fans chose up sides—mostly Garvey's. At the end of the road trip, Don called a press conference and read a statement in which he expressed his regret. He ended the statement with an odd and startling declaration: "Thank God for Steve Garvey."

Garvey's reaction was icy: "He still hasn't apologized."

And this is baseball: Sutton pitched that same night, and the first play in the field that night was a ground ball to the first baseman, who threw to the pitcher, covering for the out. As Sutton started back to the mound, he patted Garvey on the back. No one would ever have guessed that anything was wrong.

And this, too, is baseball: Sutton probably received more publicity over that encounter with Garvey than he did breaking Drysdale's club records for wins, games, starts, and strikeouts.

When Sutton came to Houston, he had already mapped out the rest of his career, something that was almost alien to me. He had by then 239 wins, and he had projected how many starts he would need over how many seasons to reach 300. He was very much like Rose in the honest and unabashed way he laid out his goals. He was way ahead of his time in that he made his feelings known to his manager—Houston's Bill Virdon—that he was willing to leave a game in the sixth or seventh inning and turn over a lead to the bull-pen for safekeeping.

He didn't have to rationalize. It was a very practical approach. The Astros had a terrific bullpen, featuring Dave Smith and Joe Sambito, and they protected a lot of leads. The other benefit was that Sutton put less wear and tear on his arm.

Within a few seasons everybody in baseball would be thinking along these terms, but at the start of the 1980s the mindset was still rooted in the past. There was a question of pride, of manhood. Pitchers wanted to complete the games they started. They expected the manager or pitching coach to come out and rip the ball from their hands. One thing you didn't do was volunteer to come out before your time.

Sutton caught some very snide criticism over this policy, as he knew he would. But he answered to his own conscience and his own schedule. I don't mean to evoke the different-drummer theme. Don wasn't driven by any desire to be unconventional. It was, in fact, his remarkable discipline and ability to stay focused that enabled him to put up Hall of Fame numbers.

I don't know if Cooperstown was on his agenda or not, but he checked everything else. He never led the league in wins or strikeouts, but he won 324 games, and held the record of 20 consecutive seasons with at least 100 strikeouts. He never won a Cy Young award, an omission we have in common. But he pitched 200 innings in each of his first 21 seasons, except for 1981, shortened by a players' strike.

In an industry where twenty is a magic number, Sutton had only one 20-win season. When he joined the 300 club, in June 1986, every other member had at least three. Now there is one other pitcher with two (guy named Ryan).

Sutton understood what the judgment would be on his career, and he anticipated, correctly, the hurdles he would have to overcome.

"In this country," he said, "we put labels on everything. The same people might make Gucci clothes and J. C. Penney clothes, but the Gucci label means it's better. You can go nineteen-nine and be brilliant and another guy can go twenty-twelve with a lot of luck—but he's still going to be thought of as better. Because twenty wins is a label; without it you're not an outstanding pitcher, you're J. C. Penney."

Don said he didn't have a problem accepting that standard, and I believe him. "I know where I fit in," he said. "Just behind Tom Seaver and Steve Carlton and Catfish Hunter. And I shouldn't even be mentioned in the same breath as Koufax or Drysdale or Bob Gibson or Juan Marichal. I may wind up with more wins, but I won't be better. I can't *dominate* a ballgame—which is the only way you can win twenty with thirty-three starts a year in a five-man rotation. I'm a technician, a workman. When I'm through, people are going to look at my record and say, 'Did *he* do that?' "

Many were surprised that Don would elect to leave the Dodgers after fifteen years of glory and distinction and occasional conflict. More were surprised that he would turn down a chance to play for the Yankees, where the lights never dim on Broadway, where the TV networks drool over any jock who can talk in complete sentences. And he was already thinking of a career in broadcasting.

But he liked Houston, and, if I remember correctly, he liked the quality of the relief pitchers. When he came to us that spring, it was fresh from the fifth one-game playoff in National League history. They needed to sweep us in the final three-game series of the season to force a playoff, and they did it. They trailed by three games on Friday and by three runs on Sunday and they caught us. It was like catching lightning in a Dixie cup.

What I remember about that series, in October 1980, was Sutton ambling out to get the last out in the bottom of the ninth, with the tying and winning runs on base. It was the kind of theatrical gesture they love in Los Angeles.

In the Houston dugout, we asked ourselves what Sutton was doing walking out of the bullpen. He had started two nights earlier and had not appeared in relief all year. Also, this development did not exactly square with the reputation he had acquired recently for being somewhat selfish.

It turned out that the answer started with Koufax, the Dodger hero of another day, the finest pitcher in the game when Sutton and I were rookies in 1966.

As the Dodgers hung close in the third game, Koufax wandered into the empty office of Tommy Lasorda to watch the final innings on television. When the disabled Reggie Smith strolled by, Koufax wondered idly if Sutton might be able to work an inning if a crisis occurred. (Never mind that the series had been one long crisis; the Dodgers had used up their entire bullpen.)

Smith offered to find out. He legged it down the tunnel to the dugout, where he found Sutton sitting at the end of the bench with his feet propped up. "Hey, old-timer," said Reggie, "can you get an out?"

His answer was a reflex. "Yeah, if I have to."

The next voice heard was Smith's, shouting down to Lasorda: "Hey, Tommy. Tommy. The old guy says he can get an out if you need him."

Sutton picks up the story: "I walked down to the bullpen and they handed me a ball and they had two catchers waiting. I hadn't warmed up ten minutes when the phone rang. I thought I was going to be an insurance policy in case the game went fifteen innings. But all I had to get was one out."

Sutton relieved young Steve Howe with runners at first and third, and retired pinch hitter Denny Walling on a roller to second base. The Dodgers won, 4-3.

That win forced a tie-breaking playoff on Monday, and Lasorda had an interesting decision to make. He had used a chubby rookie left-hander named Fernando Valenzuela in short relief in each of the previous three games, and the Astros' hitters had been helpless against him. We didn't know who he was, but all the Astros players hoped Lasorda wouldn't decide to give him a start and see how far he could go.

The Dodgers had veteran Dave Goltz as their other option. Signed to a big free agent contract, Goltz had been a total bust that season, but he was rested. Lasorda went with Goltz, hoping he would rise to the occasion.

The Astros had Joe Niekro and his knuckleball ready to go. Coming off a 20-win season, his second in a row, Niekro was masterful. Art Howe hit a three-run homer and Houston coasted, 7-1, avoiding what would have been a fourth straight loss and one of the most total collapses in baseball lore.

The Astros lost to the Phillies in a dramatic league championship series, with four of the five games going into extra innings.

We had lost J. R. Richard during the season. The 6'-8" right-hander suffered a stroke from a blood clot that had gone undetected, a dreadful experience that left a lot of guilty feelings around the club and among the fans. J. R. had complained of a dead arm, and when the doctors couldn't find the problem the reaction was predictable. There wasn't much sympathy for someone who couldn't or wouldn't pitch with his team in a pennant race.

Richard underwent lifesaving surgery, and he wasn't going to be back that season or any other. The Astros were able to overcome the setback because Vern Ruhle, a perfect example of the thinking pitcher, won twelve games in the second half of the season. He did it with a decidedly average fastball but absolute command of the mound. I doubt that many of the fans today even know the name, but it was a thrill to watch Vern Ruhle chop up the hitters.

The signing of Don Sutton was the move everyone expected to put us in the World Series in 1981. It didn't. In another script by Edgar Allan Poe, the Dodgers, our old nemesis and Don's old team, beat us in the best-of-five West Division playoff. I beat Fernando in the opener but lost the fifth game to Jerry Reuss.

When the Astros showed signs of slippage in 1982 and it became obvious that our lineup didn't pack the run-scoring punch that would help him realize his goals, Sutton asked to be traded in midseason. Having analyzed all the contending teams, Don indicated a preference for the Milwaukee Brewers, a club loaded with power hitters. The Astros obliged him.

I don't recall any shock or dismay or contempt. Don was candid and the Astros saw a chance to make a package deal for three prospects, including a fine outfielder, Kevin Bass.

Sutton helped pitch the Brewers into the World Series, and he continued on his steady course toward 300 wins. He moved on to the Athletics and then the Angels. On a clear June day in 1986, before a home crowd at Anaheim Stadium, Sutton beat the Texas Rangers, 5-1. He had become only the sixth pitcher to win 300 games and strike out 3,000 batters.

And in a closing of the circle, he went back to the Dodgers for his 23rd and final season in 1988.

I have nice memories of Sutton, playing with him, watching him adjust the mood in the clubhouse. The other pitchers were always riding him about whatever interview had been printed in that day's paper. Joe Niekro, whose blond locks had gotten a little wispy, had held the floor for a few minutes when Sutton said softly but ominously, "Are you finished? No hurry, but when you are, I'm going to start in on your . . . hair."

Knucksie clammed up instantly.

Sutton's stories usually had a point or a twist. He loved the parts of the game that were subtle, and he wasn't afraid to appear grateful. I thought he would make a terrific broadcaster, and he has.

He said the best baseball advice anyone ever gave him came from his sixth-grade teacher, who taught him to pitch when he was twelve. Henry Roper was his name. He told Don, "Change speeds and throw strikes. As long as you're throwing the ball over the plate, everybody has to work. If you walk 'em, you're the only one working."

That lesson was his ticket to stop counting soybeans. He signed with the Dodgers in 1965 for $7,500, and that spring he got to pitch batting practice to the varsity. He caught Drysdale's eye and went on to win 23 games in his first season in the minors.

When Koufax and Drysdale teamed up in 1966 for their two-man holdout, an opening was created for Sutton. "Alston was forced to pitch Bill Singer and me about forty innings," he said. "I stayed busy that spring and I made the club."

In his first exhibition game, against Detroit, Sutton struck out Al Kaline on a 3-and-2 pitch with a sweeping curve. Kaline dropped his bat and stared at him. Then he said, "Hey, kid. This is only spring training. You don't throw curve balls on three-and-two in the spring."

Sutton didn't speak. But he wanted to say, "Hey, I'm just trying to make the club." Which he did. In contrast to mine, his rookie year was the kind you paste in your scrapbook. Drysdale would take him aside and go over the hitters; even better, he would tell him what to wear and how much to tip.

He remembers his first road trip, eating alone in the hotel dining room. On two separate occasions, the waitress leaned over and said, "Your check has been taken care of," and she pointed once to Drysdale and another time to Koufax.

Anytime I pitched against Catfish Hunter, I could be certain of two things. One, my team, the Angels, wouldn't score many runs. And two, no matter what we did, his expression wouldn't change. From looking at him you could never tell if he was winning or losing, if he had given up a homer or gotten a strikeout.

This kind of self-control had to be a wonderful asset to a pitcher who worked for both Charles O. Finley and George Steinbrenner, two owners renowned for upsetting the fragile egos on their teams.

That thick Carolina drawl couldn't conceal the fact that Hunter had a big league mind. Rollie Fingers was on the mound for the Athletics late in a 1974 World Series game, and Hunter was loosening up on the side on his own, not expecting to be used, just getting the kinks out.

"Alvin Dark told me I was going in. I said, 'What are you talking about?' And I could feel my heart pounding in my chest, walking out there on the field. I'm on the mound and Dark tells me, 'This guy can't hit a curve without a paddle. What are you gonna throw him?'

"I said, 'Fastball.' He said, 'What?!! Why?'

"I said, 'Because I don't have a curve ball today.' So I struck him out on five straight fastballs. Later, Dark told me, 'Glad you didn't throw him a curve. He probably would've killed it.'"

The game has changed, he observes, as most of us do, and not altogether to his liking. Pitchers used to throw inside, below the shoulders, all the time, he pointed out, "to let a batter know he had done something you didn't like." Now you can't go inside without starting a brawl, or so it seems.

A statue of Hunter has been erected in his hometown, rural Hertford, North Carolina, a tribute to a Hall of Fame career that included a perfect game. He accomplished that feat in 1968, disposing of 27 Minnesota batters in a row for the Oakland A's. Perfect games had been thrown before, but this was the first time a pitcher had done it while wearing a green and gold uniform with white shoes.

More or less on the spot, Finley rewarded Catfish with a $5,000 bonus and a word of caution to keep his composure. The last time Finley had forked over a lump sum to Hunter, he answered to the name of James. He was nineteen years old, the bonus was $75,000 to turn pro, and his career nearly ended before it ever started.

A few months earlier, during his senior year in high school, he went rabbit hunting one day with one of his older brothers, Pete, whose shotgun accidentally discharged. When James, the youngest of ten children, looked at his foot, the left little toe was missing. Of course, he hadn't done it on purpose. A kid who will soon have $75,000 in his pants has a lot to live for, even one going to work for Charlie Finley.

But you can say quite truthfully that his career started with a bang.

"A lot of people thought I'd never play again," he said, "or that the injury would make me less effective. But it didn't. When I came back, I hit a line drive over the second baseman's head and turned it into an inside-the-park home run. The scouts decided, 'If he can run the bases like that he sure as hell can pitch.'

"Before I signed with the A's," he said, "they sent me to the Mayo Clinic to examine my foot. They assured me I would have ninety-five percent use of it. He knew he wasn't getting damaged goods."

As James Hunter, he still would have five seasons of 20 wins or more and pitch in the World Series six out of seven years—an astonishing record—with the Athletics and the Yankees. But it was Charles O. Finley, with his shrewd marketing instincts, who knew how much more notoriety he would get as "Catfish" Hunter.

Nicknames are unnecessary and often silly things, but I have learned firsthand that the fans love them and the media will go to some lengths to manufacture them. I received mine, "The Ryan Express," during my years with the Angels. It was inspired by a popular war movie starring Frank Sinatra called *Von Ryan's Express*.

Some names make good copy but never cross the line into real usage. I can't imagine anyone calling Walter Johnson "The Big Train" or Tom Seaver "Tom Terrific." I can assure you, in my years around Seaver I never once heard anyone say to him, "Hey, Terrif', how goes it?" But Catfish made the grade, even if it was entirely contrived.

Not long after he was drafted from high school, Finley paid a visit to Hertford. Finley asked him what he liked to do and he said, "Hunt and fish." Now here was the owner of a major league team talking to a nineteen-year-old prospect, trying to educate him about the big adventure that stretched ahead.

A player needs a good nickname, Finley told him, and yours is going to be "Catfish." Then he made up a story to go with it: "When you were six years old, you ran away from home to fish and by the time your parents found you, why, you had already caught two catfish and were just about to bring up a third. Got that? Now repeat it to me . . ."

Hunter went along with it so well, the story became as much a part of his career as his Hall of Fame stats.

Given his background—and that nickname—there was a tendency to label Catfish as another Li'l Abner type who relied on raw country talent. But he was aggressive, smart, and attuned to what was going on around him. He learned in his rookie year that baseball wasn't always fair.

In one of his first appearances, he pitched in relief of West Stock at a game in Cleveland in 1965. With two on and two out, he coaxed the next two batters to hit ground balls to shortstop. Bert Campaneris booted them both.

The next thing he knew, manager Alvin Dark was on the way to the mound to remove him. "I'm thinking, 'Why is he taking *me* out? I did *my* job.' "

The lesson here, of course, is that in a team sport one man pays the price for everybody—the pitcher.

I always thought that one of the things that made Catfish so effective was his level of concentration. On the mound nothing distracted him. His emotions never changed. He had an ideal temperament. "I never worried too much about base-runners," he said. "I just thought if you throw strikes and the guy hits it, you're still going to get him out. I had a coach who told me, 'Make 'em hit it. If the batter is running down the line, there's always a chance he might have a heart attack, and he's going to be out. But if you walk him, and he has a heart attack, they can just send in a pinch runner.' "

He was a linebacker in high school and he pitched with a linebacker's mentality. "I loved football," he said. "Loved the contact. And I think that part of my personality carried over to the mound. I always said I was too dumb to get scared. All I wanted to know about the hitter is where he liked the baseball, and where his power was, because I planned to put the ball someplace else. It was just that simple."

There is a slice of truth worth repeating in that humble

observation. Not everyone subscribed to Hunter's ideas, but he kept coming up with them. He was the only pitcher I can remember who never threw a breaking pitch during his warm-ups. "I never knew what kind of stuff I had until I faced the first batter," he said, "but I don't think you find out warming up, either. I just wanted to get loose. Anyway, à lot of people think you need four or five pitches to be effective, but I thought all you needed was two that you could throw for strikes. Sure, if you only have two and neither of them is working you're in for a short night.

"It helps to have a philosophy. I think too many pitchers outthink themselves. If I had a good catcher who called for a certain pitch, I usually threw it. I rarely shook him off. To win at any level you need confidence, even if you have to fake it. I always thought Blue Moon Odom would go on to be great, with the stuff he had, but he had an average career. I thought the same thing about Jim Nash, who won twelve games in a row at one time. I don't know what happened. Maybe they didn't believe in themselves enough, or realize how good they could be. You can't have doubts about yourself."

Catfish Hunter didn't. Neither did anyone else.

When Orel Hershiser joined the Dodgers he had confidence, but not everyone understood why. He didn't exactly have the stamp of instant stardom. He had been cut from his high school team. Didn't make the traveling squad as a college freshman at Bowling Green. Spent five unimpressive seasons in the minors. Then, as a rookie relief pitcher in 1984, he was about one more good pounding away from being sent down. An injury to Jerry Reuss gave him a chance to start, and he pitched well. He was on his way, a Cinderfella story.

He hadn't taken the fast track to the big leagues. Most of all, he didn't look like an athlete. If anything, he looked anemic. I'm not knocking him; I'm quoting him.

This is Orel's self-portrait: "Let's face it. I'm just a pale guy with glasses, long arms and a sunken chest. I look like I never lifted a weight. I look like I work in a flour factory. People compare me to Clark Kent and Superman, but Clark Kent at least had a good build. I'm Jimmy Olsen."

Whoever he was, the Dodgers had found another winner. Hitters got mad just looking at him. He was deceptive, a late bloomer who grew three inches (to six-foot-three) and gained almost thirty pounds (to 182) in the six months after his sophomore season. It turned out he was pretty good at ice hockey, golf, pool, whatever he tried.

In his second season he went 19-3. He was a .500 pitcher with low-scoring Dodger teams the next two years, but he was getting smarter. You hear about the "book" that pitchers keep on hitters. Some of us store information in our heads. Some keep notebooks. Hershiser fed everything into a personal computer.

In 1988 he broke one of the records I thought was unbreakable. He pitched 59 consecutive scoreless innings to better by one-third of an inning the mark held by Don Drysdale, the former Dodger. Drysdale had rejoined his old club as a broadcaster and was in the booth the night Hershiser went for it against the Padres.

He needed nine shutout innings and, as fate or luck would have it, Andy Hawkins was holding the Dodgers runless and the game would go into extra innings. (He left after ten, and the Dodgers lost in the sixteenth, 2-1.) Out of respect for Drysdale, he said, Orel offered to come out after tying the mark. I can admire his gesture. But I can't imagine a manager or a pitching coach giving it a thought, and Tommy Lasorda and Ron Perranoski ignored him.

Before Drysdale, the record had belonged to Walter Johnson, who set it in 1913.

What both Drysdale and Hershiser did, in my mind, far exceeded Johnson's achievement. Just to complete six straight games in the majors today is an oddity; to do it without giving up a run is staggering. Orel did it with a nasty sinker, an above-average fastball and curve, and by setting up the hitters with fine patience. In the record-breaking game, he retired Tony Gwynn on a ground ball to second base four times.

The Astros were one of the teams he shut out, so I saw some of those scoreless innings firsthand. At times he was overpowering. When he wasn't, he was exasperating—giving up hits and snuffing out threats; offering hope, then denying it. Sometimes he was lucky, sometimes inspired, but always unscored upon as the Dodgers pushed through September and into the playoffs.

The streak darned near overshadowed the complete season he had. In the postseason, he was both brilliant and heroic. He saved a game in relief and pitched a shutout against the favored New York Mets. Then, in the World Series, he pitched another shutout and won twice, including the fifth and final game. He was voted the most valuable player both times.

This is how his mind works: He was running out of gas in the eighth inning of the clincher, with Jose Canseco at bat and two on, and worried that Lasorda might pull him. "Now, I don't want Tommy to know I'm tired," he said, "so I have to act confident. But if I act *too* confident, he's going to know I'm faking it, so I have to strike the right balance there." He stayed in, got Canseco to pop up to the first baseman, and struck out Dave Parker to end the threat.

Thinking pitchers have at least one thing in common: pain. Pain makes you think even harder, and the pain came to Hershiser after the glory of 1988. That effort tore away at the sinew of his shoulder. He was a .500 pitcher again the next year, 15 and 15. He missed most of the 1990 season and half of 1991 after radical shoulder surgery.

The first start of his comeback, the last week in May, had some strange trappings. Hershiser picked the game he wanted to pitch, and it was against the Astros, by then my former team, loaded with rookies and doomed to finish last. He wrote a column about his injury and his pain, heavy with spiritual meaning, that ran in the *Los Angeles Times* the morning of the game. Now, players can sympathize with each other's physical problems, but no team enjoys feeling chosen. I know the Astros didn't.

Orel's return drew forty thousand fans on a Wednesday night and was given a big play by the national media. The night was charged. The Astros felt it, too. In the top of the first, they squibbed three grounders through the infield and two of their rookies lashed clean singles. Hershiser gave up four runs, one on a balk, and was in trouble the next three innings. Each time he showed his old mettle, and left for a pinch hitter after four innings, trailing 4-2.

After the game he said he wanted to take his turn in the rotation like any other pitcher, without all the hype. He said he was just a member of the pitching staff and would have to earn his way, like everyone else.

I'm sure his opponents preferred to see him in that light and maybe the other Dodger pitchers did, too. L.A. lost to the Braves in the National League West race, but the Dodgers had reason to be encouraged. Hershiser finished 7-2 and looked like himself: a tall, gawky righthander with glasses, at thirty-three trying to regain a great talent.

In September 1964, on his eighteenth birthday, Larry Dierker made his major league debut against the San Francisco Giants in Houston. I was listening to the game on the radio in Alvin, and it struck me as an exciting way to celebrate a birthday.

Dierker, tall, thin, and blond, didn't appear to have any nerves. When he took the sign or studied a hitter, he never seemed to blink. A Houston writer, John Wilson, dubbed him "the fishy-eyed guy."

Larry lost to the Giants that night, 7-1, but he struck out Willie Mays and Jim Ray Hart in the first inning to retire the side with two runners on base, giving the fans a preview of better times to come. They were hungry in Houston not only for a winner, but to see one of their bonus babies prove his worth.

I always felt a kind of bond with Dierker. I reached the majors two years after him, and when Larry retired he became a broadcaster with the Astros. He was the color analyst when I joined the club in 1980. I don't know which surprises me more, that he has been retired now for a dozen years or that I still haven't.

I relate to a story his teammates used to tell about him. On the last day of the 1964 season, Dierker came out of the bullpen to pitch in a losing cause against the Dodgers in his hometown, Los Angeles. The Dodgers led by 11-1 when Houston came up for its final turn at bat in the top of the ninth. The game had been an embarrassment, but on the Houston bench Larry felt good. He had pitched four runless innings in relief. His family was in the stands watching.

On an impulse he turned to Bob Aspromonte, sitting next to him. "Bob," he said, "you're hitting .280, isn't that right?"

Startled, not sure where the question would lead, Aspromonte just nodded.

"Gee, that's great," said the rookie. "You know, if I get the Dodgers out in the last of the ninth, that's what my earned run average will be—two-eight-oh."

Aspromonte did a double take. He looked at the scoreboard. Then he turned to his teenage teammate. "Larry," he pointed out, gently. "We're ten runs behind. There isn't going to *be* any last of the ninth."

Young or old, the pitcher is often lost in his own world. But Dierker was a thinking pitcher, always figuring, measuring, taking in information. He was not yet twenty-one when he struck out Frank Howard three times in a row. Howard, who broke in with the Dodgers, was one of the game's natural wonders, 6'-8", with a swing so wild he could knock the air out of the park.

Later, in the clubhouse, a veteran relief pitcher named

Hal Woodeshick asked Larry who told him how to pitch to Howard. Dierker said he had been tipped off by his brother, Rick, who suggested he throw the big man a breaking ball outside.

"Who does your brother pitch for?" asked Woodeshick.

"He pitches in the Pony League," said Larry. Rick was fourteen, but he watched the Dodgers on television.

Dierker was one of the rare pitchers who made the jump from high school to the majors with only a few innings in the minors. The Houston club flew him into Saint Louis during a road trip to work him out the week they signed him, and he warmed up on the sidelines during batting practice. The gates were still closed, and in the empty ballpark his fastball echoed like a canon going off. Even Stan Musial, then near the end of his magnificent career, left the batting cage and strolled over to watch.

I knew that feeling a few times early in my career and I can tell you that a kid pitcher doesn't get paid a nicer compliment. Ellis (Cot) Deal was the Houston pitching coach then and someone asked him if the unsmiling young right-hander had received a bonus to sign. "If he didn't," said Deal, "then we stole him." As it turned out, they gave him $60,000 to sign, and that was one of Houston's best investments.

In 1969, while the Mets were winning the pennant, Dierker pitched 300 innings and won twenty games for Houston. He had been limited to 100 pitches early in his career, one of the first instances of a prospect working with a pitch count.

That decision helped compensate for the fact that Houston had rushed him to the majors. Eventually, Larry developed a sore arm, and he finished his career with the Cardinals in 1977, trying to pitch his way through the pain. He told me that he knew it was time to quit when he couldn't comb his hair.

He had been the youngest player on either team the night he faced the Giants in his first start. In 1976, he pitched a no-hitter, against Montreal, and no one on the field had been around as long, twelve seasons.

Only once in his twelve years with Houston, Dierker confided, had he ever faced a batter and not known who he was. He mistook him for another player, threw him the wrong pitch, and retired him on a popup.

Sometimes you need to think lucky.

NOLAN RYAN'S
TOP TEN
LUCKIEST PITCHERS

(GOOD THINGS HAPPENED WHEN THEY PITCHED*)

1. Lew Burdette, Braves, 21-15, ERA 4.07, 1959.

2. Paul Splittorff, Royals, 20-11, ERA 3.98, 1973.

3. Dennis Leonard, Royals, 20-11, ERA 3.79, 1980.

4. Denny McLain, Tigers, 20-14, ERA 3.92, 1966.*

5. Bill Gullickson, Tigers, 20-9, ERA 3.90, 1991.

6. Charley Kerfeld, Astros, 11-2 in relief, 1986*.

7. Bill Dawley, Astros, 11-4 in relief, 1983*.

8. Bruce Hurst, Red Sox and Padres, nine straight seasons with 11 or more wins, 1983–1991, career ERA 3.85.

9. Tom Gorman, Mets, gave up two game-tying, two-out homers to Atlanta in relief, one in the 18th inning at 3:30 in the morning, and got the win after the Mets scored five runs in the top of the 19th. Game was played July 4th and 5th, 1985.

10. Doug Dascenzo, Cubs, 0-0, in relief, 1990.**

* While it lasted.
** An outfielder, Dascenzo didn't allow a run in three mop-up appearances.

The
Intimidators

The facts have grown hazy with time, but I heard the story from those involved on both sides of it, and believe this account to be more or less reliable.

First, let me clarify a term. The game that was played when I came on to the scene in the 1960s only faintly resembles in some respects the product you see today. There were clearly defined, if unwritten, rules or codes. One of these had to do with pitching inside to a hitter. You were allowed to brush him back off the plate. You might actually knock him down. Such actions were not yet regarded as grounds for court cases. Each team had its own method of handling the issue, and one or more pitchers eager to take on the account. They were known as headhunters, or enforcers, or, in the more polite reference, intimidators.

Long after Don Drysdale retired to the broadcasting

booth, his opinions on this subject were never vague. "I always believed," he said, "that it was either them or us and nothing was going to stand in my way. Take no prisoners. If you were going to lose, take down the s.o.b. who beat you, too. Make him feel the cost of victory. That was the Sal Maglie philosophy and it was good enough for me.

"I wasn't one of those guys who woke up mad on the day I pitched. I think if you dwelled on a game all day, you'd become mentally whipped. When I got to the ballpark, which was my office, and put on the uniform, I guess I worked myself into a frenzy. It all locked in when you saw that first batter staring at you from the plate."

Drysdale still holds the National League career record for hit batsmen, with 154.

"I was the kind of guy," he says, "who would hit his grandmother to win a game and sing songs at a baseball writers' dinner the next night. I had the belief, as did [Sal] Maglie, that for every one of my teammates who went down, two players from the other team had to go down. When I was on the mound, the Dodgers knew they were going to be protected. I got some terrific support through the years, at bat and in the field, and I have no doubt it had something to do with the fact that I stood up for my teammates."

Drysdale was a settler of scores, real or imagined. In 1968, before the All-Star game in Houston, his catcher, Tom Haller, spotted Rusty Staub of the Astros poking around in Don's shaving kit. Rusty was checking on whether Drysdale happened to be carrying around any of those famous "foreign substances." He resented this breach of his privacy and made a mental note of it. Later in the season, he sent Staub flopping in the dirt with a pitch high and inside.

"That's for looking in my damned shaving kit," shouted Drysdale. Rusty never said a word.

I'll say this for Big D.: with him, everything was personal. He admitted that he once threw at a Houston player because he didn't like the cartoons they kept showing in the

Astrodome on the wide scoreboard in center field. When the hitter got to his feet, Drysdale called out: "Tell them to cut that friggin' cartoon short!"

Another story that comes to mind involves Drysdale and Turk Farrell, who equaled Don in power and temper and color, if not in success. When he was with the Phillies, Farrell had the unusual honor of being sent into a game in relief of the great Robin Roberts—and for the express purpose of hitting Drysdale with a pitch.

Drysdale and Roberts had been the starters, and as the game wore on, several Phillies had been forced to dive into the nearest foxhole. Not all of them dived in time. Gene Mauch, the manager of the Phillies, considered it a personal affront when his players were plugged by an opposing pitcher.

When Drysdale came to bat, Mauch stood up in the dugout and flashed a sign to the mound that meant "Dust him." Robin Roberts, a true sportsman, shook his head. Mauch went to the mound and the answer was still no. With that he motioned to the bullpen and waved in Farrell, a big, hardheaded Boston Irishman.

"You know Robin," Turk would explain, when he told his version of the story, "he wouldn't hurt a fly."

So Mauch, who needed someone who didn't object to hurting a fly if that fly had been decking Philadelphia's hitters, found his man. "Farrell," he ordered, as he handed him the ball, "put Drysdale on his butt."

"I didn't really want to knock down Drysdale," said Turk, in the slightly injured tone of a man who saw his duty and knew he would catch hell for it. "I didn't have anything against him."

Farrell's first pitch sailed three feet over Drysdale's head, and Mauch perched himself on the top step of the dugout, cupped his hands, and yelled so they could hear him on the Dodgers' side of the field: "I said *knock him down*."

This time the Los Angeles pitcher went sprawling, and as he brushed himself off he was visibly seething. Then as now, Don was a nice-looking guy, well groomed, and he didn't like dirt any better than the next fellow.

The next pitch was closer to the plate than Farrell intended. Drysdale swung and drove it into the gap in left center for a double. As he stepped a few feet off second base, he shouted to the mound, "There's your bleeping knockdown pitch, Farrell."

Now it was Turk's turn to get mad. He wheeled and fired toward second, trying to pick off the runner, possibly. Instead the ball plunked Drysdale in the back, right between the shoulder blades. "There's your bleeping two-base hit, Drysdale," he said.

So it came to pass that the very next season, the Phillies traded Farrell to, of all teams, the Los Angeles Dodgers. The first thing he did when he joined the club in spring training was look up Drysdale. Farrell, 6'-4" and barrel-chested, feared no one. But Drysdale stood 6'-6" and had a memory at least that long.

"Well, Don, ol' buddy," said Turk, slapping Drysdale on the back. "We're teammates now."

"Yeah, it's a good thing, too. I had your name on my list." Drysdale then showed him the inside band of his baseball cap. He had half a dozen names written there in ink, his primary targets for the coming season, and one of them was Turk Farrell.

They went on to become good friends, although Farrell moved on to Houston and other teams. He was the first player with star quality the old Colt .45s produced. Out of the expansion pool they had picked such names as Bobby Shantz, the glory tot of the old Philadelphia A's, who broke in when Connie Mack was the manager. But Shantz had almost nothing left by then and they traded him to the Cards in midseason.

Farrell went on to lose 20 games in the team's first year, and as he pointed out, "You had to be a damned good pitcher to lose twenty. Otherwise the manager wouldn't keep sending you back out there."

While Drysdale, during most of his career, was known as the pitcher "with the meanest disposition on the mound," Farrell had a nature deep down like a Saint Bernard. Yet he was the enforcer on every team that employed him. Once, after Willie Mays homered twice off him, he decked Willie twice and then hit him in the back.

After the game, Mays accused Farrell of being a bush leaguer, and Turk responded by pointing out that the Houston catcher, Hal Smith, had been drilled by a pitch the previous night. (There were two catchers named Hal Smith; this was the one who played with Pittsburgh and hit a big homer in the 1960 World Series.) "Who is Willie Mays," demanded Farrell, "that you can't knock him down? The Giants knock down poor ol' Hal Smith, and nobody says nothing."

After the next day's papers had made the rounds, Farrell was beaming in the clubhouse: "The boys told me my quotes were real good."

The customs changed when the salaries soared, and hitters suddenly realized that they had million-dollar bodies to protect. But there used to be three basic reasons why a pitcher would throw at a batter: 1) he was crowding the plate, 2) in his last at bat he hit a home run, or 3) the batter before him did.

It is a part of baseball lore that Willie Mays came to dread hitting against Drysdale. As a measure of respect for Willie's power and consistency, Don threw at him a good deal and seemed to take some pleasure in doing so. The cleaning bill that Mays ran up in the years he faced Drysdale must have been substantial.

I remember hearing Drysdale compare batters to a certain kind of motorist. There are some drivers, he said, who would move over a foot to keep their distance from an oncoming car. And then there were others who veered way off to the side of the road.

Don had pegged Mays as one of those nervous drivers who swung over to the soft shoulder of the road. But Willie was also known for his baseball sense. And to start with, Drysdale threw a fastball clocked at better than 95 miles an hour. It also frequently arrived high and inside, especially when the Dodgers were playing the Giants.

The San Francisco pitchers were not shy about retaliating, especially Juan Marichal, and when the teams met the ratio got a little crazy. Drysdale had established his personal formula: "If they flip [knock down] one of ours, I flip two of theirs. If they hit one of ours, I hit two of theirs."

The Giants, it is fair to say, accepted the challenge. On separate occasions, Marichal was involved in fights with Willie Davis and Bill Buckner over pitches that low-bridged them. In one of the scarier incidents of that or any other era, Marichal clobbered John Roseboro with a bat when the Dodger catcher charged him. He was suspended and fined and finished the season ineffectively. Some thought the incident and the notoriety would be the undoing of a pitcher as temperamental as Marichal. But he returned in 1967 to win 25 games.

Roseboro was bloodied but not seriously hurt. He did file a civil suit that was in the courts for a couple of years, one that baseball tried in vain to convince him to drop for the good of the game. "That was *my* head he was beating on," John explained.

That encounter led a lot of people to wonder if there was really room in baseball for vigilantes. Today an umpire can eject a pitcher on the spot if he hits a batter under circumstances that seem suspicious. And a fine and suspension are automatic if one player threatens another with a bat.

Some of what I have written here may strike the outsider as silly and childish, even dangerously so. But it comes under the heading of job protection, of union rules. And how blatantly this business is conducted usually depends on the manager; not many pitchers operate on their own.

I suppose the old-timers did. Early Wynn was deeply offended when a rookie tried to run up on a curveball. He showed his displeasure by calling out, "What's the matter, sonny, the ball not getting there fast enough for you?" On the next pitch he dented the young man's ribs with a fastball.

True, some pitchers are more easily upset than others. The late Mel Ott, the legendary slugger of the New York Giants, had the odd habit of raising his leg like a dog at a fire hydrant when he swung at a pitch. This habit irritated Van Lingle Mungo, the old Brooklyn Dodger fireballer, who invariably would aim one at the ankle of Ott's other leg. "You bat against me like the others do," he shouted, as Ott toppled over. "None of that fancy stuff."

Now, a pitcher could be a fierce competitor without being an intimidator. Bob Gibson happened to be both. On the mound he was just plain mean, and the better he pitched the meaner he got. The first time Bill White, his former roommate with the Cardinals, faced him as a Phillie, Gibson hit him on the arm.

As I heard the story, Gibson screamed: "You s.o.b., you went for the outside ball! That part of the plate belongs to me. If I ever make a mistake inside, all right, but the outside is mine and don't you forget it."

I doubt that this was one of those private jokes between old roomies, and there was nothing to indicate White took it that way. If any pitcher of his time refused to bend to sentiment or friendship, it was Gibson. White commanded enormous respect, so much so that the owners eventually elected him president of the National League.

Do you remember 1968? That was the Year of the Pitcher. Denny McLain won his 31 games for Detroit, and in the National League Gibson worked over 300 innings and had an earned run average of 1.12. I look at that number and rub my eyes. He pitched thirteen shutouts and won twenty-two and I'm still trying to figure out how he lost nine times.

Carl Yastrzemski led the American League in batting that year with an average of .301. And the next season the mound was lowered five inches because the rulemakers thought the pendulum had swung too far in favor of the pitchers. I don't think it had. Guys like Bob Gibson just made it seem that way.

The Tigers and the Cardinals met in the World Series in

'68, and the big shootout was supposed to be between Gibson and McLain. I have heard Tim McCarver talk about catching that game, how Gibson led in the ninth 4-0 with a man on base and nobody out. He struck out Al Kaline, and the crowd in St. Louis, which had been cheering every strike, now just roared and wouldn't stop.

McCarver started to throw the ball back to the mound, then hesitated. In an article in *The New Yorker*, Roger Angell described what happened next: "Gibson, a notoriously swift worker, motioned to his battery mate to return the ball. Instead, McCarver pointed with his gloved hand at something behind Gibson's head. Gibson, staring uncomprehendingly at his catcher, yelled, 'Throw the damned ball back, will you! C'mon, c'mon, c'mon, let's go!' Still holding the ball, McCarver pointed again, and Gibson, turning around, read the illuminated message on the centerfield scoreboard, which perhaps only he in the ballpark had not seen until that moment: 'GIBSON'S FIFTEENTH STRIKEOUT IN ONE GAME TIES THE WORLD SERIES RECORD HELD BY SANDY KOUFAX.' Gibson, at the center of a great tureen of noise, dug at the dirt on the mound with his spikes and then uneasily doffed his cap."

I know that feeling of being interrupted, of being surprised, of wanting to get on with the job. He struck out Norm Cash and Willie Horton to retire the Tigers, setting a Series record with seventeen strikeouts. The next season, it seemed to me, rule tinkering began to favor the hitters.

I make a very strong distinction between the brushback pitch and the beanball. The brushback is a communications tool; it tells the hitter that you are not waiving your right to use the inside portion of the strike zone.

Nothing justifies a beanball, throwing at a batter's head. And I would like to think that no one would. When a Rob Dibble throws *behind* the hitter, head high, you can't make excuses for him. When his temper boils over and he heaves a ball from the mound into the center field seats, hitting a fan on her arm, his teammates need to show their concern. This is a pitcher who is out of control.

The problem is that gray area, when a pitch gets away and does bounce off someone's helmet or worse. A manager is certain it was an accident if a member of his staff threw the ball; he doesn't always give that benefit of the doubt to an opponent.

When Bill Rigney managed the Giants, he complained bitterly about how often Bob Purkey of the Reds threw at Mays. Willie was a more popular target than, say, Mickey Mantle or Stan Musial because he had a habit of leaning over the plate.

But as far as Rigney was concerned, it was automatic that Purkey's first pitch to Mays would be right at his ear. "Everybody knew it was coming," he said, "and it always did, and nobody ever did anything about it."

Rigney gave a good amount of thought to how he might resolve this problem. Then one year at the All-Star game he saw Warren Giles, the president of the National League, sitting with Ford Frick, the commissioner of baseball. "I told them," he said, "it was high time somebody put a stop to pitchers using my man for target practice, and I told them how I planned to do it. I said, the next time we played Cincinnati, and Purkey was pitching, as soon as Purkey came to bat I was going to send my pitcher out to play center field and I was going to bring my center field in to pitch."

Now pause for a moment and consider what effect this might have had on Bob Purkey when Rigney suddenly called time, brought in Mays, and said, "Okay, Willie, he's all yours."

Rigney never had a chance to test his idea. A few days later, a directive went out from the league office stating that no one could pitch unless he was specifically designated on the roster as a pitcher. (I don't know if the rule has been revoked, or if umpires just ignore it, but today teams on occasion bring in a position player to face a few batters and spare their bullpen when games are hopelessly out of reach.)

Of course, the reaction to Rigney's threat said a good

deal about the way baseball chose to deal with a problem.

So the illusion has been created that the rulemakers are opposed to inside pitching, just as the hockey types proclaim that they object to fighting. There are others, such as the late Leo Durocher, who regarded the duster as part of baseball's folklore. "This game," he once said, "isn't played with gingersnaps."

When the Mets came from last place to win the flag in 1969, we took it away from Durocher's Cubs. This was years after his heyday with the Dodgers and Giants, and Leo was an older and supposedly mellower lion in winter. In midseason, when the Mets had begun to make a move, we had our own beanball wars with the Cubs.

We felt sure Durocher had ordered his pitchers to throw at our best young hitters, especially the blacks, Cleon Jones and Tommy Agee. The Cubs kept knocking them down, trying to intimidate them. They won the first two games.

Can you guess who New York's enforcer was going to be? Clean-cut Tom Seaver couldn't wait to get to the mound for the opener of a doubleheader on Sunday, Thinking Man turned Intimidator.

He retired the side in order in the first inning; then Ron Santo, Chicago's most valuable player, led off the next inning. Tom's second pitch just missed grazing his head. Santo did a backflop, and the ball sailed between his flying helmet and his hair. That situation was interesting because nobody told Seaver what to do. Gil Hodges hadn't. But as a young team struggling to gain a toehold, we had to fight back. Tom knew what was expected, and he was the one who had the ball. Any of us would have done it, especially after we lost the first two.

Santo went 0-for-8 that day and we swept the doubleheader, Seaver pitching a complete game and McGraw getting the win in the nightcap in relief.

The next time the teams played, Chicago's Bill Hands hit Seaver with a pitch on his left wrist. In front of everybody, Hodges went up to Tom in the dugout and said, "You hit him.

I don't care if it takes four pitches. Hit him." Seaver finally got him on the leg. That was called sending a message.

Tom pitched the rest of that game with an aching wrist. At one point, he had to call time and tell Jerry Grote not to fire the ball back so hard to the mound. Grote could really sting you. Sometimes he just wanted to keep you alert, but more often he was so emotional he didn't realize he was punishing his own pitcher.

Years later, when Seaver was with Cincinnati, he sat down at a table where Johnny Bench was having breakfast with a friend. The friend turned out to be a retired Ron Santo, whose first words were: "Do you remember that day you knocked me down?" And they all laughed.

Don Drysdale wasn't the only pitcher on the Dodger staff with a reputation for going after the hitters. Roger Craig, who pitched against both of them, thought Stan Williams was even meaner than Drysdale. He just wasn't as well known.

Ron Fairly agreed. "In all the years I played," he said, "Stan was the only pitcher who ever scared me. And he was on *my* team."

Once, Williams threw a ball that glanced off Hank Aaron's batting helmet. After the game he apologized, and Aaron graciously accepted. "You don't understand," Stan told him, "I was trying to hit you in the *neck*."

In between bench-clearing brawls, which seem to occur at least once a year, the issue dies down and you know that the authorities wish it would disappear. But something always happens. Somewhere between 1989 and 1991, the Nasty Boys of Cincinnati happened.

Although there have been honorary members, the Nasty Boys consisted mainly of Rob Dibble and Randy Myers, the hard-throwing relief pitchers, and Norm Charlton, the southpaw who was drafted out of the bullpen to be a starter.

It may be a pure coincidence, but the Reds' pitching coach is none other than Stan Williams.

Dibble was involved in such a strange series of clashes that people began to look at him as if he were a ticking time bomb. In March 1989 he gave up a home run in a spring training game in Florida to a singles hitter. He expressed his anger by throwing folding chairs into a pond beyond the fence in center field and by beating the dugout bench with a bat, leaving several dents in it.

In May, after Terry Pendleton, then of the Cards, singled to drive in a run, he backed up home plate. Then he picked up Pendleton's bat and threw it against the backstop screen. He was suspended four days and fined.

In July, he hit Tim Teufel of the Mets in the back with a pitch, and both teams poured onto the field, fists flailing. He was suspended three days and fined.

In September, the Reds suspended Dibble for "insubordination," possibly for blasting team owner Marge Schott— "If she was a man, someone would have kicked her butt by now." He was fined an undisclosed amount.

The Reds won the pennant wire-to-wire in 1990. Either Dibble lowered his profile or the winning swept away everything else, because his slate was reasonably clean.

It stayed that way until the third game of the 1991 season, when Dibble, distressed after giving up a run-scoring single to the opposing pitcher, Pete Harnisch, threw a fastball behind Eric Yelding, the Houston shortstop. The spindly Yelding, in his first season as a regular, went after Dibble, who outweighed him by at least fifty pounds. Yet another brawl erupted, and the Reds' right-hander again drew a three-day suspension.

I haven't seen Dibble pitch in the flesh—he came into the league after I moved over to the Texas Rangers—but I do know there is a fine line between being a thug and being an intimidator.

I still have friends on the Houston team, and a few with the Reds, including Billy Doran, the former Astro second baseman who tried to act as peacemaker. He arranged a meeting between Yelding and Dibble, who apologized. "I can't say he admitted he was throwing at me," said Eric, "but he did say he was sorry it occurred."

Bob Watson, now the general manager of the Astros, who started his career there and was later a power-hitting first baseman for the Yankees, Braves, and Red Sox, took a harder line. "I have no respect for someone who throws behind a hitter's head," said Watson. "As hard as Dibble throws, he could kill somebody. I know he calls himself intimidating, but there are different ways to go about it. Let's put it this way: His style of pitching stinks."

Still, say this for Dibble: He can take the heat. When Cincinnati paid its first visit to Houston, with the president of the league, Bill White, on hand to monitor both teams, the fans booed his every move. In the process of saving a win for the Reds, all Dibble did was strike out six batters in a row, tying the major league record for consecutive strikeouts by a relief pitcher. "The pressure was on," he said. "The fans were on me pretty bad. All eyes were watching. For my own peace of mind, I had to have a good outing."

I tend to give high marks to a guy who produces in spite of pressure and distractions.

My own impression is that Rob Dibble is one of those people who can cross an intersection, and cars crash head-on behind him. He also has the knack of turning a routine moment into a controversy.

In late April, he closed out a 4-3 win over the Cubs but was unhappy with his effort. He stood on the mound and heaved the ball into the center field stands, where it hit a schoolteacher on the arm. He was suspended for four days.

In July, in his first game back after serving the Yelding suspension, Dibble fielded a squeeze bunt by Doug Dascenzo and then hit the runner in the back of the leg with his throw to first. He was ejected from the game. He said it was an accident, but the accusations flew.

Even the calm and thoughtful Billy Doran, one of the best people in the game, was running low on patience. "There's no reason for it," said Doran, referring to the throw that clipped Dascenzo. "He's going to have to grow up and understand that you have to be able to control yourself. I don't think he really knew what he was doing. I think he had a brain cramp. It didn't look good.

"Rob is as big-hearted and as nice a guy as you'd ever meet. He does things, then one second later he's sorry it happened. But sooner or later, if you keep making the same mistakes over and over again, "I'm sorry' doesn't mean anything.

"I've talked to him about it. A lot of guys have. The reason guys talk to him is because they like him. If he was a derelict and no one cared about him, we wouldn't say anything."

Up to now, these episodes haven't hurt Dibble's effectiveness, except for the eighteen days in suspensions when he was not available to his club. But I had seen the pattern before; Dibble was now in a nearly impossible position, trying to defend his character and his emotional stability.

He told reporters that he was no different than anyone else, as normal as your next-door neighbor. The writers replied maybe so, if your neighbor was Rambo.

It isn't unusual for a baseball player, or any athlete, to undergo a transformation when he gets into the arena. Don Drysdale talked about it. I know that I undergo a feeling of change that is almost physical. Your face feels tighter. Inside you feel the juices boiling.

Norm Charlton, Dibble's roommate, put it this way: "If you talk about Dibs, you're talking about two different people. On the field, he's all adrenaline, intensity, win at all costs. . . . Off the field, he's a nice guy, a family man. He's really shy. You'd think he'd be the kind of guy to grab a waiter by the tie and send his food back if it's not done right. But if he orders it well done and they bring it out raw, he won't say a word."

Hardest of all is the pressure a pitcher as emotional as Dibble puts on himself. Can he mature as a pitcher without losing the edge that has made him a winner?

Near the end of the 1991 season, when the furor over Dibble and his capers had quieted down, Norm Charlton caused a mild sensation by bringing into the open the tribal hatreds between pitchers and hitters. He did this by announcing that he had deliberately hit Mike Scioscia, the Dodgers' catcher, with a pitch.

The reason he gave raised eyebrows around the league. He said Scioscia had been stealing the catcher's signs from second base and relaying them to the hitter. Certainly, few pitchers can succeed if the hitters know what pitch is coming. But sign stealing is an acceptable part of the strategy of the game. It isn't like wiretapping the phone line a football team uses between the press box and the bench. If a pitcher thinks his signs are being stolen, the simple remedy is to change them.

Over the years, pitchers have learned to make baseballs go fast and slow; move in and out; up and down. They have learned to throw them from behind their gloves and from different angles. They have learned to do all these things with dispassion, without revealing themselves. As Joe Garagiola has said, they have the look of a house with all the lights on but with nobody home.

This sort of inscrutability lies at the center of the art of pitching. For more than a hundred years, moundsmen have kept hitters wondering, "What is he going to do next?"

Inning after inning, hitters keep coming up to the plate, flexing their muscles. Sooner or later, they are bound to get in some licks. A clever pitcher mixes his pattern of pitches to keep a hitter off-balance throughout the game. Sometimes he can do this to all nine hitters and pitch a shutout, even a no-hitter. But the odds are that, most of the time, the hitters will drive the pitcher out of the game.

The best and most confident hitters will say, "I don't care what he throws, I'm going to lean in and hit it."

This is where the brushback pitch comes in; this is where defense becomes offense. When a hitter leans in and takes a good rip, the pitcher fires the next one under his hands. Until recently, there was little downside. The hitter was aware of the tactic and was usually prepared to get out of the way.

On the surface, this would seem to be a flimsy defense. The reality is that hitters are infrequently hit by pitches. Dibble, with a fastball estimated at up to 100 miles an hour, had hit exactly *one* batter in 143 innings when his streak of troubles began.

All things considered, a good high fastball, six or eight inches off the inside corner of the plate, is a fine weapon. You send a not very subtle message at the price of a ball in the count. Sometimes the hitter will inadvertently foul it off while getting out of the way, and you get a strike or even an out. This type of pitching was accepted by both sides until the mid-1970s. The system worked because each team had the same leverage; if a pitcher got too aggressive, you knocked him down when he came to bat. You gave him a taste of his own medicine.

The rules, written and unwritten, underwent a drastic change when the designated hitter came along in 1973. Now there was no way to retaliate directly against a headhunting pitcher, at least not in the American League. In frustration, hitters began charging the mound. Who blamed them?

And soon the trend moved to the National League, where the hitters were no longer content to let their own pitchers do the policing. Today the pendulum has swung way over to the other side. Some batters charge the mound on pitches that barely miss the inside corner. They lean out over the plate in fearless defiance. Warnings about pitching too far inside, once rare, are now common. Ejections for hitting a batter without a first warning were once unheard of. Now they're routine.

In this atmosphere, pitchers have to think twice about brushing back a hitter. If you miss with a pitch and hit the guy, you might be booted from the game. If you come too close, the hitter might charge the mound. Now there is a real downside to pitching inside. But you still have to do it. You have to keep the hitter honest.

Now, here comes Norm Charlton, admitting to hitting a batter on purpose for a curious and at best marginal reason—because he was doing what he was supposed to do, stealing a sign.

None of this is meant as a putdown of Charlton, a product of Rice University in Houston, where his studies included political science and religion. But a problem is created for everyone in the pitchers' fraternity if a member casts doubt on our motives. You pitch inside not to do bodily harm or to prove your manhood, but to win games.

If a pitcher feels he must win through intimidation, I would tell him, if he asked, to do what he thinks he has to do. But, please, leave the fans a few illusions.

Of course, there are times when you simply have to know to back off and not take it all too gravely. The Pirates' Bob Walk—not an ideal name for a pitcher—once brushed back Jeffrey Leonard of the Giants with three straight pitches. Leonard shouted at him: "Don't you ever come inside on me again as long as you live—or you won't."

The next time Leonard came to bat, Walk hit him on the left arm. Leonard glared and took his base. Walk lived to face more batters.

The old-time headhunters don't exist anymore, simply because the leagues won't tolerate them. You can't help but note that when the livestock wasn't so pricey, they did.

The brand of intimidation we see today is less direct and less frequent, though the potential for serious damage still exists. With some pitchers, what you see is an act, and they take on the job as an obligation. Some are simply at war with the hitters, and they regard pitching inside—or the threat of a reprisal—as a natural business practice.

I had this lesson driven home to me by one of the game's most revered teachers, the late Leroy (Satchel) Paige. When I was with the Angels, Satch and I were invited to appear as guests on a television show in Los Angeles called "Sports Challenge."

Paige was then in his mid-seventies, but he hadn't lost his love for talking baseball. We babbled away for an hour or so backstage, and at one point he asked me if I knew what was the best pitch in the game.

I hesitated. It didn't sound like a trick question, but I

didn't want to embarrass myself by saying something obvious, and being wrong. I shook my head, smiled, and waited.

He said, "The bow tie."

I said, "I never heard of it, Satch. What kind of pitch is that?"

"That's when you throw a fastball right here," he said, and he ran his hand across his neck.

NOLAN RYAN'S TOP TEN MOST INTIMIDATING PITCHERS

1. Sal Maglie

2. Don Drysdale

3. Stan Williams

4. Bob Gibson

5. Goose Gossage

6. J. R. Richard

7. Dick Radatz

8. Dave Stewart

9. Al Hrabosky

10. Rob Dibble

The
Ace
Hardware
Men

The search for truth in baseball is an unending one. Do pitchers scuff, scrape, grease, or otherwise doctor the ball? Do hitters cork their bats? Do infielders fudge on
the tag at second base on a double play? Imagine this scene:
an outfielder dives for a low line drive, does a somersault,
and races toward the nearest umpire with the ball in his
glove, screaming, "No, no. I trapped it!"

There is a line so fine it is nearly invisible between what
is considered cheating and therefore unacceptable, and what
constitutes outwitting the opposition or winking at the rules.
Almost no one knows with certainty where the line is drawn.
It has been known to move.

In fairness, before I name any names or damage any
reputations, I ought to make my own disclosures. Have I
ever thrown an illegal pitch? In the sense of throwing a spitter, which was outlawed in the 1930s, or altering the ball by

use of a foreign object, such as a staple gun or by driving a nail into one, no, never.

But have I taken advantage of whatever edge that fate or chance may have provided? Absolutely. The rule that governs most pitchers in such cases is the rule of common sense. Baseballs do get scuffed up in the normal action of the game, and sometimes they do not get tossed out.

What you will see most of the time is the pitcher himself lobbing the ball back to the umpire and asking for a new one, because he really doesn't have the confidence of knowing how the ball will move when he throws it. You won't use one that might be a problem. But the crafty pitcher who knows how to put these acts of God to good use can bring himself a handsome reward.

Many times a ball will be returned to me with a big dark spot like a dab of shoe polish. This happens more frequently now that some hitters use bats painted black. I don't ever throw out a ball with a nice mark on it. I figure it might create an illusion, a distraction, and I never feel obligated to make the pitch easier for the hitter to see.

But I will toss out a ball that is lopsided. They get that way when a hitter just mashes one right on the button. The ball just doesn't feel right in my hand.

When I first broke in with the Mets, I didn't realize how many liberties were being taken and the tricks that were used. When I saw how much was going on, what was allowed and tolerated, I developed a philosophy: if I could help my club win, by taking advantage of a certain opportunity, I would be willing to try.

When I was with the Angels, I can remember pitching against Billy Martin and the Yankees and moving up in front of the rubber about six inches. A hole sometimes just naturally forms there from the pitcher's followthrough and how loosely the dirt around the mound is packed. This worked especially well in a key situation, if you were going against the right pitcher, say, a young and less experienced pitcher who wasn't yet attuned to what was happening.

Against the Yankees, if I had two strikes on a hitter and I felt that by moving up six inches my fastball looked quicker, I would just rock and step up in that hole and cut loose. They never noticed.

Now, probably 80 percent of the objections you get are part of the mind games that are always played between the pitcher and batter. The other 20 percent of the time, what the pitcher gets away with is borderline. Of course, some of it is wildly creative.

The classic example is Gaylord Perry. When he retired, Gaylord admitted he used so-called foreign substances, such as grease and heat rub. The ball reacted the same as a spitter, meaning that it would suddenly drop or plummet. Gaylord called it his "survival pitch." Of course, he didn't need to use it nearly as often as the hitters accused him of using it. But once he had them wondering if he had loaded the ball, the thought was there on virtually every delivery. He already had the advantage. He could decoy, just brush his cap, and psych them out. Of course, when Gaylord needed a big out, or a strikeout, I think he was very capable of throwing a real greaseball and getting away with it.

Once, Reggie Jackson thought Perry, then with Seattle, was cheating on every pitch. The umpires kept checking the ball and not finding anything. Then Gaylord struck him out and Reggie went ballistic, got himself ejected from the game, picked up the water cooler and splashed it all around. But the truth was, Perry didn't rely on slickery alone. He had a puff-ball, too. He would work on the rosin bag—no rule against that—and when he released the ball there would be a little cloud of rosin dust with it. Anything to distract the hitter, he was capable of doing.

I used to sit in the dugout all night watching him and I never could figure out when he did and when he didn't do his act.

He won his 300th game in 1982, at forty-three, pitching for his seventh team, Seattle, against the Yankees. After the game, Dave Winfield paid him a tribute of sorts when he said: "You get by with what you can get by with in life. Nobody will put an asterisk on his victories. All you can do is give him credit."

At one point during the game, he showed John Mayberry a wet one, then struck him out on a high fastball with the bases loaded.

Trying to outsmart Gaylord was like trying to fool Mother Nature, but some hitters couldn't resist. Perry was on the mound for Seattle one night when Mike Hargrove came to bat for Cleveland. When I was in the American League, the book on Mike was that he never swung at a first pitch. Gaylord knew it, so he threw a first-pitch fastball and Hargrove hit it for a home run. He screamed at him as he rounded the bases, all but accusing him of having cheated. Hargrove had to fight back a smile.

Wherever he went, for all of his years, he brought with him a temper and a persistent nature. I was in high school in Alvin when Perry, then in his second or third year with the Giants, lost to Houston one night on a bloop hit over the infield by Nellie Fox in the bottom of the ninth. A typical Nellie Fox hit. A typical Gaylord Perry reaction. He walked off the mound, picked up Nellie's bat, and broke it on home plate.

They said in the papers the next day that Fox cried because the bat was his favorite. The Houston club filed a protest with the league. There was great sympathy for Nellie because hitters are quite finicky about bats they deem as special. The commotion went on for weeks and I think Gaylord, or the Giants, finally had to apologize and compensate him, not that they really could.

Perry was single-minded and some thought narrow-minded, but he had a code pretty much his own. He won fifteen straight games for Cleveland in 1974, one short of the American League record. At forty, he won 21 games and the Cy Young award for a weak San Diego team. And three wins short of the 300 mark, he was released by Atlanta after the 1981 season and went home to his peanut farm in North Carolina.

To get his chance with the Mariners, he had to agree to a tryout and a large pay cut. When he won his 300th game, he was the first to enter that circle since Early Wynn back in 1963. I don't guess I really appreciated the value that the fans and the historians put on that number until my own count-down in 1990.

Perry had won 314 games when he retired, at forty-five, with the announcement, "The league will be a little drier now, folks."

By the mid-1980s, the big new accusation was over the "scuffball." In Houston, in 1985 and 1986, teams were constantly demanding that the umpires check the balls for scuff marks. They did it with most of the pitchers on our staff, but mainly Mike Scott, Dave Smith, and myself. The Mets and Giants would collect a bunch of baseballs for "evidence" and take them to their clubhouse. It made them feel righteous but didn't prove much because, as I said, a ball can get marked in the normal action of the game.

It would get to be a kind of ritual, a lot of it designed to upset us, get us out of our rhythm. I'd see Mike Scott rub up a ball, and Roger Craig would come flying out of the Giants' dugout, demanding that the ball be checked on the spot. It would be as smooth as a baby's bottom.

Of course, every now and then you get lucky. I was sitting on the Astros bench one night next to Phil Garner when I spotted something. I nudged Garner. "Hey, Phil, have you noticed that whenever they start a game they never roll the ball out to the mound? The umpire never thinks about it. He's preoccupied with getting the game under way." I had a warm-up ball in my hand and I said, "Watch this."

I took the warm-up ball and walked over to the end of the dugout to the concrete steps and I tore a gash in it about two inches long. Then I took the ball out to the mound and warmed up with it. The catcher was Mark Bailey and I threw the ball nice and easy so nothing unexpected would happen.

Frank Pulli was the umpire and, sure enough, he didn't

bother to check the ball. It never crossed his mind that he hadn't thrown out a brand-new game ball. W-e-l-l-l-l.

On the first pitch I threw a fastball and it broke about two feet right over the heart of the plate and Mark Bailey never laid a glove on it. The pitch went right through him and struck the umpire on the kneecap.

Pulli was hopping around behind the plate and Garner was flat on his back on our bench from laughing so hard. Then Pulli picked up the ball and instantly saw the gash in it. He glared out at me, fired the ball into the dugout, tossed another one out to the mound, and bellowed, "Ball One!" Now, the ball went right down the middle of the plate and hit him on the knee, so it had to be a strike. But I didn't feel I was in a very strong moral position to argue the point.

That was really a one-pitch joke. I knew no umpire would tolerate anything so blatant. However, certain teams got away with tactics that were not much more subtle.

When Eddie Stanky managed the White Sox, he used to take the game balls the night before and put them in a freezer, so they wouldn't travel as far. Or, if a team had a couple of power hitters, they would stick the balls in the oven long enough to preheat the center so they would jump more. They had to time the removal of them so the covers wouldn't feel warm or cold to the umpire when he rubbed them up.

It takes about thirty minutes to go through the ritual of rubbing the baseballs with a special can of mud, which traditionally came from a company that processed the mud from the Delaware River. (It seems like a curious business, and I heard a few years ago that the original company closed down. They should have diversified.)

Sometimes they would let the ballboy do the rubbing so the umpires wouldn't get their hands dirty. Naturally, if the home team heats or freezes them the kid isn't going to say anything. He's just going to roll them up and stick them in the bag.

Not nearly as much of that kind of trickery goes on today. It was more evident when you had the likes of Stanky and Leo Durocher and Paul Richards, whose roots were in the prewar game. This was their life and they were always looking for an angle. They were men who had made the passage from the low minors and never left the game, staying to become managers or coaches or scouts. Players today don't have the same appreciation of the cunning that another generation put into winning, because they didn't have to make the same journey.

I try not to get caught up in thinking the old ways were best, but on the other hand I try to pay attention to details that others might miss. The teams used to just leave the boxes of game balls in the dugout. Now they give them to the ballboy, or even assign a coach to keep an eye on them, and no one is supposed to tamper with them.

When Casey Stengel was managing the Yankees, he gave the responsibility to Ralph Houk, then his bullpen coach. Houk had been a war hero, a major who accepted the surrender of an entire platoon of German soldiers. While his back was turned one day, some kids stole the ball bag. Stengel stared at him and said, "How is it you can capture all them Germans, and you can't guard a bag of balls?"

I was with the Angels the year baseball quit using horsehide and went to cowhide, for the texture, I guess. The covers were sewn by hand at a factory in Haiti, and the first couple of years it seemed to me that the seams were a little higher than they had been. There wasn't as much uniformity. So I would go into the clubhouse the night before I was to pitch and I might go through 30 dozen baseballs, never looking at them, just sitting there and feeling them.

The ones with the high, tight seams I would save in one box and the ones with the flat, wide seams I put in another box. Then, by the end of the game, I'd have separated maybe eight dozen balls. The ones with the high, tight seams I gave to the clubhouse man and he would turn them over to the umpires to rub up for the next night's game.

Those were the balls I wanted. A lot of times a pitcher will throw out a ball because the seam feels wrong. I never had to change a ball during that period and no one ever knew they had been screened.

This wasn't doctoring the ball or cheating—this was research.

Curiously, the pitchers who are accused of misconduct are the ones who are getting the batters out and winning. In his prime with the Dodgers, Don Drysdale once had an umpire run his hands through his hair after the opposing team claimed he was putting Vaseline hair tonic on the ball. "When my wife does that," Drysdale told the umpire, "she usually kisses me."

Then there was the case of Mike Scott, who developed a split-finger fastball and turned around his career. The pitch was taught to him by Roger Craig, who later was hired to manage the Giants and constantly accused Scotty of throwing a scuffball. The split-finger is a pitch that dips and darts and in general behaves as though it has a squirrel inside it. Using it, Scott struck out 300 batters in 1986 and won eighteen games, including a no-hitter, to clinch the division title for Houston. He was the Cy Young award winner.

A suspicious breed, baseball managers often find it hard to credit sharp turns in fortune to mere self-improvement. This is true even of Roger Craig, who was in fact responsible for Scott's stardom and regarded him as his prize pupil.

Leo Durocher, then managing the Cubs, once claimed to have caught Bill Singer red-handed when a tube of toothpaste fell from the Dodger pitcher's jacket. The case was dismissed when Singer explained that he liked to brush before and after every game. Singer became a role model for young people in the fight against cavities.

No one seriously doubted that Lew Burdette threw a spitter in his long and liquid career with the Braves. He may have thrown it less than the hitters thought but more than enough to keep them guessing.

When a batter asked the umpire to check the ball, Lew would simply roll it to his catcher, who happened to be Bob Uecker on the nights that Del Crandall or Joe Torre got a rest.

The ball would dry off along the way. If Uecker had the ball at the time of the request, he gave it a quick swipe in the dirt and then handed it to the man in blue.

Other than Burdette and Gaylord Perry, I doubt that many pitchers made a living throwing the spitter or a variation of it. The reason is basic. Most pitchers find it hard enough to control the legal ones. Neither Burdette nor Perry felt he was cheating. They simply did not believe the hitters were entitled to much in the way of mercy.

A now famous episode in 1987 involved one of my former Astros teammates, Joe Niekro, then throwing his knuckle ball for the Minnesota Twins. One sight I will never forget was the look on Niekro's face, captured on videotape, when an umpiring crew in Anaheim told him to empty his pockets and an emery board went flying, followed by a scrap of sandpaper.

The vigilantes had a field day. The Angels and their fans were on their feet, howling. It was like a scene from an old Jimmy Stewart movie, with the sheriff standing in front of the jail with a shotgun cradled in his arm, warning the crowd to break up "and go home, and let the law handle this."

Joe was suspended for ten days, in one of the few cases on record where a pitcher was believed to have been actually caught with the evidence on his person. Joe said he used the emery board and sandpaper to keep his nails trimmed and flat for his knuckle ball. In his ten years with the Astros, he always had a nail file on him.

This may sound like a copout, but I don't think Niekro was guilty. If you can control a knuckler, there isn't much else you can ask a ball to do. And if he had anything to hide, if he wasn't giving himself a manicure, the last place he would take the accessories would be to the mound.

Don Sutton, another of my former pitching mates, underwent several shakedowns by umpires until he threatened to strip down to his undershirt and protective wear. Sparky Anderson, among others, accused Don of using sandpaper on the ball. Sutton let the charges work for him, believing that it was in his interest to keep the hitter guessing. "I hope the sandpaper thing keeps up," he added. "I might get a Black and Decker commercial out of it."

I remember pitching in Dodger Stadium in 1970 and losing 1-0 to Don Sutton. What stuck in my mind is the fact that in the seventh inning I reached down to pick up the rosin bag and it was all greasy. I thought, "What the heck is this?' Then it dawned on me. He was loading up the ball with Vaseline and wiping it off on the rosin bag.

Sutton was interviewed one night by Tim McCarver for a cable TV show in Philadelphia. At one point, McCarver challenged Don about his reputation for "cutting the ball." I don't think I could have handled the question with Sutton's coolness. He smiled, shifted slightly in his chair, and said: "No, I never have. The batters accuse me of it. They may think I do, and the more they wonder the better it is for me. But I don't cut the ball."

"You don't even nick it a little on your belt buckle?" McCarver pressed.

Sutton showed no irritation at all. "No," he said, "but if the ball happens to have a rough spot I *might* take advantage of it."

The hitters could never relax their vigil against Don. Pitchers are by nature nervous creatures who put themselves through a long checklist before throwing. You watched Sutton and you saw him touch his cap, brush the glove against his chest, hold it against his leg, hitch his belt, rub his neck, maybe even scratch his bottom. None of which proved that he was, in some fashion, corrupting the ball.

In his Dodger prime, Sutton was ejected from a game one night by Doug Harvey, who had inspected the ball and found a rip in the cover the size of a quarter. Don threatened a lawsuit if he was suspended for "doctoring a baseball," instead of throwing a "doctored baseball." The distinction wasn't lost on other pitchers. It went to the issue of guilt. Don insisted he hadn't defaced the ball, he simply used what was there.

As soon as the word "lawsuit" was heard the league told Harvey he was on his own.

Sutton wasn't suspended and the threat of a suit sort of faded away. But the umpires had no difficulty translating the message: Don't expect any help if a player calls his attorney. When baseball took that attitude, as I saw it, the umpires adopted a more benign policy. If it wasn't blatant, they were not going to blow the whistle.

I think Don really enjoyed seeing how far he could go. Another time an umpire went to the mound to inspect his glove, looking for a square of sandpaper. When he peeked inside, the umpire found a note which read: "You're getting warm, but it isn't here."

But suspicion is a strong force in baseball, and it is a fact of life that grounds for suspicion frequently exist. The Astros seemed to have more than their share of notoriety, including The Case of the Corked Bat. When they finally apprehended one of our guys, it was not a pitcher but a hitter, shy, soft-spoken Billy Hatcher.

There was no question the bat was corked; it split in half when he fouled off a pitch during a game and some of the cork spilled out. He was fined and suspended for twenty days. But the bat belonged to Dave Smith, the closer in our bullpen, and the question was whether Hatcher knew the cork was there. I have never asked him because I never wanted to put him on the spot.

You have to know the background to understand how crazy the story gets. The bat was one Smith used in the home run contests that went on all season among the pitchers. We divided ourselves into two teams, and we were all doing a certain amount of engineering. I had taken my bat home to Alvin, had the inside drilled out and packed it with super putty and plugged the top. The idea was to try to get more distance, and I figured the putty would be more effective than cork. If you dropped a ball made of super putty, it would bounce three times higher than the original drop. My theory was that the ball ought to spring off the bat in the same way.

What I actually did was add more weight. It was like swinging a lead pipe. I asked the team's physical therapist, Gene Coleman, about the theory behind using cork. He explained that the cork made the bat lighter and quicker, and on contact the ball would jump more. With the putty making my bat heavier, if I started my swing early enough and caught the ball just right it would take off. But the added weight was the cause, not the super putty.

Dumb pitchers don't understand the physics of hitting. But that's how it all got started on the Astros. So there were corked bats in our racks and there were bats with power putty in there. And when Billy Hatcher knowingly or unknowingly picked up a Dave Smith model and it came apart, the front office went bonkers. Dick Wagner, then the general manager in Houston, now in San Francisco, called down and told Dennis Liborio, who was in charge of the clubhouse, to get rid of all the pitchers' bats that had junk in them.

Dennis was running around the clubhouse grabbing bats, thinking the league president, the FBI, or the border patrol was going to burst in, confiscate all our bats, and lock up the place. It would be like Eliot Ness raiding a distillery in Chicago.

You could argue both sides of the Hatcher case. I have had teammates borrow my bats, looking for one that felt good, trying to shake off a slump. Realistically, the way hitters are about bats, if he picks up a used one from a pitcher, he figured to know what was in it.

But you want to give a Billy Hatcher the benefit of the doubt. The incident cost him a major amount of momentum. He had been hitting .328 and when he returned to the lineup his average slipped 40 points. He is a sensitive fellow and the attention was very disruptive. He was embarrassed by it and he lost some of his intensity and focus.

Skeptics questioned the validity of his earlier average, and you could see his confidence sink. He was traded to the Cubs and then to the Reds. He reestablished himself and erased many of the doubts when he hit .750 for a four-game World Series record as the Reds swept Oakland in 1990.

I was happy for Billy. And the pitchers discontinued their home run contests in Houston.

As long as I am giving equal time to the hitters in the Bending the Rules category, I can't overlook a fellow I rank among the game's true characters, Norm Cash.

I always had a soft spot for the Detroit first baseman after he brought a table leg to the plate during my second no-hitter. But there was one encounter when neither of us laughed.

Corked bats had been a part of the game long before I broke in, but my first experience with one involved Cash. I was pitching for the Angels in the early 1970s, and he hit a fly ball to center field with a runner on third. I had to back up home plate because the ball was deep enough to score the runner.

After the play, as I started to walk back to the mound, I passed Norm's bat and I could see that the end of it was plugged. It didn't take a carpenter to tell the center had been hollowed out and filled in with a wooden plug.

I thought about what I should do on the way to the mound. I knew it was about as legal as opium, but it wasn't clear to me how to best turn this to my advantage. So the next time Cash came to the plate, I walked off the mound and yelled at the umpire to check his bat. "It's corked," I said.

The umpire didn't seem to understand what I was talking about, so I repeated myself. "Look at the end of his bat, it's corked."

Meanwhile, Cash was looking at me as if he couldn't believe this was happening. He didn't appear angry, just puzzled, as if I had accused him of something meaningless, like wearing his socks too high. The umpire picked up the bat, turned it around, and saw immediately that it was plugged. He just tossed it over toward the dugout and told

Norm to get another one, and that was the end of it. I'm sure that Norm was using the same corked bat the next day.

What I should have done was wait until he hit one into the upper deck off me, and then made my protest to the umpire. I can only blame this lapse of judgment on my youth.

I want to be careful not to send out the wrong message here, but I think young people understand the difference between breaking a rule and looking for an edge. There is a certain amount of action in baseball that falls into a gray area—like the phantom tag at second and the first baseman cheating on the throw that doesn't quite reach him, coming off the bag as if he has already caught the ball.

The umpires will tolerate a scuffball or a corked bat as long as no one forces their hand. My complaint is when they enforce a rule selectively, or penalize one player as an example to the rest. For the most part, I believe the umpires would prefer not to get involved in what they—and many fans—see as the game of cat and mouse between the pitcher and the hitter.

NOLAN RYAN'S
TOP ELEVEN PITCHERS
WITH THE RIGHT SCUFF

(OR SO THE HITTERS CLAIMED)

1. Gaylord Perry

2. Lew Burdette

3. Kevin Gross

4. Don Sutton

5. Bill Singer

6. Joe Niekro

7. Mike Scott

8. Don Drysdale

9. Rick Honeycutt

10. Dave Smith

11. Nolan Ryan (but don't tell anybody)

Heat
Wave

Fastball pitchers are to baseball what millionaires are to *Fortune* magazine, a topic of tireless speculation and comparison. This is true of most things athletic; speed and power have always intrigued and excited us.

The pitchers I admire most tend to be the ones who were just ahead of my time. I don't think you can fairly judge your peers until you have the benefit of time and distance. But this isn't unusual, either. You never feel as important as the stars of the class ahead of yours in high school.

So the names that hold the most magic for me are still Koufax and Drysdale and Gibson and Marichal. Each of them probably threw in the mid-90s in his prime, but speed on the radar gun, miles per hour, doesn't mean as much to me as what the ball does. The true power pitchers had fastballs that would rise and explode. "Every pitcher's best pitch is the fastball," Koufax once said. "It's the fastball that makes the other pitches effective. Hitters must look for it and try to adjust for a breaking pitch. While they are looking for the breaking pitch, the fastball is by them."

I hesitate at trying to rank them. Koufax may have thrown the liveliest fastball ever. Drysdale threw a heavier pitch, and few hitters could touch him when he brought the hard one inside. Gibson had that deadly combination of speed and pinpoint control. I loved what Johnny Keane, then managing the Cardinals, said when he started Gibson on two days' rest against the Red Sox in the 1967 World Series: "I had a commitment to his heart."

On velocity alone, Marichal was their equal, but he isn't remembered for his power because he had such a complete inventory. He used six different pitches and he could throw each of them at three different speeds. In effect, if a hitter tried to anticipate what Marichal might deliver, he had eighteen guesses. Everything about him was the picture of power, especially that booming leg kick.

Of my generation, Tom Seaver, Steve Carlton, J. R. Richard, and Goose Gossage were the ones who could blow the hitters away. A current list would include Roger Clemens, Dwight Gooden, Lee Smith, and Rob Dibble, out of the bullpen.

The fastball is such a central part of baseball lore that the players keep inventing ways to describe it. In Bob Feller's day they were called fireballers. Other expressions include gas, heat, smoke—you may detect a trend there. One year the popular phrase was "bringing it." The latest is "bad cheese."

If you really want to start an argument, and possibly a stabbing or two, raise the subject some night in your neighborhood bar. Who was the swiftest pitcher of all time?

Among others, there would be votes for Walter Johnson, known as The Big Train in his heyday with the Washington Senators, the 1920s; Cleveland's Bob Feller, Herb Score, and Sudden Sam McDowell; and Ryne Duren of the Yankees.

Johnson and Feller set strikeout records that lasted for decades. Score was a pitcher of high drama, a southpaw, handsome, almost unhittable his first two seasons, when he won 16 games and then 20. His career was shortened when a line drive hit him in the head, affecting his vision. McDowell was another left-hander feared by batters, a fastball-curveball pitcher who threw at warp speed.

Duren may have been the first relief pitcher to rely almost entirely on his fastball. When he warmed up in the bullpen, it sounded like a cannon going off. His wildness was a part of his threatening image. He wore glasses as thick as Coke bottles, and when he went to the mound he consistently threw his first pitch against the backstop, which discouraged hitters from digging in.

Once, Duren walked three straight hitters on twelve pitches, forcing in a run. He stormed up to the home plate umpire and demanded, "Where the bleep are those pitches?"

The umpire raised his hand to his chin. "Well, dammit," fumed Duren, "I've got to have that pitch." Meaning that he considered it close enough to be called a strike.

The high hard one, you reflect, is the basis for many a baseball myth. And when you poked around, wondering who was the fastest gun, you kept hearing about one pitcher whose legend grew to almost Paul Bunyan proportions but who never won a game in the major leagues.

His name is Steve Dalkowski, and you heard it wherever you went, even in the low minors. There was no one who could touch him, they said. The myth was that he threw his fastball at 120 miles an hour, and only one thing kept him from going on to Cooperstown. He couldn't get the ball over the plate.

He had an almost cult following, an underground fame, that must have been something close to what Tom Wolf wrote about Chuck Yeager in *The Right Stuff*: his name was virtually unknown to the public, but every pilot who felt the wind beneath his wings knew who he was.

Dalkowski had been in the Baltimore Orioles farm system and once roomed with Bo Belinsky, one of the game's noted playboys. Bo helped spread Dalkowski's fame and so did Paul Richards, who could work wonders with a young pitcher, and Earl Weaver and Billy DeMars. Every pitching coach Baltimore had tried to improve his control and get him to harness that raw power. The Orioles built their teams on pitching all through the 1960s, and they stressed the fundamentals as no other organization did. But no one could push the right button with the mystery pitcher his friends knew as Dalko.

Over the years I talked to a lot of scouts who said that Dalko had the greatest arm they ever saw. Whether he did or not is hard to say because minor league records really don't count for much.

Your first surprise about Steve Dalkowski is finding out that he wasn't very big, 5-8 or 5-9, probably not over 165 pounds. I don't doubt that he threw exceptionally hard, and that impression may have been reinforced by his appearance, the fact that he was left-handed, small, and wore glasses.

So what did he do? In Stockton, California, he threw a ball through the fence in right field and shattered the wood. In Wilson, North Carolina, he threw a wild pitch through the welded mesh screen sixty feet behind the catcher. Thirty years later the hole was still in the screen, regarded as a sort of shrine among the town's baseball fans.

Once his catcher didn't get the glove up in time and a rising fastball hit the umpire in the face mask, shattering it in three places. There was a story that one of his pitches nearly ripped a hitter's ear off, and they had to sew it back on. I don't know, but that's what they claim.

This much is fairly well documented: he struck out Ted Williams in spring training, just blew the fastball past the hitter with the quickest bat in the game. In the minors his catcher was Cal Ripken, Sr., who isn't given to invention or tall tales. If anyone asked Ripken how fast Dalkowski was, he answered, "Nobody else was close."

I don't know if Paul Richards discovered Dalko or signed him for the Orioles, but he contributed mightily to the legend. Richards, who had been an ambidextrous pitcher in the minors and a skinny catcher in the majors, sent Dalkowski to the Aberdeen Proving Grounds the night after he pitched a complete game. This was long before the radar gun had been discovered.

At Aberdeen, they borrowed an instrument, a tubelike device that could measure the speed of an object in flight, and set it up on a tripod at home plate. The experiment must have been a frustrating one, because it took Dalko forty minutes before he could get a fastball close enough to the tube to measure it. He was clocked at 98.6 miles an hour—and he wasn't pitching off a mound, just flat ground. Using the same machine, Bob Feller was timed at five miles slower, and he was fresh and sober at the time (witnesses could not say the same about Dalko).

This was where the talk began that Steve could stop a radar gun at 120. Maybe so.

He was still a kid, but he had the beginning of a drinking problem, and maybe it was partly from trying to fulfill all those expectations. Richards decided he needed a steadying influence, so the Orioles sent him to Florida to play under a veteran manager. There he started hanging out with Belinsky, whose credo was live for the moment. The manager wound up having a heart attack.

Legends have a way of growing because so often the essential details can't be disproved. But Dalko's numbers are in the Baltimore files, there to be interpreted like the strange writings on the walls of Middle Eastern caves.

He spent nine seasons, all in the minors, and averaged thirteen strikeouts and thirteen walks per nine innings. In 1960, in Stockton, he struck out 262 batters and walked 262 in 170 innings. Now that is consistency.

He threw 283 pitches in a complete game at Aberdeen, and in his next start was knocked out of the game in the second inning. By then he had thrown 120 pitches. In another game, he struck out 18, walked 21, and pitched a no-hitter.

As Sandy Koufax was becoming the dominant pitcher in

the majors, Steve Dalkowski finally appeared to be finding himself. Some thought that he might have read that Koufax, who had been plagued by wildness as a rookie, took a little off his fastball and started throwing strikes. In 1963, at Elmira, he suddenly found home plate. He still rang up the strike-outs, and now he began to win.

The Orioles brought him into spring training with the big club the next season, and every time he warmed up the play-ers would swarm around the batting cage to observe the arm that had inspired so much awe. That was the spring he struck out Williams. He struck out the side in his first two appear-ances in exhibition games.

Then, against the Yankees, he fielded a bunt laid down by the opposing pitcher, Jim Bouton, later of *Ball Four* fame, and made a whirling throw to first. But that awesome left arm was gone. No one knew that anything had happened at the time, and it may have been one of those injuries no one could then diagnose. Still, it was sad and it was permanent. Some pitchers get a sore arm and it goes away in a week. Dalkowski got one that lasted forever.

Ron Shelton, who was once a minor league pitcher and eventually directed and cowrote the film *Bull Durham*, put it this way: "Zeus quietly took back his thunderbolt, and Dalko returned to the minors to wander around for a couple more years."

He wound up his career in the Mexican League, then went home to Stockton, where he worked at a series of odd jobs—bartender, forklift operator, ditch digger. No one will ever really know what Dalkowski, the little man with the overpowering arm, might have accomplished. But 30 years after he lost his last chance at getting to the majors, they still talk about him, and that is a kind of immortality.

"I've been told that I'm a mix of Seaver and Ryan. I like that. When I was in junior high I used to go to the Astrodome and watch Nolan and Joe Sambito. I patterned myself after Seaver and Ryan. Both are workhorses, have great forms, great styles, strong legs. Both are my type of pitcher." Roger Clemens said this after winning the Cy Young award in 1986. One of life's uncomfortable moments has to be handling this kind of compliment, having one of the great performers in your field announce that you were a boyhood hero of his.

Roger and I happen to have a few things in common. We both grew up on the outskirts of Houston, Roger in the suburb of Katy and me in the town of Alvin. We run across each other fairly often, especially at the winter awards banquets, where Roger has been a regular since his blockbuster season of 1986. I am aware of the comparisons and have no strong feelings about them. Clemens has been described as "Ryan with an attitude." But he isn't the next me or the next Seaver. He is already in his own category, and barring injury he will break the records of a lot of pitchers.

He already holds the strikeout record for a game, twenty, and three hundred wins is on his horizon. In 1991, he became the fifth and youngest pitcher to collect three Cy Young awards, and the first American League starter in a decade to do it without winning twenty. Clemens, 18-10, led the league in strikeouts and earned run average. This tells me that in the age of pitch counts and bullpens that are six deep, voters are no longer looking as closely at victory totals.

When Roger gained his first Cy Young in 1986, his twenty-four victories led the majors; he was the winning pitcher in the All-Star game and carried the Red Sox to the World Series. He repeated in 1987.

This isn't meant to be boastful, but offhand I can think of just one record that appears beyond him. It isn't likely that anyone on the scene today will threaten my mark of over 5,000 strikeouts. The way the game is played, not many pitchers are going to be active at 45, throwing fastballs for a living.

I doubt that Roger plans on pitching that long. The game takes more out of him than it did me, mainly because I have a high tolerance for aggravation. I have survived because I was able to keep my life relatively uncomplicated. Roger is another story.

I've had a good relationship with Roger and I worry about him some, the distractions of being a star in a media-intensive city such as Boston, the pressures that are often self-inflicted. Clemens has to be explained. He doesn't ask to be, but he has the temper, a bit of impatience, and a salary that will soon jump to $5 million a year. Those are the things that make you more visible than you want to be. But the people who see only the obsessive side of him, the drive to be perfect, won't get to know him. They mistake shyness for surliness.

He matured in 1991 after a couple of lingering episodes that would have sidetracked a person of weaker character. You can go back to October 1990 and the fourth game of the League Championship Series, Boston against Oakland.

To begin with, Clemens was trying to avoid a sweep of his team while pitching with a tender shoulder. The concern for his health even extended to the opposing pitcher, Dave Stewart, who said, "I hope he isn't taking any risks of hurting his career." How many sports can you name where the rivals are so solicitous of each other's security? What a guy, Dave.

As matters unfolded, plate umpire Terry Cooney reduced the chances of Roger doing permanent damage to his arm by ejecting him in the second inning. You could pretty much tell from his reaction that Roger was not all that hot to be protected. From the mound, he said some things not usually heard in the reading room of the Betsy Ross Society.

Television viewers across the country drew their own conclusions as the TV camera zeroed in on Clemens's angry face. He had disapproved of the call on the last pitch, and now he was off the mound, shaking his head as he often does, letting off steam. He was talking to himself and if he cursed, initially, at least, he did so in a generic way. What he said to Cooney, most observers agreed, was: "I'm not (expletive deleted) talking to you . . . keep your (expletive deleted) mask on." But Cooney jawed back and the dialogue quickly went downhill from there.

I could not help but think that if the boxer Gerry Cooney had Terry's reflexes, he would have been the heavyweight boxing champion.

Whatever the dejected Red Sox may have thought of the umpire's vision, they had to concede that the man has fantastic hearing. From 65 feet away, over the roar of 50,000 fans, Roger's words found their way to Cooney's ears. As the uproar spread, Clemens was accused of bumping a second umpire.

Clemens was ejected with one run in and Tom Bolton had to hustle out of the bullpen to give up a two-run double. Roger's exit was soon followed by his team's. Stewart never wavered on his way to a 3-1 win, his second of the series. The Red Sox scored one run in each of their four losses. Meanwhile, the Athletics, with such muscle men as Jose Canseco and Mark McGwire, who can make a baseball scream, accomplished the sweep without hitting a home run. This is greatness.

After the commissioner's office finally finished its investigation, including testimony from a lip reader who defended Clemens's language, he served a five-day suspension early in the 1991 season and paid a $10,000 fine.

Give Clemens credit for being the intense competitor he is, and pitching with pain. It may not be smart medicine, but it makes for fine drama.

No pitcher had ever been ejected from a playoff game, and that was more fodder for Roger's critics in Boston, who have him tagged as a hothead. Labels can be hard, if not impossible, to shake in baseball. You can get away with being goofy, but if the impression gets rooted that a player is *difficult*, the clubs always have their periscopes up, looking for signs of boat rocking.

I react to the stories about Clemens as a friend and a fan. I want him to get good press, but I don't feel licensed to offer advice in the field of human relations. When someone asked Roger what we talk about, he replied: "Nolan likes my curve and tells me I ought to use it more."

That is about as much shop talk as passes between us. When we pass each other on the field or run into each other at a charity dinner, we talk about whatever has been ailing us—my back, his elbow. We sound like two geezers sitting around a doctor's office. I might ask about the new house he's building in Houston, and Roger might ask how the cattle business is doing. We can be pretty boring.

In the off-season, Roger was involved in an odd scuffle in a Houston nightclub called Bayou Mama's Swamp Bar. He had gone to the aid of his older brother, Gary, who wound up in a fight with two strangers. In the confusion, Roger jumped on a police officer's back, according to some of the witnesses. I might not recommend this method of breaking up a fight, but it occurs to you that it might be nice to have Roger Clemens for a brother.

One point needs to be made. Roger is no night crawler. He stays as close to home as anyone. To the extent that this disturbance gave a different impression, it was mostly bad luck and bad timing.

It might be entirely coincidental, but Houston's legal system is famous among pro athletes around the country. One year four New York Mets, Tim Teufel, Bob Ojeda, Ron Darling, and Rick Aguilera, were arrested for getting into a brawl with a couple of off-duty policemen working security at a club called Cooters. Ricky Sanders of the Redskins, Dale Ellis of the Seattle SuperSonics, and Dave Winfield, then with the Yankees, have appeared in a Houston courtroom. Carl Lewis, the world's fastest man, was arrested early one morning for driving sideways across an esplanade.

And in perhaps the most publicized incident of all, James Worthy of the Lakers picked a number out of the yellow pages before a game and called an escort service. It happened to be a sting operation, run by the Houston Vice Squad. In fact, most of the escort services in town had been taken over by the Vice Squad. Houston probably has the only police department in the country that is cost-efficient. Worthy was booked, arrived late for the game but helped the Lakers win, and settled the case by doing community service.

What puzzles most Houstonians about this activity is how athletes manage to get arrested in a town where most of the natives can't find anything to do after ten o'clock.

The charges against Clemens were dismissed, but he took some heavy needling in the press and on the roast-and-toast scene. And, of course, the baseball gossips wondered if these back-to-back controversies would cause him to stumble when the 1991 season started.

He was so distracted that he won his first six starts and had an earned run average under one. Even though he was sidelined for nearly a month with injuries, he won eighteen games and the Cy Young award. As he always did, he tried to dominate every game. He tried with all of his pride and intensity to keep a faltering Boston team in the pennant race. That he could not do.

You don't need to look very closely to know where Roger is vulnerable. "Sometimes," says his pitching coach, Bill Fischer, "he forgets that he's a human being. I have to remind him that even a pitching machine throws a bad one every once in a while."

At twenty-nine, he is already closing in on 150 wins, halfway to 300. If you want an insight to the potential he still has, consider the night he struck out 20 Seattle Mariners, in May 1986. He allowed three hits and *did not walk a batter*. His manager, John McNamara, who had witnessed perfect games pitched by Catfish Hunter and Mike Witt, called it "the most awesome pitching performance I have ever seen."

Two qualities make Clemens rare among power pitchers. First, his fastball explodes down in the strike zone. "He was throwing so damned hard, the ball just ran in and exploded. Basically, I had no chance," Jose Canseco said after striking out four times against Clemens. Second, there is his control. The only others who could match him were Koufax at the end of his career and Bob Gibson.

When your fastball travels at 97 miles an hour and you can work in and out, the best of hitters will be overmatched. For a brief period, after surgery to remove a cartilage fragment from his right shoulder in the winter of 1985, Clemens seemed uncertain that he could regain his speed. In the spring, he kept going to his curve.

Fischer took him aside and growled. "You're throwing all breaking stuff. How hard do you think you're throwing your fastball?"

"Eighty-four," he guessed.

Fischer handed him the readings from the radar gun. "Ninety-three. Constant." His confidence quickly returned.

There is a touch of irony to the story of his rise to the majors. He pitched for one season at San Jacinto Junior College, near Houston, and was scouted by the Mets. But the pitching coach at the time—a man named Bob Gibson—was not suitably impressed, and Roger accepted a scholarship to the University of Texas. The next season, 1983, he led Texas to the college baseball title.

And that was how close the Mets came to signing, in consecutive Junes, Roger Clemens and Dwight Gooden.

At a social gathering in Houston, a night or two before the New York Mets opened the 1984 season, a writer mentioned to Davey Johnson that he had covered my first big league start. I had lasted one inning in a loss to the Astros near the end of the 1966 season.

Coincidentally, added the writer, he had been in the press box for my next start, also in the Astrodome, and first big league win, in April 1968.

Johnson, who played college ball at Texas A&M and feels at home among Texans, became animated. "Are you working Saturday night?" he asked.

The writer said no.

"Well," said Davey, "you ought to come out to the stadium anyway. We're starting a kid named Dwight Gooden.

Someday you may want to be able to tell your grandkids that you saw both Nolan Ryan and Dwight Gooden in their major league debuts."

As thoughtful as the tip may have been, the results for Gooden were the same as mine nearly 20 years before: he was driven from the mound and the Mets lost.

But the season ahead was going to be a spectacular one for the teenager from Tampa. He would win 17 games and finish with 276 strikeouts and an earned run average of 2.60. At nineteen, he was the Rookie of the Year.

He averaged nearly twelve strikeouts per nine innings, the highest in history—not only for a rookie but for anybody. The fastest pitcher on the planet? He was already a contender.

In New York, the media and the fans quickly anointed him "Dr. K.," a partial tribute to basketball's Julius Erving ("Dr. J") and a play on the scorecard symbol for a strikeout.

I long ago lost track of how many times I have been asked why a "K" was adopted. The answer is: a sportswriter for the New York *Herald* named M. J. Kelly introduced the notation in 1868 to avoid using an "S," which he thought might be taken as a reference to the shortstop. Kelly simply chose the last letter of the word "struck." And that is why Gooden is not known as Dr. S.

By 1985, there appeared to be no limit to what Gooden would accomplish. He posted a 24-and-4 record, 268 strikeouts, and an ERA of 1.53. He demonstrated a maturity on the mound that seemed unreal. He was something not exactly common among pitchers, a splendid athlete, quick with his glove and his bat.

A month into the 1986 season, he had beaten the Astros on two hits for his thirteenth career shutout. He had driven in two runs with a triple off Bob Knepper. He was not yet twenty-two.

Gooden was what baseball always had promised but so seldom delivered: a phenomenon. It wasn't simply the way he had overpowered the league; Tom Seaver, Vida Blue, Fernando Valenzuela, Mark Fidrych, and others had captured the fans in their impressive freshman seasons. What made you marvel over Gooden was the fact that he made the jump virtually out of high school: he had pitched a season in A ball. Not only did he have the poise of a veteran; his rivals treated him as one.

The fans began bringing placards to Shea Stadium with the letter "K" on them to follow his strikeouts. A section of the bleachers began to be identified as the "K Korner."

When a specimen of this caliber arrives, you check for possible weak spots. Gooden was 6-3 and 198, healthy and still growing. If you questioned anything, it was whether he could maintain the pace, and in New York, where the fans are often so eager to devour their young. Would he fall victim to the too-much-too-soon syndrome? Would the big-city bright lights get him?

He was in awe of nothing. He had been around major leaguers all his life, going to the spring training games in Tampa with his father. He had a solid family base and he was eager to learn. He didn't force the strikeouts, didn't get caught up in the scorekeeping. The strikeouts would come, he said, but "winning is the big thing. If you throw a lot of pitches, before you know it your arm's gone."

It took me a few seasons to reach that conclusion, but it took more for me to do anything about it. Gooden was already starting to look for more outs on the first pitch. From the other dugout he came across as a young man who was in control. He was quiet, modest. The veterans on the Mets noted that he didn't enjoy talking about himself.

The Mets protected him from the press, a smart move, giving them access only after games he pitched. But wise observers held their breath. "We don't have pitching stars anymore," said Frank Cashen, the Mets general manager. "They're more like meteors."

Would he be immune to the kind of calamity that too often awaited the golden children? The signs began to creep in. He began to show up late for appointments or miss them altogether. He missed the Man of the Year banquet in his honor in Tampa. And, before his twenty-second birthday, the marketing people moved in. They copyrighted his nickname, put his endorsement on dozens of products.

All too suddenly, the answer was at hand. No, he wasn't going to cheat the fiddler. He was arrested in Tampa in January 1987 after being stopped for what was described as a routine traffic violation. Somehow, it escalated into a charge of battery on a police officer and resisting arrest. Photographs of Gooden showed him with both eyes swollen shut. The police report said that they spotted a Mercedes weaving through traffic; Gooden, the driver, and a friend were "combative." Witnesses said they saw the police beating two men who were on the ground, not resisting.

Now his whole private life was front-page news: a child, a broken engagement, a bad scene at an airport, a minor car accident. Rumors began to float, but not many were prepared when the reality came. In April, Doc Gooden checked into a rehab clinic in New York for treatment of cocaine abuse. He had requested the treatment himself.

His teammates were shocked, even those who had dealt with drug problems of their own. One early reaction in New York was of fans feeling betrayed. The famed Stage Delicatessen scratched the young pitcher's name from its menu. You could no longer order a Dwight Gooden and get a sandwich consisting of open-grilled salami, melted Swiss cheese, and hot sauerkraut for eight dollars and ninety-five cents.

As one social critic noted, it was just another example of a town without pita.

He was treated for 28 days and then went to the minors to pitch himself back into shape. When he made his return to Shea Stadium, no one knew what to expect. Dick Young, for years the curmudgeon and conscience of New York sporting teams, urged the fans to express their disapproval of Gooden's fall from grace by booing his appearance.

When he headed to the mound to warm up, the crowd gave him a standing ovation. He won that night, was 8-and-1 at one point, and finished with a 15-7 record.

He is once again among the upper tier of pitchers in baseball, but he no longer does things that no one had ever done. "He was great at nineteen and unbelievable at twenty," said Davey Johnson. But unspoken was the thought that might have been part of the answer. Baseball—the Mets, celebrity, all of these—had stolen his youth.

Nolan Ryan's
Top Ten Pitchers
with the Nastiest Sliders
(the fastball's sidekick)

1. J. R. Richard

2. Ferguson Jenkins

3. Bob Gibson

4. Steve Carlton

5. Tom Seaver

6. Mickey Lolich

7. Ron Guidry

8. Sparky Lyle

9. Goose Gossage

10. Rollie Fingers

Flakes, Jokers, and Hot Dogs

Once every few decades or so a player seems to fall into America's lap and the fans hug him to their hearts. It happened with Dizzy Dean back in the thirties. Some do it with ability and presence. Bo Belinksy grabbed the headlines for a couple of seasons in the 1960s, and he did it without the benefit of winning.

And some are supernovas who flash across the baseball skies and then for whatever reason are gone before their time. The most striking example was Mark (The Bird) Fidrych, who became the most appealing and talked-about player in the game in the 1970s. No one had seen anything quite like him. He existed in a world of his own, which by itself would not have made him unusual in baseball. But his antics were unrehearsed.

In every generation, we have heard the lament that there is a shortage of the kind of characters who have given the game so much of its texture. Old hands would ask, Where have they gone, Rube Waddell and Rabbit Maranville and Boots Poffenberger?

I had little idea who they were or what they did, but their names alone suggested enough color to paint a barn. I knew about Dizzy Dean and the Gas House Gang, Lefty Gomez and Yogi Berra and Jimmy Piersall.

As far as I know, the word "flake" has been around for as long as the sport itself. Jim Brosnan—who was judged a character because he not only read books but wrote them—drummed it into the public consciousness in a book called *The Long Season*. The term "flake" is from "snowflake"—there are no two alike.

I don't know of any player who felt offended by being called a flake. The term may fall short of flattery, but it is the nature of most athletes to want to be viewed as different. Nor do you hear any strenuous objection if a player is pegged as a little nutsy. Odd as this may seem, the real resistance is to being identified as a hot dog, which means a showboat, a guy who plays to the stands. Early in their careers, Willie Mays raised some eyebrows with his basket catches, Pete Rose by running to first base on a walk, and Joaquin Andujar with nearly his every move. I've heard that the book Rickey Henderson is writing is titled *Confessions of a Hot Dog*.

Fidrych was a rookie right-hander with the Detroit Tigers in 1976, and I think it is fair to say that no one on our club—the California Angels—knew anything about him. I read some of the early news stories with a little skepticism. My first reaction was that it doesn't take a whole lot to get Detroit fans excited. Here was a kid who talked to the ball, who got down on his hands and knees to landscape the pitcher's mound. If a teammate made a big play behind him, Mark would clap his hands and jump up and down and yell. You hadn't seen so much emotion since the last time Monty Hall asked a contestant which curtain she wanted. He also happened to win nine of his first ten starts.

The first time he pitched against us, we started exchanging looks in the dugout, as if to say: "What is it with this turkey?" What I saw was a gangly kid with curly blond hair that bounced over his ears. He dropped to his knees and smoothed out the little holes on the mound like a kid in his sandbox lost in an imaginary world.

He held the ball in front of him and you could see his lips flapping. Of course, it was his way of focusing on the task. I have never seen a pitcher who was so hyper, so uninhibited. The crowd went daffier with every gesture, every reaction.

Ralph Houk, then the Detroit manager and a baseball man I always respected, called Mark "the best young pitcher I have ever had in my career." Remember, Houk had been a coach, manager, and general manager with the Yankees during the heyday of Vic Raschi, Whitey Ford, and Mel Stottlemyre.

I have to draw a line here: Fidrych wasn't just a "rookie sensation." There is a new one every year, sometimes several. And as we get over the newness they go on to stardom or blend into the crowd. But The Bird made the kind of impression that lasts, far out of proportion to the length of his career.

When our teams met, I checked in with Rusty Staub. The Tigers were a weak club at the time, struggling to become mediocre. But Fidrych had filled their stadium in his last three starts at home. I mean sellout crowds. One night in the Angels clubhouse we caught the end of one of his games on a national telecast of "Monday Night Baseball." He beat the Yankees, 5-1, and the camera showed a fan hopping around in a feathered yellow costume. The 50,000 fans in Tiger Stadium refused to leave after the last out. They kept calling for him. Finally, Rusty went into the clubhouse and said, "Bird, get your shirt on, you have to go back out there."

Fidrych said, "Aw, no man, it's too much."

Staub, who had won the game for him with a three-run homer off Mike Cuellar, his former teammate with the Astros, insisted: "Mark, you gotta get out there and give those people what they want. You gotta keep it going for all of us."

He said he would if Rusty walked out with him. Staub said he would go as far as the dugout, and then he was on his own. The compromise worked.

When Fidrych reappeared, he was in his socks, his hair was wet and dangling in long, electric curls. He wore a sheepish grin as the fans cheered. Some teenage girls who had rushed down to the box seat railings all but swooned. The TV interviewer asked the usual senseless postgame questions: "Have you ever seen a crowd like this before?"

"What can I tell you?" said Mark, with a shrug.

What indeed. Here was a young man who had pitched hardly at all in the first six weeks of the season. When he finally made his major league debut, in relief, he only had to face the Oakland As, in their park, with the score tied, the bases loaded, and nobody out in the bottom of the eleventh. He gave up a sacrifice fly that lost the game.

Suddenly he was the hottest thing to come out of Detroit since bucket seats. He had the narrow face and unruly hair of a rock guitarist, and the disposition of a guy who feeds pigeons in the park. He also would develop a winning touch, which led the entire Detroit team to more or less adopt him. They nicknamed him "The Bird" after the character on the kids' TV show "Sesame Street."

"What happened with Mark," said Staub, who had been in the league nearly fourteen seasons and had nearly another ten to go, "is the greatest thing I have seen since I turned pro."

Rusty himself wasn't a character unless you count the fact that he was a gourmet cook and had a collection of fine wines. But he was the most prized of the bonus babies Houston corralled in the club's first season or two, while I was still tearing them up for Alvin High.

Staub was a red-haired, nineteen-year-old outfielder and first baseman, batting cleanup in the majors. Houston fans felt toward him as they would a young relative visiting from New Orleans. They wanted to take him home to dinner.

"The difference," he said, with a laugh, "is that I hit .224 my first year and they stopped fussing over me. But with

Mark, everybody pulls for him. The players were all rooting for him in the spring to make the team. He was doing the same things then, but the writers hadn't discovered him."

Talking to a baseball may strike some people as, well, peculiar. You don't really need to worry until the ball starts talking back. Of course, I know a lot of pitchers who talk to themselves. Little pep talks or warnings, where not to put the ball, reminding yourself who the hitter is and what he likes. The writer George Plimpton called it "The Inner Voice."

As near as I could tell, nothing The Bird did was contrived. I have seen a lot of players reach the majors and do weird things to be noticed. But you knew instinctively that he had been this way his whole life. I don't think it ever occurred to him that he might need to protect himself.

When he made the team in the spring, he celebrated in his own way. According to what Mark told his teammates, he and his girlfriend snuck into the ballpark in Lakeland. He climbed the flagpole, alone, and slid down the other side. Then they made love on the pitcher's mound.

"Some of the older players," said Staub, "we try to protect him, just keep the sharks from getting to him, the guys with the fast deals. But nothing bothers him. When it got out that he was only making $16,000 a year, somebody started a drive: 'Send a buck to The Bird.' But Mark stopped it. You have to know how he talks. He said, 'Hey, I'm making more money now than I need. If they gave me a raise, I'd probably get cocky and pitch lousy.'

"He drives a subcompact and if he really could live the way he wanted, he'd drive a truck, work in a garage, and drink beer all day."

Those tongue-in-cheek words were painfully close to the truth, as would become apparent all too soon.

I don't like to see the word "tragedy" used in connection with baseball. It's too big a word, better reserved for wars and plane crashes, fires and floods and other natural disasters. But the sudden ending to The Bird's career was the saddest misfortune.

His career amounted to roughly that one brilliant and entertaining year, before the injury hex finished him. Yet it is hard to imagine anyone accepting a setback as Fidrych did, with no brooding or bitterness. We would all, I think, like to take our losses with the tranquility he did. His attitude seemed to be: "I was lucky to be here, hadn't expected it, enjoyed what there was, let's get on with life."

I may not be doing justice to what churned inside him. But this is what I saw, what I sensed. The Bird plays in an occasional Old-Timers' Game. That gives me a jolt; he is younger than I am. With the exception of a rare appearance by Joe DiMaggio, Fidrych gets as big a hand as anyone. The fans remember him; they are acknowledging what they missed.

The Bird owns a farm in Massachusetts, where his roots are. He has more than 100 wooded acres, where he raises pigs and a few cows and drives a pickup truck. "I'm in love with my land," he says. "I got it all from playing ball. It gives me prestige. Someone says, 'What you got?' I say, 'One hundred and twenty-one acres of nice land.' "

I had been in the majors ten seasons when Fidrych had his dream year. What happened to him was what happened to nearly every pitcher up to that time who complained of a sore arm. They tried heat and ice and massage, and if those didn't work they told you to rest the arm or pitch through the pain. Not much was known about rotator cuff injuries, and the doctors hadn't yet developed what became known as Tommy John surgery.

He didn't have an agent and the fan in the upper deck didn't need four beers to gaze down at Fidrych and imagine he saw himself. On the TV screen, his face seemed to glow. He became the second rookie in history to start an All-Star game, went 19-and-9 for a next-to-last-place team and led all major league starters in earned run average (2.94). Almost by himself, he boosted Detroit's attendance by more than 400,000 over the previous year.

Bird T-shirts, buttons, and records were big sellers. In

Detroit, the fans named babies after him and the state legislature demanded that the Tigers raise his pay. I can't imagine Texas politicians doing that.

At twenty-two, he threw a fastball close to 90 miles an hour, had a nice curve and the control of a veteran. If he had come along ten years later, his rookie season would have been worth a million dollars in fringe deals.

Then it all fell apart, in one of those freakish accidents that make you shudder at the thought of how randomly fate yanks on our strings.

Fidrych was just shagging fly balls with Staub the next spring, 1977, in the outfield in Lakeland. "You want this one, Rusty?" he asked.

Staub said, "No, kid, you take it."

He went streaking after it with his usual exuberance, and suddenly he felt a pop in his left knee. He had torn a cartilage. He tried to return too soon from the injury, and ten days after he came off the disabled list he felt another pop. This time the pain was in his right shoulder. He finished with six wins and four defeats, and his teammates remember his rage and helplessness at season's end.

I don't know how he did it, but he managed to break the washer and dryer in the clubhouse. Then, typical of The Bird, guilty over his display of temper, he brought his tools in, got on his knees, and repaired them.

He went on and off the disabled list, back and forth to the minors for rehab. He started three games in 1978 and went 2-and-0. Then he was 0-3 and 2-3 and Detroit let him go. He spent three more seasons in the Boston farm system and then in 1983 he retired. In 1985, the doctors operated on his rotator cuff and cleaned out the shoulder and he no longer found himself waking up at three in the morning in pain. But the next time he faced a batter it would be in an Old-Timers' Game.

The Bird had a message for every young player who made a grab for the brass ring. "I got no regrets," he said. "I got memories. I'll always keep them alive. Grab [the fun] while you can, 'cause you never know when it's gonna disappear. You can't think about it; you gotta just go until something happens."

The two pitchers I have known as teammates who were so unlike what had been written about them, not at all what you expected, were Joaquin Andujar and Dennis "Oil Can" Boyd.

Andujar would play the clown on the plane or in the clubhouse or around the batting cage, but he demanded to be taken seriously as a pitcher. It confused and annoyed him if the fans, the press—or his manager—failed to distinguish between his two personalities.

Andujar was signed by the Redlegs out of the Dominican Republic, and came to the States in 1970 with a vocabulary that consisted mainly of "hot dogs" and "french fries." That was about all he ate his first two months in baseball.

Drafted by the Astros in 1976, he was in the majors a year later, launching a career that would be called, among other things, "tempestuous."

It is a pity that Joaquin (pronounced wha-KEEN) became better known for his tantrums and one-liners than for his gifts as a pitcher. He made a contribution, of sorts, to his new language when he announced, referring to the uncertainties of baseball, "There is one word in America that says it all: 'You never know.' "

He liked to refer to himself as "One tough Dominican," and he did wind up in a number of fights, including one with his best friend, Cesar Cedeño. When he was a young minor leaguer with the Reds, he and his roomie, Ray Knight, both had short fuses. They used their fists often. I don't recall anyone saying that Andujar ever won.

I'd rate him with anyone as a competitor. He kept his teammates sharp and awake because we never knew what he might do next. After one loss he jumped into the showers in full uniform. A switch hitter, he sometimes would bat from the right side against right-handers and from the left against left-handers. He was once thrown off a plane for refusing to remove his stereo tape-player from the aisle. It was the first time I ever heard of a passenger being ejected for failing to conceal a stereo.

In Houston in 1980, Bill Virdon used him as a reliever and spot starter and he was erratic all year. Traded to St. Louis, he came under the friendly wing of Whitey Herzog, who put him in the rotation and left him there. Joaquin was the kind of pitcher—as most are—who needs to take a regular turn, who can be effective if he is used every fifth day or less. He was strong enough to pitch on less rest than most of us.

In St. Louis he was reunited with Hub Kittle, the Cardinals' pitching coach, who had been in the Houston organization and had managed Andujar in the winter leagues. He also spoke fluent Spanish. We tended to forget how difficult it was for some of the youngsters from Latin America to adjust to our culture and that small world called major league baseball.

I don't know that he changed many opinions in 1982, but he was close to brilliant as he pitched the Cardinals into the World Series, winning his last seven games down the stretch. He beat the Braves in the playoffs and the Brewers twice in the World Series.

He was still thought of as eccentric, a nine on the emotional Richter scale. But now everybody knew he could pitch.

A year later, he was back on the roller coaster. He couldn't rely on his best pitch, the slider, and when you have this problem two things will happen: Your control begins to go and you get beat.

At one point he lost ten in a row and had a 3-11 record. His slump was a combination of bad luck and bad pitches, as most slumps are. When we faced the Cardinals, Herzog was trying hard to deflect the criticism of Joaquin. "We've been shut out four times when he pitched," said Whitey, adding: "Of course, some of those shutouts were by 7-0."

It may not be vividly remembered, but an umpire tossed Andujar from a World Series game the year before Roger Clemens had that experience. But the tough Dominican wasn't the starter. He was the fourth man out of the bullpen in a seventh game that the Cards were losing by nine runs. He had started and lost the sixth game on a close call, and the umpire who made it was now behind the plate. Andujar was an explosion waiting to happen.

After he had won twenty in both the 1984 and 1985 seasons, St. Louis traded him to Oakland, and the signal seemed clear: Andujar was big trouble; his talent was not worth putting up with his temper.

I think the decision was more practical. The Cardinals believed he was wearing down. In '85, he won only one game after the third week in August, and his earned run average ballooned. The heat and humidity and artificial turf wore him down. "I know he's crazy," said Herzog, "but he really does have a heart of gold."

That's how I think of him. He moved on to the A's and then made a second stop in Houston, on his way out of the league.

When Dennis "Oil Can" Boyd joined the Texas Rangers in midseason 1991, I had heard the stories and knew his reputation. But the fellow who joined the Rangers was quiet, even-tempered, and eager to redeem himself.

He had the limber build and elastic arm of a Satchel Paige—although I'm not comparing *anybody* to Satchel in skill or savvy or endurance. Satchel pitched in a different league.

But it is hard for me to square all the troubles Boyd had over the years with the low-key, educated man who sat a few lockers away from mine. "People think I'm some kind of psycho or something," he said when he arrived from Montreal. "That's not true. People just don't know me."

If they did, they would have learned what a remarkable history Dennis and his family have. He was born in Meridian, Mississippi, where his father, Willie, pitched against the Aaron brothers and Willie Mays. Satchel Paige passed through town on several of his barnstorming tours, and a generation of Boyds learned to play ball at the Lake Erie

Ballpark on Tenth Avenue. Oil Can was one of six brothers, the rest of whom played for the local semipro team.

Each of them pitched at one time or another, but arm injuries or workaday pressures kept the rest from getting a chance. When Oil Can reported to the Red Sox in September 1982, he called home from the Boston Sheraton Hotel and said, "We made it. We *all* made it."

If people were quick to form an impression of Oil Can Boyd, the early one was favorable. The Boston fans liked what they saw on the mound and how he came across in his interviews, a friendly, quotable southerner with the best new nickname in the league. It seemed that in Meridian beers were called oil cans. During the summer, Dennis and his friends would sit around the neighborhood gas station knocking back a few cold ones. That was how he picked up the name.

He also had a Doberman that acquired a taste for beer. They both cut down, but how would you like to encounter a Doberman kicking a six-pack-a-day beer habit?

A psychology major at Jackson State, he knew that to stay in the majors he had to wage a constant battle to conquer his temper. When he was seventeen and pitching in a semi-pro game, he blew up after a bad call by an umpire and surrendered a double that broke up his no-hitter and cost him a run. He swore at the umpire, who threw him out of the game. "I took my uniform off and left the park in my underwear," he said. "I sat in my daddy's car, crying, kicking, cussing, and fussing."

Later, his father told him there had been several big league scouts in the stands. They all left when they saw him lose his composure. He didn't know if the scouts would ever come back. Of course, they did.

That intensity was his edge on the mound. Off the field, he struggled to get the genie back in the bottle. To me he was a prime example of how hard it is in baseball to reverse that negative momentum. Players tell each other that nothing matters except what happens "between the white lines." That is absolute nonsense. What you say and where you say it can ruin you faster than a fat pitch over the middle of the plate.

In Boston, Boyd joined a staff that already had Roger Clemens, Bruce Hurst, and Bob Ojeda. He quickly moved in as the number two pitcher behind Clemens. In 1986, he was 11-and-6 at the All-Star break when he learned that for the second season in a row he had been left off the squad, this time by Kansas City manager Dick Howser.

He lost it. He was so confident he would make the team he had already purchased plane tickets and reserved hotel rooms for his entire family. He went screaming through the clubhouse, as I heard it, cursing just about anyone who got in his way. He climbed into his car, gunned it out of the parking lot, and drove around until he had calmed down. "I didn't want to be bawling in front of my locker," he said. When he returned to Fenway Park, the clubhouse man told him he couldn't go in. He had been suspended.

So began a three-week period that branded him. He got into a dispute with two undercover narcotics officers in a Boston suburb. He was described as having serious financial problems. Drug rumors started. He checked into a hospital and proved himself emotionally stable and chemically clean. Every test was negative.

In a span of thirteen days, Boyd's picture appeared on the cover of the *Boston Herald* tabloid eight times. I'm not suggesting that every time an athlete gets into trouble the media has a field day. But every athlete needs to learn the lesson of staying out of harm's way.

His career in Boston never recovered. He missed most of 1987 and chunks of the next two seasons with what eventually would be diagnosed as a blood clot in his right shoulder. It was the same condition that ended J. R. Richard's career—and nearly killed him.

The doctors found an anticoagulant that allowed Boyd to pitch, but his performance was inconsistent and the Red Sox gave up on him. He was traded to Montreal and then to the Rangers. Today, he is still making adjustments, trying to regain his form. He weighed a scrawny 156 pounds when he came to Texas, and it amazes me that he was ever thought of as a power pitcher. He has a great feel for changing speeds and setting up hitters. When he is in that mode, he's hard to beat.

He is a mellower Oil Can Boyd today, and I think he has finally controlled a temper that was once too big for his body.

Of all the sports, only baseball actually encourages humor, allows time and room for funniness. I'm not sure why this is so, but it is. When two athletes collide in football, even with all the pads and armor, what jumps into your mind is a train wreck. The blooper reel makes you cringe. When baseball players run into each other chasing a pop fly, the picture you get is the Three Stooges: Larry, Curly, and Moe. The ball, almost with a mind of its own, bounces away. The blooper reel makes you laugh.

Bad baseball, like truly bad opera (I'm guessing here), can be funny. Bad football can be only upsetting, sad, maddening.

When Mickey McDermott was a pitching coach for the Angels, the story followed him around of a day in May 1948, when he was a skinny, baby-faced left-hander for the Boston Red Sox pitching in his third or fourth big league game. He was that familiar type, wild and fast, the kind who can throw a grape through a brick wall—if he can hit the brick wall.

McDermott and a veteran named Mickey Harris tied a record by walking seventeen Cleveland batters. Harris had issued the first eleven passes and was on the bench cheering McDermott on to greater things when the ninth inning rolled around.

With two out and a full count on Pat Seerey, the voice of Harris could be heard above the rumble of the crowd. "Throw it away," he yelled to McDermott. "Throw it away, Mick. We'll break the record."

Needing just one more wayward pitch to register walk number eighteen and inscribe his and Harris's names forever in the lore of the game, McDermott dutifully heaved a fastball a foot above Seerey's head.

Unfortunately, this is a story without a happy ending. Seerey, a notorious bad ball hitter, swung at the pitch and missed, striking out.

I can relate to that story. I can smile at the futility of the moment and also sympathize with the players. I know how it feels to be young and have no command of your pitches, unable to get yourself together, disoriented with what you are doing. Your arm doesn't feel attached to your body.

I can remember my first season with the Angels, when Del Rice was a rookie manager. In the first inning I walked the bases loaded and I'm behind in the count 3-and-0 to the next hitter with nobody out. I glanced into the dugout and there was Rice, standing over the trainer's medicine trunk, drinking straight out of a big container of Maalox. I'm on the mound, taking that in and thinking, "So, how am I doing, Del?"

The twist is that I came back and struck out that batter and then the next two. Now I had faced six guys, walked three and struck out three, and retired the side. I ducked into the dugout and plopped down beside the manager and Del *wouldn't even look at me.* He just stared straight out across the field. The expression on his face said, "I don't get paid enough to put up with this." He was fighting his demons.

Twenty years later, I still can see him standing there, gulping down that Maalox. Would have made a great TV commercial.

And yet many times I have seen players who looked into the dugout with the bases loaded, tight spot, and started to laugh. On the bench, you knew there was some joking going on. My attitude is that the world won't fall off its axis if I give up a hit or a run. I would much rather not, but you have to keep it in perspective. There are those who find the fun in pitching and those who make it labor and pain. They remind me of certain golfers who believe that any show of emotion weakens them.

There are pitchers you like to watch or be around; or you like to hear the stories that are told about them. And there are the special few, such as Larry Andersen, who manage to weave in their own brand of humor with a touch of locker-room philosophy. They contribute something original to the atmosphere and to the team. Of course, if they couldn't pitch they wouldn't be around to enjoy.

When Andersen landed in Houston he was well traveled, making not much above the major league minimum, and hoping a little magic would occur to extend his career. It did. His slider came to life, and he became one of the National League's most consistent middle relievers. He eventually signed with the Padres as a free agent for a contract in seven figures.

But mainly what he had going for him was an off-the-wall wit that wouldn't let him surrender. The only time he would take a serious approach was when it was time to go to work. You could see him change when he began to take off his jacket to warm up. He was a valuable presence in the clubhouse because he kept the air fresh; he filled what I call the dead time, and there is plenty of that in baseball. He was genuinely funny, always looking for a new gag. It was Andy who found the Conehead masks for Dave Smith, Charley Kerfeld, and himself to wear the day the Astros clinched the division title in 1986. In the Astrodome, with its space-age environment, they looked right at home.

That year and the next, he appeared in 120 games, winning nine out of the bullpen in 1987. After kicking around for years, he finally found a home. Off the mound, he provided us—and the media—with endless hours of puzzlement. He emerged as a collector of Thoughts to Ponder, or Unexplained Mysteries of the Universe.

His specialty is the little teaser that keeps you awake in the middle of the night. For example:

Why is there an expiration date on sour cream?

Why do people park in a driveway and drive on a parkway?

Why do green olives come in a jar and black olives in a can?

"You ever wonder about things like that?" he asked me one day. "I wonder about things like that."

His list grows longer:

Why does your foot smell and your nose run?

Why is it called a shipment if you send it by car and cargo if you send it by ship?

Why do fat chance and slim chance mean the same thing?

What do they package Styrofoam in?

Was Robin Hood's mother known as Mother Hood?

What do they call a coffee break at the Lipton Tea Company?

To his surprise and satisfaction, when Andy's teasers appear in print he often hears from a source. "I got a case of teabags from Lipton's," he reported one day, "and a note that said they call it a tea break."

The thirty-seven-year-old right-hander has lots of questions but almost none of the answers. The last time we talked he hadn't figured out a way to make money from this hobby, but he was working on it.

Of course, the possibilities are endless, as well as timeless. He calculated that he had close to fifty questions that defy science. Every so often an effort to solve one will succeed and, with regret, he removes it from the file.

"I started out wondering how a fly lands on the ceiling," he said. "Did it fly upside down or do a spin at the last instant? Eventually I ran across a story in *Reader's Digest* that said some researchers actually figured it out. They beamed a light on the ceiling and set up a camera, and when a fly came to the light and landed they filmed it in a slow-motion sequence. He extended his two front feet and flipped his body underneath."

We sat together in respectful silence in the Houston dugout that day, both of us acting as if I actually knew what he was talking about. "Yeah," said Andy, "people are starting to mail me questions now. I throw most of them away, the ones that are too far out. I just hope the people who sent them don't think I'm on the same wavelength they are."

How can you tell when you are running out of invisible ink?

Why is it that it's the day that breaks when it's the night that falls?

Why do they call it "freezer burn"?

Aside from his oddball questions, Andersen has spent time coming up with paradoxical phrases. Some of his favorites: jumbo shrimp, plastic glasses, marine land, and a baseball mind.

All he really tries to do, of course, is keep his teammates loose and let a little tension out of what can be a pressure-filled profession. "If your whole life is baseball," he says, "you're just setting yourself up for failure. Even the best hitters make an out two times out of three. And this is not a game you can play your whole life. So if you get injured or something, you feel like you've failed. I refuse to look at myself like that. But you see a lot of young kids coming up who think they've got to make the team or they've failed. That puts a lot of undue pressure on them and it becomes even harder to perform.

"I've seen big-name players who seem to have everything. Million-dollar contracts, big house, and expensive cars. They can't enjoy it. They put so much pressure on themselves that they can't relax and have a good time. Life's too short not to have a good time.

"The one thing I try to do," he said, "is make sure I don't offend anybody. That's the furthest thing from my intention. I just think guys get too wound up before they get into a game. If you went out there just to pitch and didn't have any fun, you'd end up being a total basket case. For myself, if I'm not being screwy or off the wall, I'm in trouble."

Andy's humor is verbal and mental—I'm trying to stay

away from words like intellectual or cerebral; I don't want my neighbors in Alvin to start worrying about me.

Bill Lee wasn't the first big leaguer to wear a full House of David-style beard. Nor was he the first to have a nickname ("The Spaceman") that suggested he was from another planet. But Lee wasn't just a guy with a mind like an eight-lane freeway, including loops. A hard-throwing lefthander who could start or relieve, he was the classic flake. He almost succeeded in bringing the sixties counterculture into baseball.

Lee meditated, made a trip to China, admitted he used marijuana—said he sprinkled it on his pancakes—and negotiated with the commissioner to settle the dispute he knew it would raise. He agreed to pay a $250 fine with the provision that he could donate it to a charity of his choice. He sent the check to an Indian mission in Alaska.

It was an old baseball story—he appealed to the fans because he was different and to the writers because he was so quotable, and the club tolerated him as long as he won. But Lee gave it a twist. When he was no longer winning, he predicted, "I'll wind up face-down in the Charles River."

In the end, it wasn't losing that caused his teams, Boston and Montreal, not to tolerate him. It was the stink he caused when the clubs persisted in trading away his friends. Each time, he went on strike, first when the Red Sox dealt Bernie Carbo to the Indians. Lee staged a one-day walkout, explaining: "They keep saying we're all supposed to be a family here. If you're a family, you don't send your children to Cleveland."

He did it again when the Expos released Rodney Scott. He peeled off his uniform, stalked out of the clubhouse, and spent the day shooting pool in a Montreal tavern. When he reported to the ballpark the next day, the front office had his release papers waiting for him. He signed them "Bill Lee, Earth '82."

When I pitched against him, I had to concentrate all the harder because The Spaceman could distract you with whatever he was doing. We had an odd kind of bond. He considers me his opposite—for all I know, he may have been paying me a compliment. But he thought my power style of pitching was contrary to Newton's Law, insisting that I "was trying to make the ball go up in a world that is basically going down." I tried not to think about it.

But he once said, "If Nolan is the 'Ryan Express,' then I guess I'm the Marrakesh Express." He was always taking off for India or China or Alaska, occasionally by plane. It must have been a trip to be on Bill Lee's team. He once asked the equipment man if he could have the number "733," and the guy looked at him, baffled, and said they didn't carry any such number, why would he want it? "It's Lee spelled upside down," he explained. Well, not quite.

He was funny and tough and he had an opinion about everything, which is guaranteed to cause an outbreak of acid indigestion among baseball's management types. The risk is that people won't remember that he actually could pitch—he won seventeen games three years in a row and then, with his arm nearly gone, won sixteen for the Expos on nothing but wit, wits, and pluck.

But he certainly had a nice touch with a phrase. Once, as Detroit's Al Kaline walked to first after taking a close pitch, he shouted at the Tigers star: "Swing the bat, for Christ's sake. You're not a statue until you have pigeon shit on your shoulders."

And as much as baseball considered him a rebel or a misfit, he could be eloquent in describing the essence of pitching. "The mound is my personal zone," he said. "I compete with myself in an attempt to place each pitch more perfectly than the one that preceded it. I could always relate to Kirk Douglas in *Young Man with a Horn*, trying to strike that note that nobody had ever hit before. I was always trying to throw the perfect sinker."

By most standards, certainly baseball's, Bill Lee would be considered an intellectual. George Kimball, the Boston sports columnist who covered him in his time with the Red Sox, was once assigned to ghostwrite a World Series column for him. After several days of hitting the New York hot spots with "The Spaceman," George found himself with writer's block and a deadline just an hour and a half away. When he got to his desk, though, he discovered two stories neatly stacked there. Lee had written George's column as well as his own.

I doubt that many pitchers would pull a writer out of a ditch, but Bill Lee was one who did.

I suppose there are several reasons why, in my mind, I make a connection between Lee and Al Hrabosky. They were both colorful, eccentric lefthanders from California whose careers were nearly parallel. Hrabosky, "The Mad Hungarian," made it to the majors with St. Louis in 1970, a year after Lee. The 1982 season was the last for both of them.

Hrabosky appeared in 545 games, all but one of them in relief, and pitched over seven hundred innings, which tells you right there that he was a closer. He was awfully good at what he did, saving 94 games. When he figured in the decision, he won 64 percent of the time.

I am not sure whether his antics on the mound were calculated, or whether they came naturally. But Al knew, and that was what mattered. It is a bit of shock today to see him in his role as a broadcaster, without the mustache he copied from Vlad the Impaler. On the mound, he called on the powers of the gypsy war gods, or so he said.

When he glared at a hitter, he called it, "The laser beam of hatred."

Today he says: "I know it sounds schizo. I know that I'm basically playing a role, but out there I really was the Mad Hungarian. I believed in him 100 percent. The Mad Hungarian was an insanely demented maniac, a dangerous lunatic who would do anything to win."

If there is a little redundancy in that thought, it was

Al's way of emphasizing a point. He describes himself as having been a sensitive child who suffered one baseball-related trauma after another. He flunked his Little League tryouts and never even made his junior high baseball team. His instincts were better suited to football, but he stopped growing at 5'-11" and 185, not the ideal dimensions for a pro linebacker.

That was his position in the eighth grade. "I really liked to inflict pain," he says. "But I couldn't control my madness. My coaches would take bets on which quarter I'd get thrown out and I never disappointed them."

He was in a class by himself in 1975, when he was 13-3 for the Cardinals and led the National League with twenty-two saves. He did not just march to a different drummer, he was out there in front of the band.

"A lot of guys questioned my sanity," he says. "Fine. I wanted them to think I was crazy. Hate, rage, destroy. It all has a reason. The emotion, the adrenaline, gave me more power, greater confidence. And that insane look on my face when I turned around . . . it helped me crush a batter's ego. I wanted them to think I was so crazy, so sick, I just might stick the next one in their ear. What I discovered was a thing called controlled rage.

"What I would do, I guess, is get myself psyched on hatred. Like, did the batter get a hit off me? Did he humiliate me with a run batted in? And the fans. Did they hate my guts? Are they giving me a standing boo-ovation? The more they booed, the more psyched up I got."

Still, the ego of a pitcher can be a fragile thing, and the reign of the Mad Hungarian began to fade two years later, when Vern Rapp took over as manager in St. Louis and issued a ban on all facial hair. He ordered Hrabosky to answer any questions from reporters with a "no comment."

We all know the story of Samson, and while Hrabosky didn't shrink away overnight, he was no longer happy in St. Louis. He would wind up with the Royals and finish in Atlanta.

I've never worn a beard or mustache, but I don't suppose I would enjoy having someone tell me I can't. So I sympathized with Al after he shaved off his whiskers and complained: "How could I intimidate a batter when I looked like a damned golf pro?"

To me, Sandy Koufax was the ultimate
pitcher: power, curve, control. He was the
one you would pay to watch pitch.
(Houston Post *photo.*)

Koufax often works with the young Dodger
pitchers at the end of the season. I visited
with Sandy during the '81 playoffs.
(*Photo by Joel Draut.*)

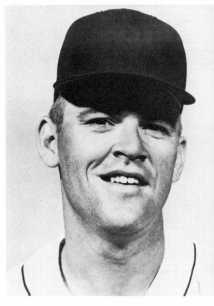

Jim Bouton gets a laugh out of Mickey Mantle (left), but Mick didn't find Bouton's book, *Ball Four*, so funny. (Houston Post *photo*.)

Denny McLain had a rising fastball and devil-may-care attitude. He served up a fat one for Mantle's 535th homer. (Houston Post *photo*.)

Don Drysdale ran a two-for-one special: If you knocked down one of his hitters, he'd knock down two of yours. (*Photo by Ray Covey*.)

It was an adventure to be young and pitching in New York. Koosman and I are listening to Tom Seaver; it figures. (*Photo courtesy of Ruth Ryan.*)

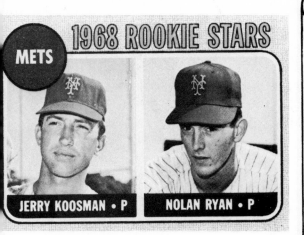

just wanted to make the Mets in 1968, but Jerry Koosman keeps telling me *his* rookie card is worth 1,200 and climbing. (*Truitt Photographics.*)

Babes on Broadway: Jim McAndrew and me either ending or starting the season, I'm not sure which, in the late sixties. (*Photo courtesy of Ruth Ryan.*)

Detroit's Mickey Lolich wasn't really fat. He was strong and had what we call in Texas a farm boy's body. (Houston Post *photograph.*)

He says he wasn't an "all-time great," but Jim Kaat was one of the all-time survivors. He had that tough sidearm twister. (*AP photo.*)

When baseball people talk about serious heat, Sudden Sam McDowell's name always comes up. At times he was unhittable. (Houston Post *photo.*)

If everything was riding on one game, the Cardinals' Bob Gibson would have been the choice of money to pitch it. (*Photo by Ray Covey,* Houston Post.)

Blue Moon Odom had great potential. I remember when the A's used him to pinch run in the World Series; he was out at home. (*AP photo.*)

There were times when Vida Blue amazed me. In the years I saw him, he won without having command of his breaking ball.
(*Photo by Michael Boddy, Houston Post.*)

I enjoyed pitching against Catfish Hunter. He never showed any emotion, not even while he was pitching a perfect game.
(*AP photo.*)

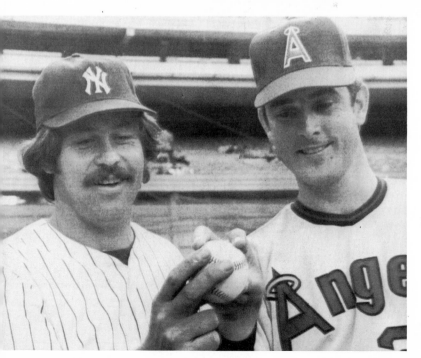

Al Hrabosky thought his facial hair helped convince the hitters he was mean. You couldn't disprove the theory by looking at him. (*Photo courtesy of Rawlings.*)

Sparky Lyle labored for the A's and the Yankees, so I don't think turmoil bothered him much. (*AP photo.*)

Rollie Fingers helped change the way managers used the bullpen. He appeared in seventy or more games in four straight seasons. Give that man a towel. (*UPI photo.*)

Burt Hooton pitched in the shadow of Sutton and Fernando, but won big games for the Dodgers. (*Photo by Joel Draut,* Houston Post.)

Hitters would tell me they started thinking about facing J. R. Richard days before the game. He was a menacing sight. (*Photo by Manuel Chavez,* Houston Post.)

With his beard in full bloom, Bill Lee lived up to his nickname, The Spaceman. Clean-shaven, he seemed almost normal. (*Photos by Peter Brosseau and Mac Juster/Canadian Press.*)

Jim Palmer might have laughed with a bat in his hand, but he was all business on the pitcher's mound. We had our own rivalry going in 1973. (*AP photo.*)

I faced Ferguson Jenkins in both leagues. Few were more consistent. He won twenty games six years in a row for the Cubs. (*UPI photo.*)

As Yogi Berra (left) is supposed to have said, you can observe a lot just by watching. Danny Darwin (center) is a study in intensity when he pitches. (*Photo courtesy of Ruth Ryan.*)

Hey, I can hit, too. I'm being greeted by Art Howe and Alan Ashby after homering in my first at bat with the Astros. (*UPI/Bettmann photo.*)

Some serious shop talk going on here: That's Mel Wright, then the Astros' pitching coach, in the middle as Sandy Koufax makes a point. (*Gulf Photo.*)

Our four-man rotation in Houston in 1980 was as good as any in the National League: Joe Niekro is in front; J. R. Richard and Ken Forsch are to my left. The bats are just props. Mine's corked. (*Photo courtesy of Ruth Ryan.*)

You couldn't get mad at Fernando Valenzuela even when he was beating you. He was definitely the fans' favorite in Hollywood. (*Photo by Joel Draut,* Houston Post.)

There was no happier story in baseball when Mark (The Bird) Fidrych broke in with the Tigers. And, suddenly, it was over. (*AP photo.*)

I wonder how many pitchers hurt themselves trying to imitate Juan Marichal's leg kick? I rank him with Koufax and Drysdale. (*AP photo.*)

When Ron Guidry came to the Yankees out of Southwestern Louisiana, he ranked near the top as a pitcher who threw "bad cheese." (*AP photo.*)

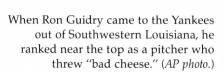

Phil Niekro proved that you could win by throwing nothing but knuckleballs. What he didn't know about pitching probably wasn't worth knowing. (*AP photo.*)

The knuckler saved Joe Niekro's career. He was a big winner in the early eighties, but got more attention over his manicure kit. (*UPI photo.*)

When I was with the Mets, we knew that Tug McGraw had the kind of confidence that made you believe. He didn't hide his feelings, either. (*AP photo.*)

After he retired, Gaylord Perry admitted throwing a spitter and a greaseball. But he swore he was innocent this time when the umpires ejected him. That's Rene Lachemann, the Seattle manager, pleading his case. (*UPI photo.*)

Steve Carlton and I kept swapping the strikeout record in 1983. He had just gone ahead when this shot was taken, tipping his cap to the crowd. (*UPI photo.*)

Bruce Sutter had such command of the split-finger, the hitters would go to the plate looking for it and still come up empty. (*AP photo.*)

Tom Seaver was the only pitcher I knew who could look good slipping and falling on his fanny, as he does here. (*UPI photo.*)

Twenty wins with a twist: Rick Sutcliffe did it in 1984 while pitching in
both leagues, with the Indians and
Cubs. (*AP photo.*)

Pitchers get as much advice as
politicians. George Bush was the
vice president when he gave
Dwight Gooden a pointer at Shea
Stadium. (*AP photo.*)

Goal-oriented is the way I would describe Don Sutton. On his way to three hundred wins, he thought in terms of years, not games. (*AP photo.*)

After he joined the Rangers, I learned that Oil Can Boyd in private wasn't the moody, troubled guy people thought he was. (*AP photo.*)

A fellow Texan, Doug Drabek started in Little League and went all the way—to the Cy Young Award in 1990. (*Photo by John Makely, Houston Post.*)

Others had success with the split-finger fastball, but Mike Scott perfected it. The no-hitter he pitched against the Giants clinched the division for us in Houston in 1986. (*AP photo.*)

Big, strong, smart, durable, and tough in the clutch—Jerry Reuss was all of these. As a lefthanded practical joker, he was hard to beat, too. (*AP photo.*)

The death of Donnie Moore of the Angels raised sad and difficult questions for players and fans alike in 1989. (*AP photo.*)

Neither one of us ever dreamed we would pitch twenty-five years in the big leagues. Tommy John came back from major arm surgery to do it. (*AP photo.*)

Steve Howe made it to the Yankees after stints in rehab and the minors, but still has to battle ongoing problems. (*AP photo.*)

One of the most reassuring sights a starting pitcher can behold is still Goose Gossage coming in from the bullpen. (*AP photo.*)

If I had to pick the most dominating pitcher in the game today, it would be hard to overlook Roger Clemens, with his three Cy Young awards in six years. He may retire the trophy. (*Photo courtesy of the Texas Rangers.*)

When Clemens is on the mound, you can count on some serious heat. My young friend from Katy is hard on the hitters and on occasion the umpires. (*AP photo.*)

Twice Bret Saberhagen won twenty games followed by a losing season. He didn't lose his stuff or his cool. Now he has the comeback thing down pretty good. (*AP photo.*)

Behind that smile is a nervous dad. I have never been as distracted before a start as I was when I pitched for the Rangers against my son Reid, a University of Texas freshman, in an exhibition game in April 1991. (*AP photo.*)

The Minnesota fans showered Jack Morris with confetti after the '91 World Series; I'd like to know that feeling before I retire. (*AP photo.*)

I'm pleased with the way my wife and kids raised me. Left to right: Reese, Ruth, me, Wendy, and Reid. (Photo by Bob Mader.)

Nolan Ryan's
Top Ten Pitchers
Who Can't Be Cloned

(ONE OF A KIND)

1. Satchel Paige

2. Bill (Spaceman) Lee

3. Bo Belinsky

4. Al (Mad Hungarian) Hrabosky

5. Mark (The Bird) Fidrych

6. Larry Andersen

7. Tug McGraw

8. Sparky Lyle

9. Denny McLain

10. Joaquin Andujar

NOLAN RYAN'S
TOP TEN
COLORFUL PITCHERS

1. Vida Blue

2. Dallas Green

3. Jim Golden

4. Bob Lemon

5. Mark Lemongello

6. Blue Moon Odom

7. Don Black

8. Whitey Ford

9. Kevin Brown

10. Gil Blanco

| NOLAN RYAN'S |
| TOP TEN LEAST |
| LIKELY LOOKING PITCHERS |

1. Bobby Shantz

2. Fred Gladding

3. Terry Forster

4. Charley Kerfeld

5. Kent Tekulve

6. Ryne Duren

7. Jumbo Elliott

8. Mickey Lolich

9. Hoyt Wilhelm

10. Johnny Hutchings

The
Bulls
in the Pen

Think about the very term, bullpen, and what it brings to mind: a gate swinging open and an angry bull charging out to confront the matador. And there you have the essence of relief pitching.

Bill Lee's vision is less threatening than mine. "The ultimate relief pitcher would be a Tibetan monk," he says. "Standing on the mound, he would raise his hand and direct the ball over the plate simply by using mind over matter." Whatever the model, relievers have always had their own world out there. These pitchers earn their pay not game to game but batter to batter. You don't need to be in the league very long to collect a dozen stories about relievers who ordered out for pizza, who set part of the stands on fire, who walked across the street to a tavern during a lull in the action and gulped down a quick beer. Explaining how they spend their time is one of the challenges of the job. "A lot of long relievers," said Jim Bouton, "are ashamed to tell their parents what they do. The only nice thing about it is that you get to wear a uniform like everybody else."

But if pitchers belong to a separate community, a brotherhood—and we do—then relief pitchers have an underground of their own.

No area of the game has undergone a more distinct change, or evolution, since the early 1960s. It takes a certain temperament to be a relief pitcher. What not everyone agrees on is what goes into that temperament.

"We're parasites," said Dan Quisenberry, who spent most of his career with the Royals. "We live off the people who spend two hours on the field. In the bullpen there is no definite mood. Anything goes down there as long as you remember three basic rules: no women are allowed, don't do crossword puzzles in the open, and hide the food."

It occurs to me that if he doesn't start out with one, the baseball firefighter ends up with a fatalistic attitude. "I've seen the future," said Quisenberry, "and it is much like the present, only longer."

When Jeff Reardon was with the Expos, the fans once booed his wife at a charity function. "I was upset at the time," he said, "because booing a wife is inexcusable. But it comes with the territory. When a reliever messes up, that's it. Game's over. You're the goat. If you're the type to let things bother you for long periods of time, this is the wrong job."

There have been ones with angry blood, the Richard (Goose) Gossage and Sparky Lyle type, and those with icy blood, such as Elroy Face, Dennis Eckersley, and Bruce Sutter.

I have known pitchers who wound up being effective in the bullpen because of a paradox: They were too nervous to start. I remember a left-hander named Hal Woodeshick who failed as a starter with the Tigers, Indians, and Senators, then had a second career out of the pen in Houston and St. Louis. He walked in his sleep the nights before he was due to start. Once his roommate woke up just as Woody was about to climb out of his hotel window. When they finally decided to switch him to short relief, his worries were over. He didn't have time to get nervous.

The oddity here is that you think of one of the first requirements of relief pitching: a zombielike emotional state. But that idea is a trifle off-center. The ones I've been around, the good ones, have a lot of lava flowing inside. They have learned to channel it, and that is what gives them the edge every good fireman must have.

I used to hear Whitey Herzog say, "A manager is as smart as his bullpen." Herzog would add that he wasn't very smart when they fired him in Kansas City. He didn't have a closer with the Royals. Then he became almost a certified genius in St. Louis, where he had Bruce Sutter and Todd Worrell, among others.

Toss out the strike season of 1981 and only one team in the last ten years has made it to the World Series without a reliever who saved at least nineteen games. The Boston Red Sox were the exception in 1986, and the weakness of their bullpen cost them the sixth and seventh games (although the memory that lingers is of a ground ball trickling through Bill Buckner's legs).

In the mid-1970s, when I was still with the Angels, there were only a handful of star relief pitchers in the game, most notably Bruce Sutter, Rollie Fingers, Sparky Lyle, and Goose Gossage. In the 1980s, something that no one would have thought possible took place—three relief pitchers won the Cy Young Award. (Starting pitchers were not offended, just surprised. Those guys had their own award, we thought. Actually, Rolaids had sponsored the Relief Man Award since 1976.)

The three were Fingers, with Milwaukee in 1981; Detroit's Willie Hernandez in 1984; and Steve Bedrosian of the Phillies in 1987. Their recognition was simply a measure of how crucial relief pitching had become. "If Ty Cobb had had to hit against some of these guys," said Pete Rose, "he might have batted .315" (instead of his lifetime mark of .363).

Today every team needs an ace, a star in the bullpen. And nearly every team has had one: Jeff Reardon, Tom Henke, Dave Righetti, John Franco, Lee Smith, Lance McCullers.

The role of the relief pitcher has made the complete game an almost obsolete stat. There was once an attitude that the middle reliever could be a marginal guy, someone who might or might not hold down the score in a game you were losing, hoping your team would make a comeback. No one thinks that way anymore. They are now called "setup men," and they often have to protect a lead for two or three innings because most teams have no starting depth. The extra starters have been replaced by the specialists. So a manager can no longer afford to let the middle men take them out of a game, allowing his closer to go days at a time without seeing action.

Tracing the beginnings of this trend isn't difficult. I would go back to the early 1970s, when Dick Williams in Oakland and Sparky Anderson in Cincinnati found new ways to use their staffs.

Williams relied on three setup pitchers to prepare the way for his ace, Rollie Fingers, while Sparky became known as "Captain Hook" as he maneuvered three or four relievers around an unreliable rotation. Sparky's theory was: "If I have the bullpen and you don't, then you only have six or seven innings to beat me." To Quisenberry, this is the frontier school of managing: "A manager uses a relief pitcher like a six-shooter. He fires until it's empty, then he takes the gun and throws it at the villain."

A team without reliable setup men forces the stopper to pay a heavy price. Managers reach a point where they won't trust anyone else in the bullpen and they go to the guy with the hot hand day after day. They abuse him until he blows out. It happened to Steve Bedrosian in Atlanta and Tippy Martinez in Montreal. Bedrosian came back. Martinez pitched in seven straight games in 1983, including both ends of two doubleheaders. He was never the same.

Even the great ones have no security. During the winter

meetings in 1980, Fingers was with three teams in four days. St. Louis got him from San Diego, and Whitey Herzog had him fly in to meet the press. The next day he was traded to Milwaukee. So he and Bruce Sutter were teammates for about a day. But it worked out okay. They would have killed each other to get the ball.

When Dick Howser took over the Yankees in 1980, he set the pattern for using relievers that many managers follow today. He brought in his stopper, Gossage, only when New York was ahead and almost never for more than six outs. In addition, he only had the Goose warm up five times that year without sending him to the mound.

Few things wreck the morale, or the arm, faster than getting up and down, warming up for most of a game and never going in to pitch. I've seen managers ruin a pitcher doing exactly that.

Most of the pitchers I've talked with over the years would do somersaults off the nearest curbstone to play for a manager who has been a pitcher. This is one reason Roger Craig, who broke in with the Dodgers and once lost 20 games for the Mets, is so popular in San Francisco.

Herzog was an infielder who didn't quite make it in the majors, but he has studied pitching. I know how Todd Worrell felt when he had his best seasons under the manager they called, with affection, the "White Rat," a reference to his hair, not his character. "Whitey always said that a relief pitcher makes a manager," observed Worrell, "but a manager makes a relief pitcher, too. The managers who understand pitching know how many times a pitcher warms up and how many pitches he has thrown in the bullpen."

Teams today chart every pitch, in some cases including warm-up pitches, and have guidelines for everyone on the staff. The Phillies rarely used Bedrosian for more than an inning. Lee Smith's limit was generally five outs.

I can't be certain when teams started counting pitches, but the first time I ever heard of it was with Paul Richards, who did it with his young throwers in Baltimore and Houston. When Larry Dierker broke in with the Colt .45s right out of high school, Richards had him on a 100-pitch limit. That made an impression on me because I was just finishing high school myself.

And about fifteen years later, when I was having a little arm trouble, Dick Wagner, then the general manager with the Astros, slapped a 100-pitch limit on me. I hated it. For one thing, it was an arbitrary limit. I might have been tired one night after 50 pitches, just getting loose on another after 75. We had several meetings that season and I never could convince Wagner that I knew my arm better than he did.

But the pitch count had more to do with starters than relief pitchers. Yet it was the gauge that told managers when to begin looking for help.

I am no longer surprised that young pitchers sign their first pro contract with the expectation that they will go to the bullpen. When the Mets, and Gil Hodges, stuck me out there it was because they didn't know what to do with me. I never felt that they had any permanent notions of keeping me in relief. For one thing, they didn't have nearly enough confidence in my control. It still amazes me that Hodges brought me into the third game of the 1969 World Series in a tight spot and left me in when I easily might have walked in a run.

If you were a starter and threw hard, the only way you could accept going to the pen was if a team had a set rotation and you knew there wouldn't be an opening any time soon. The Chicago Cubs drafted Lee Smith out of high school in Castor, Louisiana, and tried to custom-tailor him into a relief pitcher.

To begin with, Lee had never heard of the Cubs before they drafted him. Smith, who was 6-6, told Mike Roarke, the Chicago pitching coach, that he didn't care for the idea and thought he would go to college and play basketball instead.

Roarke, a tough ex-catcher and a former college football player, told him: "Your fastball is a helluva lot better than your jump shot, so get your butt out to the bullpen."

The first time I saw Lee Smith enter a game for the Cubs,

I had to rub my eyes. He threw the ball 100 miles an hour or better, and he got it over the plate. It was the right move, but he remembers his reluctance. "I thought the big man always started," he said.

Not anymore.

Baseball will never be as specialized as football, but the bullpen by committee is definitely here to stay. It's easier to find someone who can go through a batting order once than it is to find a Roger Clemens or a Jack Morris who can complete a lot of games.

Whatever the right makeup might be, the right stuff is even more important. Some managers like them unflappable, and some don't mind if they are a little goofy. Tug McGraw liked to sit on flagpoles. Moe Drabowsky once used the bullpen phone to order takeout food from a Chinese restaurant. Rollie Fingers showed little or no emotion.

But they all had the right stuff.

There are names so right, so perfect for baseball that no one could have made up a better one. Babe Ruth, of course, was the all-time best baseball name. Mickey Mantle, Joe DiMaggio, Mel Ott, Yogi Berra—can you imagine any of them playing anything but baseball, anywhere but in New York?

The Mets (and later the Phillies) had Tug McGraw. That name says to us: a scrapper. Mischief. *Our Gang.* I doubt that anybody ever in his life called him Frank.

When Tug first came to the Mets, baseball people considered him a flake. The more traditional managers are often made nervous by this breed of player. But the more success McGraw had, the more his antics were tolerated, and he became a personality in New York and Philadelphia. Gil Hodges, a no-nonsense guy, kept trying to rein him in, and his maturity grew out of the four or five years he was associated with Gil.

Hodges took a protective interest in him. He drilled into him the concept of what was acceptable and what wasn't. If Tug had been with a less forceful manager in those years, his unchecked energy might have swept him right out of the league.

His screwball made McGraw a pitcher, and one timely slogan made him a character and a hero.

Tug did most of his growing up in front of the fans. He was spontaneous, impulsive, excitable. "Fans did not have any trouble reading me," he said. "My attitude was, 'This is a great life. I'm more than willing to share it with you.' " He wore his emotions on his sleeve like a patch.

His instincts were keen. Once, pitching against the Dodgers in Los Angeles, a piece of strategy backfired and he took out his frustration on the next hitter. He plugged the likable Bill Russell, touching off a brawl.

I can't say what makes one such moment larger than another. Maybe it has to do with the fans reacting to what is seen as a blatant, unsportsmanlike act. There was the time Pete Rose injured Bud Harrelson of the Mets with a slide at second base that was more like a rolling football block. On his next trip to New York, Pete received death threats.

McGraw concocted a plan to disarm the crowd when the team made its next visit to Dodger Stadium. He appeared on the field for batting practice wearing a combat helmet and military fatigues. Russell got into the spirit of it by showing up with a giant, comic boxing glove on one hand. The Los Angeles fans lapped it up. They knew show business when they saw it.

With Tom Seaver, Jerry Koosman, and McGraw carrying them down the stretch, the Mets won the pennant in 1973 in another fairy-tale finish. They won it under Yogi Berra, who had taken over as manager after Gil Hodges died of a heart attack.

The Mets were in last place in their division on Friday, August 17, thirteen games under .500 after a loss to the Reds, seven-and-a-half games behind the first-place Cardinals. That night the president of the team, M. Donald Grant, visited the clubhouse and made a short speech, telling the players they had to believe in themselves.

Moments later, McGraw jumped on a chair and started shouting, "You gotta believe! You gotta believe!" Some of his teammates thought he was clowning or mocking Grant. But Tug said later that his wife had said the same thing as he left his house to drive to the ballpark.

The words became his mantra and the team's battle cry. He would start chanting it as he pulled into the parking lot. The newspapers picked it up, and fans, even nuns, began writing it on signs to hold up at Shea.

The division was so weak that year, the race so close, that five teams were still contenders going into the last week—and only the Mets were over .500. They wound up winning it with 82 wins. In the final six weeks, McGraw won five games and saved eleven. He led the cheers, too: "You gotta bee-leeeve!"

Tug had the ability to whip the crowd into a frenzy, just by dashing—as he usually did—from the dugout to the bullpen, or coming off the mound pounding his glove against his thigh to celebrate another win.

There was a funny story behind that gesture, and Tug told it to Marty Sutphin, an editor for the Associated Press. He was pitching in Triple-A in 1968, a starter then, and he threw a two-hit shutout the day after he got married. At the end of each inning, as he returned to the dugout, he tipped his cap to his wife in the stands. But each time she would shake her head. Later, she explained: "You tipped your cap to a lot of women when you were single. I want a special sign."

And the thumping-glove sign was introduced.

The Mets beat the Reds in the playoffs and lost to Oakland in seven games in the World Series. Two years later, they began breaking up the club and fired Berra in midseason.

Not long after he was traded to the Phillies, McGraw had surgery to remove a benign tumor from his back. He quickly returned to form and had the city of Philadelphia in the palm of his left hand. He pitched in five more playoffs and one more World Series.

That one was at the expense of our Houston team in 1980. He appeared in all five of the league championship games, including the last one, which the Phillies rallied twice to win, 8–7, in ten innings. Had I not let a three-run lead get away from me, the Astros, not the Phillies, would have been in the World Series against Kansas City. I think that was the only time I have been unable to hold back tears in the clubhouse after a game.

The Phillies went on to beat the Royals in six games, and a Philadelphia barge line renamed one of its boats the *Tug McGraw*.

There were only a handful of pitchers who mastered the screwball in the last 25 years, and the three best were Fernando Valenzuela, Mike Marshall, and McGraw. The pitch set up everything else for Tug, his curve and slider and the fastball he could throw at three speeds. He called his cut fastball—where you take a little off—"the Peggy Lee," because hitters would watch it cross the plate and ask, "Is that all there is?"

He struck out Willie Wilson in the ninth inning with the bases loaded to save the last game of the 1980 World Series. After the game, he was asked if relief pitching was primarily mental. He said no. "If it was, I'd be in the trainer's room soaking my head in ice. I've never been paid a dime for my brains."

He held the club record for games saved for both the Mets and the Phillies when he retired on Valentine's Day of 1985.

In the 1970s, the approach to relief pitchers, how they were measured and valued, the psychology of how they were used, underwent yet another major change.

Two things had happened. In 1969, an official statistical category was created called the "save," and it established a new standard of excellence unrelated to wins and losses. Now every stud in the bullpen wanted to be the late-inning guy, the finisher.

The other factor was the declining importance of the complete game. In Cincinnati and later Detroit, Sparky Anderson won pennants while yanking his starters at any time, using his staff as a kind of relay team. He drove his pitchers nuts, and around the leagues a lot watched what he was doing with some foreboding. But Sparky thrived on his reputation as "Captain Hook," and the bottom line was that in most seasons his teams stayed in the race.

The 1974 World Series was the third straight in which no starting pitcher completed a game. The era of the relief specialist had arrived.

Sparky Lyle broke in with the Red Sox, struck gold with the Yankees, and finished with the Rangers and Phillies. He defined the new order when he joked, "Why pitch nine innings when you can get just as famous pitching two?"

Closers, such as Lyle, Mike Marshall, Rollie Fingers, Al Hrabosky, Bruce Sutter, Goose Gossage, and Jeff Reardon, began appearing in 50, 60, 70 games almost routinely. They were called on to protect a lead, pitch an inning or less, and to do it day after day. There were pitchers whose basic responsibility was to retire one hitter when the left-right percentages dictated it.

Pitchers have replaced other pitchers for as long as the game has existed. (In the late 1800s, when the rules did not permit substitutions unless a player became hurt or ill, one fielder was designated as the "change" pitcher.) In 1911, Mordecai (Three Finger) Brown started 27 games and relieved in 26. There were the legendary early firemen: Fred (Firpo) Marberry with Washington, Brooklyn's Hugh Casey, and Johnny Murphy and Joe Page with the Yankees.

But the bullpen became a priority in the 1960s, and financial parity with the starters arrived in the next decade.

Lyle emerged as an all-star in 1973 and the best in the game in 1977, when the Yankees went to the World Series in spite of the kind of turmoil that destroyed most teams.

Sparky had an ideal temperament for a relief pitcher, although no one really agrees on what that is. He was feisty, stubborn, proud, with a funny bone and a kiss-my-foot attitude. Those qualities served him well when the egos clashed in Yankee Stadium, as they constantly did in the heyday of George Steinbrenner, Billy Martin, and Reggie Jackson. The New York writers began to refer to the stadium as "The Bronx Zoo," which became the title of Lyle's bestselling book about the 1978 season.

Sparky had the cockiness that managers often prefer in a closer. He was outspoken, even defiant. After he struck out Willie Mays on three pitches in the 1973 All-Star game, he was asked by a reporter if he felt badly about fanning Mays. "Hell, no," he said, puzzled. "Why should I feel bad?"

He was told that Mays, who had announced that he would retire at the end of the season, was making his last All-Star appearance.

"I don't know what you're getting at," said Lyle, "but I felt real good about striking him out. Real good. I'm sorry I didn't get the chance to strike him out twice."

When a pitcher constantly goes into a situation where the game is on the line, where one mistake is all he gets, he tends not to be very sentimental.

Sparky impressed me because he was a leader on that Yankee team, and he did it by being himself. Relief pitchers are not often in a position to provide leadership. They are physically and sometimes emotionally at a distance because they can't be certain when they will be playing. It is even harder on a team that had as many factions and as much turbulence as the Yankees of Steinbrenner and Martin.

I have been on clubs that had personality clashes and a certain amount of petty bickering. Most teams do. The Angels were just cleaning up their clubhouse when I joined them. The Red Sox, the Dodgers, and the Mets have their histories of unrest and dissension. The Oakland A's, and Charles Finley, proved that you can win pennants without a love fest.

But for continuing looniness the Yankees were in a class of their own. In the 1970s you sat spellbound, waiting for the next episode. That season Reggie Jackson and Billy Martin had to be separated in the dugout. Catfish Hunter argued with Martin, Sparky with Jackson, and Jackson with Mickey Rivers and Thurman Munson.

No owner meddled more in the daily operation than Steinbrenner. He screamed at the players, called them into his office, second-guessed the manager. But the big problem with the Yankees was that they no longer had a nucleus of players who had grown together.

I'll give this to Sparky: He didn't hold much back. He had mixed feelings about Martin, especially after the Yankees traded for Goose Gossage and tried to use Sparky in long relief. But he was loyal to Billy and resented the fact that Reggie was not.

Once, Jackson loafed on a pop fly that fell in front of him for a single and Martin made a point of embarrassing him. He went to the mound to change pitchers, and at the same time he sent Paul Blair to right field to replace Reggie. That day Reggie had refused to come out early to shag flies and work on his fielding, so you can guess what frame of mind Billy was in.

This was in front of a full stadium and a national television audience, and Reggie felt that the manager had tried to humiliate him, which he had. In the dugout, he confronted Martin: "What did I do?"

Martin said, "You know what you did."

"You have to be crazy to show me up in front of all those people," Reggie yelled at him and then, according to Sparky, he insinuated that Billy was old.

Martin snapped and went for Jackson's throat. Elston Howard and Yogi Berra had to wrestle him to the other end of the bench, while Reggie shouted at him, "You better start liking me. If one of us is going to go, it isn't going to be me."

It was hardly a secret that Reggie had, or thought he had, a direct line to Steinbrenner. The next day the word spread that Martin was going to be fired. Sparky went to Billy and said he just wanted him to know that if he lost his job because of the incident, he was going to pack his bags and go back to New York for the rest of the road swing. He did it because the manager was right to remove Jackson. His message was, if you can't discipline a player for giving a sorry effort, "then you might as well have made Reggie the manager."

A few weeks later, Steinbrenner did fire Martin, in the middle of the race, and brought in Bob Lemon. Scorched by the fan reaction, George then announced that Martin would be rehired for the 1980 season, after a nice rest.

I don't know if Sparky made a protest or not, but the Yankees rallied to win the pennant, and after the season the club traded him to the Rangers. As Graig Nettles put it, "He went from Cy Young to sayonara."

Nolan Ryan's Top Ten Pitchers Who Take the Worry Out of Being Close

1. Rollie Fingers
2. Bruce Sutter
3. Goose Gossage
4. Sparky Lyle
5. Dan Quisenberry
6. Hoyt Wilhelm
7. Elroy Face
8. Tug McGraw
9. Mike Marshall
10. Dave Smith

The
Young
and the
Restless

Pitchers are the shooting stars of the game, more visible than the position players because the "W" or the "L" appears next to their names. When things go bad, the flameout seems all the faster and more devastating.

Some come back, most do not. The list of those who don't keeps growing: Mark Fidrych, J. R. Richard, Steve Blass, Randy Jones, Steve Stone, LaMarr Hoyt, Pete Vuckovich, John Denny.

Then there are those like Frank Tanana, who make hard transitions. When we were with the Angels, he had the nastiest stuff of any lefthander I had seen since Koufax. Then he hurt his arm and made it back as a total junkman; his fastball couldn't blacken your eye. He adopted a calmer life-style, too.

John Candelaria, Mike Flanagan, Bert Blyleven, and Rick

Sutcliffe were others who, in the last decade or so, saw brilliant seasons followed by disaster, their careers threatened.

No one can be certain where it goes, the talent or the desire of a young pitcher cut down in the high noon of his career. But I can tell you, few sights are any sadder.

In the spring of 1991, Charley Kerfeld, just a big, happy moose of a guy, was getting a last chance with the Texas Rangers. At twenty-seven going on seventeen, he had been traded by the Astros and released by the Braves. By coincidence, one of the rookies in camp was a pitcher, Brian Bohannon, who had been a batboy in Houston during my earlier years there.

Bohannon was rehabbing an injury, and as we ran wind sprints one morning I couldn't take my eyes off his haircut. It was flat on the top, almost shaved on the sides, and real long in the back, almost ponytail-long. In a half-kidding way, I said, "Hey, Bo, what's the deal with that haircut?"

He said, "What do you mean?"

I said, "I mean, why do you have your hair cut like that?"

The question apparently puzzled him. He wrinkled his face and said, slowly, "Well, I have to have my own identity," and he spaced the word so that it came out, i-den-ti-tee.

I nodded and said, "I want you to do me a favor this morning."

Politely, he said, "What's that?"

I said, "Go over and ask Charley Kerfeld about having your own i-den-ti-tee. About four years ago I had this same conversation with him. On St. Patrick's Day 1987, he came to the ballpark with lightning bolts shaved into the side of his head and they were painted green. I asked him about it and he said, 'I am searching for my i-den-ti-tee.' Bo, I want you to go ask Charley how he feels about his i-den-ti-tee now. Ask him if he wished he hadn't done all those things because of how he has been labeled."

Bohannon just stared at me, as if wondering what in the world my point was and what could it possibly have to do with him. But later in the day, in the clubhouse, I yelled over to Kerfeld: "Charley, do you remember a few years ago, telling me about how you had to have your own i-den-ti-tee, and that was why you dressed and acted the way you did?"

Kerfeld slowly nodded his head. I said, "And do you remember me saying there might come a time when you wished you hadn't called the club's attention to yourself? How do you feel about it now?"

He said, "Well, I wish to hell I had listened to you back then." Here it was, four years later, and young Brian Bohannon was going through the same cycle. Baseball does repeat itself.

In 1986, Kerfeld was one of those rookies who just explodes on the scene, which isn't easy to do out of the bullpen. But he had a flair, an appeal that reminded you a little of what Fernando Valenzuela had done for the Dodgers in 1981, rolling out of a village in Mexico to flatten National League batters like a tortilla.

Charley went 11-and-2 in his rookie year, as Houston lost to the Mets in the playoffs, losing the last game in sixteen innings, 7–6, in what some of the writers called the greatest game ever played.

Kerfeld looked like a huge marshmallow, 6'–6" and about 250, but he threw hard and enjoyed himself and the fans fell for him. Oh, no one was ready to say that Charley was cut from the same cloth as Dick (The Monster) Radatz, who was big and fast and wild. Nor did they rush to compare him to Ryne Duren, who had even more impressive credentials. He was big and fast and wild and nearsighted.

Duren, the ace of the New York Yankees' bullpen in the mid-1950s, used to psych out hitters by throwing his first few warmup pitches against the screen.

Kerfeld played games with no one but himself. Still, it is hard to overstate the value of having an ogre in the bullpen, a fellow who by merely standing up and adjusting his knickers can send a shiver of fear through the opposing dugout. Charley was a figure of promise. You had the feeling that, without overtrying, he could be a throwback to the old-timey pitchers who would sneak out the bullpen gate to go chase a fire engine.

He tried to show the Astros what kind of heart he had in 1986. He shed 45 pounds over the winter, slimming down from a peak of 286, a feat of remarkable discipline. This is a guy who ate pizzas as though they were pretzels.

Charley had made great sacrifices for the team. There was a wonderful moment in the middle of a game against the Braves when he leaped off the bench to pitch the ninth, banged his head against the railing, and ricocheted back into the bench, almost knocking himself out. I laughed so hard I darn near needed oxygen.

But the next spring, the stories about Charley all had to do with his life-style. He had the lightning bolts shaved into the side of his hair and painted them green for St. Patrick's Day. He invited women to share a bath with him in a tub filled with Jell-O. He wrestled with Hulk Hogan. He collected T-shirts featuring the Simpsons. He drank enough Miller Lite to qualify for his own beer commercial. He played Beastie Boys and AC/DC tapes loud enough to break Plexiglas. And when he had trouble finding the plate, the Astros shipped him to Tucson, their Triple-A farm club in the Pacific Coast League.

He was twenty-three, the only major leaguer ever born in Knob Noster, Missouri. He pitched five no-hitters as a schoolboy and managed to win one of them, so erratic was his control.

"I would strike out nineteen or twenty guys," he said. "Sometimes I'd strike out all the batters, but I'd also have eight walks and four hit batsmen and a whole bunch of wild pitches."

Drafted by the Astros in the first round in 1982, Charley ascended through the minors to reach Houston at the end of the 1985 season. The next year he splashed into prominence.

He wouldn't merely enter the game; he would splatter into it like a bag full of water tossed from the top of a tower. He would stomp and stagger around the mound, then leer at the hitter through eyeglasses as murky as last night's beer bottle. The comparison to Duren did have merit. Charley was nearly blind in his left eye. "I try to get the most hideous-looking glasses I can find," he said.

He had a touch of Duren and Radatz and Mark Fidrych in him. He told reporters that the thoughts uppermost in his mind were about girls and money.

As if his forthright manner wasn't noteworthy enough, he did something in the 1986 league playoffs that endeared him to a national television audience. Pitching at Shea Stadium in the eighth inning of a tight game three, Kerfeld threw Gary Carter a low fastball. Carter hit a bolt right back to the mound.

Undaunted by a delivery that left him stumbling toward the first-base dugout, Charley whipped his glove behind his back and caught the ball with a sensational grin. "I've tried that a thousand times," he said later, "and caught the ball maybe twice. It was a great feeling, especially because I hate Carter and there were 55,000 people in the stands. No, make that 55,000 animals from the zoo."

Humility wasn't his strong suit. Embroiled in a contract dispute, he settled when the Astros agreed to provide him with 37 boxes of orange Jell-O, orange because he was mourning the team's decision to drop its notorious rainbow-colored uniforms; the number 37 because it had been worn by some of baseball's more imaginative souls, such as Casey Stengel, Jim Piersall, and Bill (Spaceman) Lee, late of Boston, Montreal, and the planet Pluto.

"I always liked Bill Lee," Kerfeld told me. "He said what he wanted and wasn't afraid of the repercussions."

The ball club grew increasingly upset with his antics, partly because the one who made them public was Charley. He told reporters that he had decided not to use the orange Jell-O for clubhouse pranks, such as pouring it into teammates' shoes. Instead, he planned to go swimming in it with a girlfriend, who had offered to bring the whipped cream.

"But then," he said, "we got sick of each other and dropped the idea."

Then it was the front office's turn. He gained 25 pounds and lost nine miles per hour off his fastball and his pitches were getting mashed. He practiced his windup in front of a mirror. He talked to me and he talked to Mike Scott, looking for advice. Then he went to Houston and talked to a palm reader named Madame Zelda. "Basically," he said, "she took my twenty-five dollars and said everything would be fine in five days."

Three days after visiting Madame Zelda, Kerfeld was demoted to Tucson. On the phone answering machine in his apartment in Houston, he left this message: "I ain't here and I ain't gonna be here. I'm going, going, gone."

In Tucson, he had a run-in with his manager, drew a suspension, and drew comfort wherever he could find it. He took note of the rise and fall of Bret Saberhagen, who at twenty-one was the youngest American Leaguer to win the Cy Young award and the World Series MVP trophy. The next year, Saberhagen suffered through injuries and a 7–12 finish.

By the All-Star break in 1987 he had won fifteen games and people were laughing at his jokes again. Noted Kansas City's veteran reliever, Dan Quisenberry: "When everything was going good and Bret was loosey-goosey, everybody said, 'What a great temperament for a pitcher.' Then it was, 'When is he going to get serious and stop taking everything as a joke?' Now everybody loves his loosey-goosey attitude again. You'd be amazed how much funnier people think your stories are when you put up big numbers."

But for Charley the numbers didn't come and the laughter died. He commuted between Tucson and Houston but couldn't recapture the form of his rookie season. Somewhere along the way he developed shoulder and elbow problems and underwent surgery. He still had the mischief and charm and the self-deprecating humor, but the anything-goes spirit was tempered by two and a half years of pain.

If this sounds like a requiem for a heavyweight, I can

only hope not. Kerfeld isn't the type to just fade away. He was with the Astros the first two weeks of 1990 and, as pitchers often tell themselves, he was only a pitch away.

"My worst moment," he says, "was opening night. My first night back. I really wanted to do well and I got so close. One pitch. I was one pitch away. Got it one more INCH over the plate than I wanted. If I got that guy out, things might have done a three-sixty in my favor."

The guy was Barry Larkin, whose bases-loaded triple off Kerfeld in the eleventh inning beat the Astros that night. The Reds went on to lead the pennant race from wire to wire to win and sweep Oakland in the World Series. Kerfeld wound up back at Tucson.

"The reality," he said, "is that I didn't make the pitches I had to make. You come into the majors from an itty-bitty small town, and you want to experience so many things. I've seen the good and the bad in a short time, how quick you get to taste stardom and how quickly it goes."

After his release by the Braves, I helped arrange his tryout with the Rangers in spring training. I talked to him during the winter, told him what he needed to do to get in shape, how he needed to throw strikes to make the club. He reported twenty pounds overweight. I didn't get to see him pitch, but Bobby Valentine told me he couldn't remember Charley ever getting ahead in the count.

He wound up in the Mexican League, hoping to find his fastball and his confidence. As I analyze his case, I think much of Charley's problem was created by his size. Growing up, he was so much bigger than everyone else, the expectations were inflated. He was expected to be the team leader, bully and enforcer. In fact, he is the classic Ferdinand the Bull type, extremely insecure. He was just so formidable as a kid, he slid by on his size and ability and never had to learn to pitch.

When I was still in high school, catching a game or two at the Astrodome, but thinking seriously about going to a junior college and playing basketball, Bo Belinsky was breaking in with the Los Angeles Angels. He was dating Mamie Van Doren and Tina Louise and other starlets, as they were called then, and enjoying the patronage of Walter Winchell, the famous gossip columnist with the staccato radio delivery.

Bo also managed to fit a little baseball into his busy social calendar, and for a time he gave the old game a rather vigorous shaking up.

By the time I signed with the Mets, Belinsky had been traded from the Angels to the Phillies and then to the Astros. Wherever he went, he became a terrific crowd pleaser and a popular presence in the clubhouse, especially among those single players who were eager to join Bo on his excursions into the world of romance.

It was Belinsky who, pressed for an example of what made him happy, replied: "Happiness is a nice pad, good wheels, and an understanding manager."

Back then, the standard gag was whether or not baseball would interfere with Bo's career. He was left-handed and graceful, with a lively arm. Some scouts thought he reminded them a little of Koufax, but not for long. He was handsome in a dark, dramatic kind of way, glib and suave and quotable. When he appeared at his first press conference after being traded to the Astros, he ended the lunch by raising a champagne glass and offering a toast:

"If music be the food of love, by all means, play on." The press all but fell out of their chairs. They had found a pitcher who quoted Shakespeare.

If only he could have pitched.

But by any measurement, he was one of the game's wonderful characters, and he left with no regrets. "People keep telling me I wasted my talent," he said. "I don't see it that way. I figure I got more ink for doing less than any pitcher who ever lived."

When I joined the Angels in 1971, they were still telling stories about him, how he teamed up with Dean Chance to drive Bill Rigney, the manager, and Fred Haney, his boss, to the edge of sanity.

A rookie drafted out of the Baltimore farm system, he reported a week late to the Angels spring training camp at Palm Springs in 1962. He called a news conference to announce that he had been detained by a billiards tournament. Then he demanded a raise.

But that was just for openers. In May, he pitched a no-hitter against the Orioles and went on to win his first five games, all but standing baseball on its dignified ear. Within a month he had acquired a pink Cadillac, a famous blonde fiancée (Miss Van Doren), a business agent, a lawyer, and Walter Winchell's readership. All on an annual salary of $7,000.

He might have conquered the world. "Instead," said Bo, "the no-hitter I pitched actually cost me money. I had to buy drinks for everyone. It was like making a hole-in-one."

It was all downhill after that. He fell prey to the neon lights of Hollywood, finished his rookie season with a record of eight wins and ten losses, and became stamped as the playboy of the Western world.

He reported punctually the next spring, with Mamie Van Doren as his fitness director. He ended the season pitching in Hawaii. "He needed the rest," Mamie explained.

When the Angels decided to farm him out, Bo responded with his own flawless logic by asking for a raise. By removing him from Los Angeles, he pointed out, the club was cutting him off from extra sources of revenue. Secondly, he argued, his reduction in status to a minor leaguer hurt his image at the banks.

By now it was clear that Bo's relationship with the Angels had become a sort of Tom and Jerry cartoon, in which he matched wits with the front office and lost. It was Haney's belief that Belinsky needed the stability and sense of purpose that matrimony would bring, and like a kindly uncle he nudged him accordingly. He expressed alarm about Bo's taste in women, and he declared in public that if the young south-paw would tend to his knitting, he could become "a great asset to his team, to baseball, and to himself," which was asking a lot of any man.

Bo conceded that a good portion of his problems in Los Angeles stemmed from his discovery of a limitless supply of beautiful women. "No guy," said the streetwise native of New Jersey, "should be sent to Los Angeles without the proper orientation course." He had swell memories of the first winter he spent there.

"As luck would have it," he said, "the East and Midwest caught the coldest winter in years. Dames I knew in New York, Baltimore, and Chicago wrote to me, wanting to come out to California. They asked me such things as where would I recommend they stay?

"Several times I thought of sending them Fred Haney's address, to show him the nice girls I went out with."

His three years with the Angels were a dizzy and excit-ing whirl. On one road trip, Bo and Chance pulled up in a taxicab at three in the morning to discover the entire team, including Rigney, standing on the sidewalk in their night-clothes. The hotel had been evacuated because of a fire alarm.

The Angels traded him to Philadelphia, which had also acquired first baseman Dick Stuart as part of a rebuilding program that went nowhere. Although now located just 30 miles from his hometown of Trenton, Bo was miserable dur-ing the two seasons he spent with the Phillies. He felt useless and complained that his manager, Gene Mauch, couldn't relate to him. Mauch had been enthused about the acquisi-tion, predicting that Bo would provide the club with at least a dozen wins.

He had a good spring but early in the season complained of a pain in his ribs. He was told it was a muscle kink and he had to pitch through it. By the time x-rays showed that the rib was cracked, Bo's summer was in trouble, and so were the Phillies.

Sent back to the minors, he was claimed by Houston and

soon was basking on the sun-kissed shores of Cocoa Beach, near the club's spring training complex. Somehow he acquired a stray dog, which he named Alfie, after a womanizing character played by Michael Caine in a popular motion picture. Houston was soon to learn what Bo was all about.

For a brief period, there were scare stories issuing out of Florida that he was a new man. There were wild tales about Bo the dog lover, and how he had forsaken the pleasures of the flesh. In bed by midnight. No soft stereo in the background. No king-size four-poster. Even Bo believed it.

"I'm living the good life," he would tell visiting journalists. "I am making the milkshake and eight hours of sleep scene."

But it was at best a temporary adjustment, brought on by the conditions around him. Anyone familiar with the nightlife in Cocoa could understand why Bo adopted a dog. His friendship with Alfie, a shaggy black and white mongrel who wandered into camp one day, became part of the team's lore. Alfie was flown back to Houston as the club's new mascot and soon had nearly as much publicity as Rin Tin Tin. The clubhouse man provided him with a sandbox between Bo and another relief pitcher, Barry Latman, who moaned: "How am I going to explain to my wife that I locker next to a dog?"

It generally comes as a jolt to anyone who looks up his record and realizes that, for all the headlines he inspired, Bo won a total of 25 games as a starter in his first five seasons in the majors. He earned his reputation as a Romeo and party animal, and there was little written or said about him that he resented.

Bo was never one to enjoy the splendor of the morning hours, and he seldom accepted phone calls in his hotel room before 1:00 P.M. In Los Angeles, he once slept through the early innings of an afternoon game.

The importance of attitude in sports was established long ago. Those who hit it big are propelled by an inner motor that pushes them almost relentlessly. What stirred inside Belinsky's skull wasn't known, but it was obvious that as a competitor he chose to sleep until 1:00 P.M. He was not one of those who raced through life. He strolled leisurely, stopping to sniff the flowers.

Now a guy who adopts stray dogs, shoots pool, dates ladies named Mamie and Tina, and quotes the classics can't be all bad. Even Gene Mauch conceded that Bo was a charming sort of rogue. "You can't help but like the guy," said Gene, plucking at another strand of gray hair as he filled out the deportation papers.

Belinsky was by no means a buffoon. He had a caricaturist's talent for capturing the essence of things. For example, his opinion of Philadelphia: "Philly is a town where you can see *Ramar of the Jungle* four times on the late show. Soon as I pop into the hotel, flip on the TV, and see the jungle scene, I say, 'Hey, Ramar, I'm back in Philly.' "

Hawaii, he sums up, "is where the goodies are." And: "Oklahoma City [then the home of Houston's top farm team] is nice if you bring enough Alka Seltzer."

In short, Bo was an original, and not even the lords of baseball, with their subtle pressures, could change him. They tried to stifle Bo, sit on him, shut him up, smooth him out until he blended in with the fences. But in the end the only one who was able to stop him was Belinsky himself.

His second spring as an Astro, he jumped the team to sunbathe on the beach with a lady he had discovered in the centerfold of *Playboy* magazine. Jo Collins (39-24-38) had started out as the playmate for September, and wound up as the Playmate of the Year for 1969.

For Bo, the days grew short when he reached September. The Astros suspended him, and rather than accept a demotion to Oklahoma City, Belinsky demanded his release so he could return to Hawaii. In time, happily, Bo got his wish and pitched for the Islanders until his contract was acquired by the Pirates, and again by the Cardinals, and finally by the Reds.

Teams and managers tend to believe that they can reform and reshape a problem player who appears to have talent. Jo thought so, too. They were married and had a few fun-filled years traveling baseball's byways, became the parents of a daughter, then were divorced. Bo was through in the majors after 1970, appearing in three games in relief for Cincinnati, with no wins and no losses.

"If you get involved with gorgeous women like I did," he said, "it's tough keeping up with them. The money you spend is incidental. It's all the time you have to invest. Then if it leaks out that you're going with someone in the limelight, that puts added pressure on you. If the ballclub finds out they throw it in your face."

Of course, in Houston as elsewhere, the younger players were intrigued with Belinsky and his record. He became more philosophical as the seasons slipped past. "The first thing I would tell any young player coming up," he said, "is the importance of conditioning. He can't do his best if he doesn't get enough rest every night. Smoking is no good either. It cuts down your wind."

At that precise moment, Rusty Staub, just coming into his own in Houston, walked by and asked, not unreasonably: "Then what are you doing with that cigarette in your hand?"

"Do as I say," retorted Bo, "not as I do."

"That isn't much of answer," said Staub.

"Okay," conceded Bo with a shrug, "so I'll never be a superstar."

He never was. And no one knows whatever became of Alfie.

I try to be fair when I look at the case of Denny McLain and Pete Rose and others whose falls were steep, who went from idol to inmate. I try to separate their legal problems from how I knew them as competitors. But I don't condone what they did. I don't believe in making exceptions. No matter how much success you have in sports or anywhere else, you still have to abide by the laws of society. That may sound simplistic. But when you enjoy the kind of adulation they did, you come into contact with a wild variety of people, and the temptations can be enormous.

Denny McLain wore number 17 when he won 31 games in 1968, at the age of twenty-four. He was thought of as a kind of Studs Lonigan character, charming his way out of the trouble he seemed to keep inviting.

In March 1985, as major league teams were assembling for the rites of spring, he was wearing number 04000-018. His was just another number at the federal penitentiary in Talladega, Alabama. His uniform was a drab, tan, prison-issue jumpsuit, with black socks and blue sneakers.

At one point, he stood before a federal judge, who was preparing to sentence him to 23 years in prison, and said: "I don't know how you get to where I am today, from where I was seventeen years ago."

That was my first full season with the Mets, 1968, and Denny McLain was the hottest name in the sport. He had it all—fame, fortune, and a rising fastball. He was the first pitcher in thirty-four years to win 30 games and two years later set another record by being suspended three times in the same season. He was accused of investing in a bookmaking shop and placing his own bets on basketball games by using a phone in the press room at the Tigers spring training camp in Lakeland. Had baseball ever seen a more audacious character? At least that was how the public saw him then: a rogue, a renegade, an imp.

It was a winding road that led from Tiger Stadium to a prison cell in Alabama. He was forty-two when he went behind bars, weighing at least 80 pounds more than when he was featured on the cover of *Time* and sat on a sofa next to Johnny Carson's desk, the first pitcher since Dizzy Dean in 1934 to enjoy a 30-victory year.

In a trial that lasted four months, ending in March 1985, he was convicted on four counts of extortion (loansharking), conspiracy, and drug trafficking. He denied heatedly that he ever sold or dealt in drugs. His attorney predicted that he would be "an absolute winner on appeal," and he was, but he spent more than two years behind bars before the decision was overturned.

I pitched against McLain after I went to the Angels, and he was playing out the final scenes of a career shortened by a shoulder injury. I saw him as a battler and liked his candor. But the charges against Denny sobered a lot of people in baseball. This was self-destruction carried to new extremes.

He managed and briefly pitched for a fledgling prison baseball team. Then the pain returned to the arm he wrecked pitching on two days' rest for the Tigers during the pennant races of 1967 and '68. His arm was ruined by cortisone shots. He still can't lift it above his head.

He quit managing the prison team because the media interest bothered some of the inmates and, of more concern, some of the administrators. "I don't know much about him," said the assistant warden in Atlanta. "To me, his career started on the day he was sentenced in Tampa."

Even the most distant fan should find a familiar ring to the name of Denny McLain, and detect echoes of the later, less severe—but no less degrading—plunge of Pete Rose. In McLain's magical season, he lost only six times and led the Detroit Tigers to their first world championship in 23 years.

McLain was a "closer." He had the killer instinct. Once a game started, no competitor of his time wanted to win more fiercely. He would get stronger as the game progressed. At his peak, he was like the character in *Mad* magazine, Alfred E. Neuman, whose motto was "What—me worry?" Nothing bothered Denny. Nothing distracted him. Not his opponents. Not the crowds. Not the pressure of a pennant race. Not even bad debts or gambling threats.

"What made him special," said Jim Campbell, then the general manager of the Tigers, "was a sense of confidence that I have never seen in any other pitcher. He *knew* he could beat your ass and then he went out and did it."

One example: On August 16, 1968, McLain was pitching against the Boston Red Sox, trying to lock up his 25th victory. "The year went so fast," he says now, "I remember very few ballgames. The most significant thing I remember was one night in Boston. I had men on second and third and nobody out. I had to face Dalton Jones, Carl Yastrzemski, and Ken Harrelson. We were winning the game, two-oh.

"Mayo Smith, our manager, came to the mound and said, 'Let's walk Dalton Jones.' I said I'm not walking anybody. Even if he hits a home run, it's only three-two. Smith says he wants to walk him. I said I'm not walking nobody."

The manager returned to the dugout. Three pitches later, McLain struck out Dalton Jones. Yaz stepped in. On three pitches, Yaz struck out. Here came Mayo Smith again.

McLain: "He says he wants to walk Harrelson. I say, 'Mayo, you must be out of your mind. I'm not walking Kenny. He hasn't hit me since he came into the league. This guy is *out*.' Then Bill Freehan [the catcher] comes to the mound and says don't throw him any breaking balls. I said, 'I'm sure as hell not throwing him any fastballs. I'm gonna throw him three sliders.' "

Which he did. And on three sliders, Harrelson struck out. In the dugout, Mayo Smith walked over and with a rueful grin said, "Denny, we'll never have another argument on the mound."

McLain said, "We didn't have one then. We were going to do it my way, no matter what you thought."

He usually did things his way, which at least in part explains how he got to where he was.

McLain won 16 games as a rookie in 1965, then 20, 17, 31, and 24. He won two straight Cy Young awards as the best pitcher in baseball. He won most of those games with an arm that needed liberal doses of cortisone before he could even warm up. "What else could I do?" he said. "Baseball was all I knew or wanted."

McLain did not win a game in the heat of the 1967 pennant race, which the Tigers lost on the last day of the season. He injured a toe when, depending on whose story you believe, he kicked a clubhouse door or tried to walk after his foot had fallen asleep. A third story has a stranger bouncing up and down on the toe, crushing it, to remind McLain of some gambling debts.

By 1970, all he led the major leagues in was trouble. Before the season, Commissioner Bowie Kuhn suspended him for his role in the bookmaking parlor three years before. When he returned, he was suspended by the team for dousing two sportswriters with a bucket of ice. And, finally, he was suspended again by Kuhn, that time for carrying a gun.

McLain, who had won 92 games in four seasons, was 3-and-5 for the Tigers that year. In the winter, they traded him to the Washington Senators, whose owner, Bob Short, was looking for a big name to boost attendance. McLain had another of his 20-game seasons in Washington—he lost 22 and won 10—and the next year he was in Oakland. He pitched in only five games for the A's and fifteen more for the Braves, who then released him.

He was a very human hero, while he was a hero. I think that other pitchers who played with or against him may want to remember him for one gesture. Mickey Mantle was struggling to hit his 535th career home run to pass Jimmy Foxx and move into third place on the all-time list behind Ruth and Mays. He had gone a stretch without one as the Yankees faced Detroit in the final days of the 1968 season.

McLain had a big lead over them in the ninth inning as Mantle stepped to the plate, hitless, for his last turn at bat. McLain motioned for catcher Bill Freehan to come to the mound for a conference. When he returned to his position, Freehan whispered to Mantle: "Denny said to tell you the first pitch will be a fastball down the middle."

Mantle was suspicious. "Does he mean it?"

"I wouldn't put it past him," said Freehan with a shrug.

Mantle took a called strike waist-high.

On the mound, McLain grinned and gave a slight nod with his head. He was going to groove another one. Mantle jumped on this pitch and drove it high into the upper deck in right field in Yankee Stadium as 50,000 fans went wild. In a gesture not everyone saw, McLain touched the bill of his cap as the Yankee slugger circled the bases.

At twenty-eight, just five seasons after he had enjoyed a Hall of Fame year, Denny was finished as a major league pitcher. "His arm had so much cortisone in it," said Joe Burke, who had run the Rangers and the Royals, "he wasn't effective anymore. He was still a great competitor. He just didn't have anything left."

He pitched his last game for a semipro team in Ontario in the summer of 1973. "I knew how my arm felt," he says. "I knew it was over. I didn't complain."

He had the Irish mug of a Jimmy Cagney and he looked like a Dead End Kid in a church loft as he stroked the keys on an electric organ. He saw himself as an easy rider kind of guy who cut a few corners and then got stuck with the bill.

To begin with, he was a street kid from Chicago who ran numbers on the city's South Side. His boyhood dream was not to play baseball but to become the world's greatest organist. "I didn't get interested in baseball," he says, "until the baseball people came around offering bonus money and the organ people didn't."

After the 1968 season, he made $25,000 playing the organ in Las Vegas. (The next year, I was one of the Mets offered $10,000 to appear with the comedian Phil Foster, telling jokes, singing, and trying to dance in a chorus line. That was a substantial payday to me, but I turned it down. I told Ruth I wasn't an entertainer. I didn't want to stand up in front of a roomful of people doing something I didn't know how to do.)

But McLain was no amateur. In the off-season, he signed a contract to endorse the newest Hammond organ. No one had been in such demand since Ethel Smith was knocking them dead with "Tico Tico."

McLain's father was thirty-five when he died of a heart attack on his way to watch his young son pitch. Denny went to work for ten dollars a day taking bets as a numbers runner on the South Side. That was his childhood.

In 1977, there was a pathetic picture in the paper of a pawnshop owner holding the Cy Young trophies Denny McLain had hocked to scrape up a few dollars. He thought it was as low as he could sink. And he was wrong.

In late 1988, the appellate court reduced his sentence to time served, citing the presiding judge for prejudicial conduct. McLain went back to Michigan, rejoined his wife and four daughters, one adopted, and worked for a time in the marketing department of a minor league hockey team. Later, he landed a job as a sports talk show host in Detroit. Slowly, he has begun to rebuild his life.

I doubt that the public will ever see McLain as a sympathetic character. But you concede that he has been a complicated one, haunted by his father's early death, a street kid with a musical talent who became for one season the best pitcher in half a century of baseball. He threw his arm away because he thought the party would last forever.

It never does.

NOLAN RYAN'S
TOP TEN MOST
DUBIOUS DISTINCTIONS
A PITCHER EVER SUFFERED

1. Most runs allowed in a losing no-hitter, four, all unearned, by the Yankees, behind Andy Hawkins, against the White Sox, July 1, 1990.

2. Most runs allowed while arguing a call, two, by David Cone, Mets, against the Braves. After covering first, Cone objected to a safe call by umpire Charlie Williams as two other runners crossed the plate.

3. Most pitchers used without retiring the same batter, six, by the Chicago Cubs. San Francisco's Jay Alou hit safely off each of them, Dick Ellsworth, Lew Burdette, Don Elston, Dick Scott, Wayne Schurr, and Lindy McDaniel.

4. Most managers served under in one season, Dock Ellis, seven, with three teams, 1977: Billy Martin, Yankees; Jack McKeon and Bobby Winkles, Oakland A's; and Frank Lucchesi, Eddie Stanky, Connie Ryan, and Billy Hunter, Texas Rangers.

5. Smallest shoe size by a major leaguer, Art Herring, size three. He pitched for four teams from 1929 to 1947.

6. Most consecutive starts without having a run scored to begin a career: four, by Jim McAndrew, Mets, 1968. The rookie right-hander gave up just six runs in his four starts and lost them all, as the Mets failed to score in any of them.

7. Most hit batsmen to open a game, three, by Dock Ellis, Pirates, against the Reds, 1974. Dock loaded the bases by hitting Pete Rose, Joe Morgan, and Danny Driessen. He then walked Tony Perez to force in a run. With a 2-and-0 count on Johnny Bench, he was taken out, having thrown eleven pitches, none for strikes.

8. Most balls called on a pitcher while warming up: three, by John Boozer, Phillies, against the Mets, 1968. When Boozer entered the game in relief, he spit on his hands before his first toss, and an observant umpire Ed Vargo cried out, "Ball one," claiming he had violated the spitball rule. Manager Gene Mauch protested that his pitcher had not yet faced a batter. Vargo said it made no difference. The defiant Mauch told Boozer to wet his hands twice more. Vargo called ball two and three, then ejected both the manager and the pitcher. All the while, the batter, Bud Harrelson, was still in the on-deck circle.

9. Most times traded or released by the same team: Bobo Newsom, by the Washington Senators, five times.

10. Poor timing: Don Larsen's wife filed for divorce on the day he pitched his perfect game in the World Series.

The Marathon Men

There are pitchers for a day (Don Larsen's perfect game in the 1956 World Series), and pitchers for a month (Orel Hershiser's 59 consecutive scoreless innings), and pitchers for a season (Denny McLain winning 31 games).

Then there are the fortunate few who stick around for the very long run, who go on year after year, defying the calendar and the odds. Tommy John, Joe and Phil Niekro, Gaylord Perry, Steve Carlton, and Charlie Hough—and I probably should include myself—pitched well into our forties. I doubt that we are going to see that kind of longevity from many of the pitchers starting out today. Teams won't stay as long as they once did with a struggling or hurting pitcher making millions a year. For the player, the trend will be to sock it away and get out early rather than endure the pain and the pressures.

John lasted 26 seasons without ever having overpowering stuff and in spite of a series of injuries, including one that should have ended his career before he really found himself. Niekro retired at forty-eight. Four years later, managing the Richmond club in the Atlanta farm system, he offered to activate himself when his staff came up short. The Braves turned down the idea, but Phil went so far as to check out whether pitching in the minors would affect his Hall of Fame eligibility. It wouldn't.

Niekro's baby brother, Joe, was literally right behind him, retiring a year later in 1988 after being released by the Twins. Joe was in his prime at forty-three, with 22 seasons on his timecard. The Niekros had realized their dream of pitching together, when Houston traded Joe to the Yankees late in the 1985 season. He arrived in time to watch Phil win his 300th game.

Carlton maxed out at age forty-four and 24 seasons, and they nearly had to tear the uniform off him and put up roadblocks at the stadium gates.

To have a career of such duration takes a certain amount of good timing, good health, and an unwillingness to quit. Tommy John did it largely on the strength of the third condition. I can't imagine anyone overcoming the hurdles he did to last as long.

After nine seasons in the majors, he had a losing record at 84–91. After twelve, he had won as many as fifteen games only once. You lose track of the comebacks he made. He pitched for six teams, was released once, was a free agent three times, and retired once to coach college ball.

What impresses me most is that all of his big winning, his pitching in five playoffs and three World Series, came *after* experimental surgery that saved his career. He was with the Dodgers in 1974 when the doctors removed a tendon from his right forearm and transplanted it to his left elbow. The medical and baseball opinions were unanimous: he would never pitch again.

He was out all of 1975, then won 20 games in three of the next five seasons, once with the Dodgers and twice for the

Yankees. The procedure became known as the Tommy John operation.

Three things a pitcher doesn't want named after him are a surgical operation, a disease, and a memorial trophy, but it worked out fine for John, an irrepressible type. His style of pitching helped him come back. He never threw hard, but he had a deadly, heavy sinker, a decent slider, and exceptional control. I put him in a category with Randy Jones as left-handers who rarely give the hitters anything juicy to hit.

While he was with the Yankees, Tommy had another misfortune: his young son fell out of an upstairs window and was for a time in critical condition. He made a full recovery, and I think the players in both leagues followed the little boy's progress. Nothing stopped Tommy, which tells you about his faith and dedication.

John had another quality that is helpful to a long career, a sense of humor. Once he was asked if a pitch Toronto's George Bell had smashed 400 feet for a homer had been out of the strike zone. "It was after he hit it," said John.

And when he decided not to hang on until he reached 300 wins, retiring just twelve short, he said: "I'm not a goal-oriented person. The only thing that burns inside me is Szechuan cooking."

With his modest disposition and the oddities of his career, he was an easy target. Bob Costas, the NBC sportscaster, joked about his agelessness: "This guy is so old that the first time he had athlete's foot, he used Absorbine Senior."

John joined the Dodgers in 1972 as I was making my way to Anaheim. In 1977, two years after his surgery, he responded with a 20–7 season. When his contract ran out in 1978, I followed the story in the papers, knowing his negotiations could foreshadow mine a year later. It was revealing to see the line the Dodgers adopted. Peter O'Malley had succeeded his father as head of the club, and he said flatly that the Dodgers did not guarantee "large-dollar" contracts to players who have been injured. O'Malley added, "Tommy also has an age problem. He probably will be able to pitch at

36 and 37 . . . he likens himself to Gaylord Perry and Warren Spahn, but we still feel baseball is a young man's game."

Objections duly noted. Signing with the Yankees, he was 21–9 in 1979 and finished 22–9 a year later.

When he made his last comeback at forty-three, after two or three subpar seasons, the advice he needed came from Tom Morgan, the pitching coach who had been so instrumental in turning my career around with the Angels. He stopped by Morgan's house one morning and they just played catch. As the writer Thomas Boswell later described it: "What Morgan saw was a frightened old pitcher trying to be so fine—allowing himself two inches of error, not a foot—he was cutting himself off, not extending, not pulling down through the ball at the last instant. The old knack returned almost instantly."

Tommy John would have fit easily into the chapters here on southpaws and thinking men. I prefer to include him in this one. He was a pitcher with enormous grit and staying power. He ran the full course and he ran it well.

In my mind, Joe and Phil Niekro formed baseball's closest and most enjoyable brotherhood. They may have lacked the country charm of the Deans, and they didn't have the intensity of the Perrys, Gaylord and Jim, but they were the only knuckleballing brothers in the history of the game, both started and relieved, and they represented a combined total of 46 seasons and 539 wins. They hold the sibling records in both categories, outlasting the Perrys by three seasons and ten wins.

The Niekros talked about the knuckler as though it were a family heirloom, and in a way it was. Phil learned it from his father, who had learned it from a fellow coal miner in a semipro league. When Phil was a kid—hard to picture Phil as a kid—his dad would come home from the mines, sling him over his shoulder, and carry him into the backyard, where they would lob knuckle balls to each other.

Phil never considered baseball as a career until the Milwaukee Braves signed him for a $500 bonus while he was pitching against teams of coal miners in Ohio. I'm not certain how strict the protocol is among knuckle ball pitchers, but Joe was less of a purist than Phil; he started his career as a slider-sinker pitcher and went to the knuckler because Phil was having success and he needed another pitch to salvage his career.

I didn't realize, until I went to the Rangers and played with Charlie Hough, that among the specialists in this art form there are two types. There is a Joe Niekro, who can still slip a fastball or another pitch past a hitter. And there are the purists, such as Charlie and Phil and Wilbur Wood, who wouldn't throw anything else unless the knuckler just flat wasn't working and they were desperate to get the ball over the plate.

"To me, the knuckler is one of the toughest pitches to learn," Joe told me, "because there are not many guys in the system who can teach it. And kids want to impress scouts and they want to throw hard. In high school and college, everyone is looking for the 92-mile-an-hour fastball. But the knuckler is also the best pitch in the game because you never know where it's going and it doesn't tax your arm.

"There was a stretch during the 1940s when there were several knuckle ball pitchers in the majors. Then they kind of disappeared until Hoyt Wilhelm, Wilbur Wood, Phil, and myself came along. The pitch has been in our family for a long time."

I saw Wilhelm at the end of his career, but I couldn't appreciate the beauty of what he was doing. I thought he had developed a trick pitch to prolong his time.

Phil's knuckler fluttered and moved so much that the Braves almost let him go because no one could catch him. He had pitched on teams in the minors where the catchers simply refused to play when his turn rolled around. He had lost more than a few games when a third strike rolled back to the screen while the winning run crossed the plate.

All-star catcher Joe Torre grew to hate that pitch. Paul

Richards was the general manager in Atlanta in 1967 when he decided to take Phil out of the bullpen and make him a starter. But first he needed a catcher, so he made a trade with the Phillies for Bob Uecker, who has become famous by joking about what a pitiful hitter he was. When he put on the big glove, though, nobody laughed. Uecker could catch.

The first day he walked into the Braves clubhouse, there were two telegrams waiting for him. One was from Torre, and it was from the heart: "THANK YOU VERY MUCH. GOD BLESS YOU."

The other said, simply: "LOTS OF LUCK. YOUR BUDDY, PHIL NIEKRO."

Torre laid out a carpet of white towels leading to Uecker's locker. Uecker caught every game Phil started the rest of the season, and he went through a ritual of his own: Before the game he took four aspirin for the headache he knew he would have when it ended.

Once, after Niekro had beaten the Pirates, 2–1, Atlanta's trainer, Harvey Stone, looked up from rubbing his arm and casually remarked to a reporter that Phil could probably pitch the next night.

Paul Richards overheard him. "No, he couldn't," said Richards.

"Why not?" asked the writer. "He needs more rest?"

"No," said Richards, "but Uecker does."

Phil's new career was on its way, and at least partly because Uecker had told him what he had to hear: "Just throw the damned thing. Don't worry. I'll take the responsibility for chasing it down."

I don't believe the job was any easier for Alan Ashby, Joe's batterymate in Houston. With the knuckler, the catcher tried to keep his right hand, his throwing hand, behind his back, in order to reduce the risk of breaking a finger. Even so, I think Alan managed to break them all at least once.

Between them, Joe and Phil caused the insurance rates for catchers to rise wherever they went.

You didn't have to be around either of the Niekros very

long to understand how much love was there. Whenever Atlanta and Houston played, and Joe and Phil hooked up, there was an extra tension in the clubhouse. Their parents never wanted them to oppose each other, and the brothers had to call and comfort them. Every season one would agitate the front office to make a trade for the other.

Then it finally happened in New York, where Phil won his 300th game in his last start of the 1985 season at Toronto. On that day, Phil decided to live out his own peculiar fantasy.

It was funny, because we had all heard the brothers express virtually the same thought. Phil: "Sometimes, I think of what it would be like to be a successful, conventional pitcher, and then I'd say, no. I'd rather have it this way. The mystery of it. It's so much fun being a knuckle ball pitcher."

And Joe: "One of my fantasies was to face a Mike Schmidt and say, 'Okay, Mike, here comes a ninety-six-mile-per-hour fastball, now hit this.' Of course, I could never throw it."

So on the day he went gunning for number 300, Phil Niekro made up his mind that he would win without throwing his best pitch. He would prove that he was a pitcher, the genuine article, and that he hadn't lasted all these years because of a gimmick. When he warmed up, he told his catcher he thought he wanted to start off the first few hitters with hard stuff.

He sailed through four innings without throwing one knuckler, and the Yankees led, 3–0. By now his teammates were wising up, and in the dugout the puzzlement was fairly general. Joe asked him, "When are you gonna throw one?" Phil didn't answer.

In the sixth, with Phil working on a shutout and leading by six runs, a grinning Willie Randolph trotted to the mound from second base. "What the hell is going on?" he asked.

"Not gonna throw one," said Niekro.

"Go for it," yelped Willie.

By the ninth inning, with the Yankees up 8–0, everyone in the park knew that the old man hadn't yet thrown a knuckle ball. Before he started to the mound, he turned to Joe and told him if he lost the shutout he was going to take himself out of the game. He wanted Joe to finish it and share the 300th win with him.

Joe told him, in effect, to get out of here.

Phil had two out in the ninth, Tony Fernandez on second, and Jeff Burroughs at bat with a 1–1 count when he threw his only two knucklers of the game, both for swinging strikes and the final out. He didn't compromise, he simply acknowledged that it would be inappropriate to close out the biggest game of his long career without using his signature pitch.

It was a storybook time for the Niekro brothers, but it all dissolved the next spring, when the Yankees gave Phil an unexpected pink slip before the club broke camp. The Yankees traded an unhappy Joe to Minnesota, where he made news with his ten-day suspension for carrying a concealed emery board and scrap of sandpaper. Still, he wound up in his only World Series with the Twins in 1987, pitching two scoreless innings in relief.

Phil lasted two more seasons and squeezed off eighteen more wins before the Indians cut him. He went to Toronto and then back to Atlanta to pitch one inning in a symbolic final game with the Braves.

He was two years short of fifty, and he didn't go gently. "They released me because of my age," he complained, "not my talent. Same thing with Tommy John."

The paths of all three were strikingly different. Tommy rode the roller coaster. Phil forged ahead with blinders, always ready to be tested. Joe went with the flow, to five teams in his first eight years, an unhurried man who enjoyed himself. On the Astros, he was celebrated for his ability to relax. "It takes him ninety minutes," our traveling secretary, Donald Davidson, once said of Joe, "to watch '60 Minutes'."

I agreed with Joe. Being impatient doesn't make the time pass faster, and sometimes you don't want it to go any faster.

As the years have piled up, I've noticed that most pitchers don't want to single out their wins or records when they assess their careers. Maybe it sounds too selfish. But I can remember hearing Don Sutton say, "I want to be remembered as a guy who almost never missed a turn, who gave my team a lot of innings, who kept them in the game."

I used to enjoy eavesdropping on Don's interviews, because he was smooth with the press and his answers were sharp. Still, I know how much those 300 wins meant to him, and how carefully Don kept track of where he stood in the Dodgers' record book.

I've said the same thing myself, and I'd like to think I mean it. But after a time you get kind of programmed, and I'm no longer sure that we don't just say what sounds correct. It is still true, however, and always has been, that you can't control whether you win or break a record. All you can really do is keep going out there and stay as long as you can.

A pitcher I compare to Sutton and Tom Seaver, in terms of lifetime achievement and mental approach, is Jim Palmer. He pitched nineteen seasons, and he pitched most of them in pain. He also did something the rest of us didn't come close to doing. He spent his entire career with one club, the Baltimore Orioles. So I mark him down as a marathon man, although he could just as easily fit in there with the brainier members of the class.

He was also a true highball pitcher who was awesome once he found his groove. He won 20 games eight times out of nine seasons from 1970 to the end of the decade. He pitched over 300 innings in four of those years, and 296 innings in two others. He was a three-time Cy Young Award winner, his first one in 1973, the season I won 21 games for a fourth-place club, pitched two no-hitters, and struck out 383 batters to break the record held by Koufax.

This may come off as envy or jealousy, but I guess that was as close to a feud as I've ever had with another pitcher. I'm not sure why, or even if Jim was aware of it, but I had the feeling he was a critic of mine.

He had a typically brilliant Palmer year, with 22 wins

and nine losses and an earned run average of 2.40. So I couldn't argue with his selection or my finishing second. But it bothered me when a reporter asked him about the closeness of the vote and he said something that sounded to my ears like: "Ryan goes for strikeouts and I go for outs."

I always considered them the same thing. I marked Palmer as a prima donna and made no effort to get to know him. Still, I wanted to include him in this book because he was openly curious about the mental processes of other pitchers. So was I, but I don't think Jim thought so until fairly recently.

Frankly, we didn't clear the air until Jim was interviewed (by my co-author) for this book. I wasn't entirely wrong, but it became clear to me that Jim didn't question my loyalty to the team. He just didn't consider me, in my early years, to be a real smart pitcher, and the evidence is probably on his side.

What he said was: "One of the things that it takes a while to learn is that your good fortune isn't always dictated by how you perform, but how the team plays. You're not in total control. You do your best and the rest is up to them. It took me five or six years to accept the fact that whether I won or lost wasn't entirely up to me.

"Nolan, in some cases, was a little different than most of us because he was a strikeout pitcher. He had more control of his destiny on a given night. Sometimes, though, I think he tried to do too much. We each have our personality traits. I think Ryan had to be fairly stubborn because he did it his way his whole career. Personally, I think he's a better pitcher now than he has ever been. He throws the ball over the plate more. He made believers out of a few skeptics."

Jim may or may not have been one, but this is a compliment that pleases me. The reader may conclude that I am hiding behind this book to accept it, but I can only say that the feud, if there ever was one, is over.

I like what Palmer has to say about being in shape: "You don't think about it once you're on the mound. You have made a contract with yourself. If you are serious about it, you are going to be as well conditioned as you can."

Jim had a routine all his own. He played tennis left-handed in the middle of the day, when it was hot and humid. "I figured it was good cardiovascular exercise and gave me an advantage over the other guy. I don't know if that really was the case, but it's what I thought."

One way or another, he managed to pitch at an exceptionally high level until one year short of his fortieth birthday. Then he tried to come back six years after he retired, after he had made a successful transition to radio and television and advertising.

He didn't succeed—the Red Sox hit him pretty hard in his debut—but I admire him for trying. This was at a time when George Foreman had returned to boxing after ten years and Mark Spitz was trying to make an Olympic comeback after nearly two decades away from the pool. No one can explain how Foreman, overweight and overage, reestablished himself as a heavyweight contender by going the distance against Evander Holyfield. George is unique.

I followed all of their stories, maybe with more interest than most of the public. But I can say this: It's easier to stay at your game and maintain the level of your performance into your forties than it is to lay off for a few years and try to come back. As the boxer Willie Pep once said, "First your legs go. Then your reflexes go. Then your friends go." No, you can't turn back the clock.

Palmer was exceptional because he tore his rotator cuff at twenty and still had a full and rewarding career. "Pain was pretty much a part of my pitching for the last fifteen or eighteen years," he said. "I was accused of not wanting to pitch with pain. But I pitched 4,000 innings and probably 3,600 of those were after I tore my rotator cuff. So I had pain all the time.

"I learned early that if a pitcher has any kind of arm injury, people are going to be slow to accept that because, if you are any good at all, they don't want you to be hurt. They want you to be doing the job you're paid to do. It's a very fine line between being hurt and not pitching, and pitching through the pain."

You get a fair insight into how Palmer's mind worked when you learn that he is a native New Yorker, and that he practiced a technique called "visualization." I guess many of us do, we just don't know it had a name.

"A lot of times," he said, "pitching is like being on a roller coaster. You have to be strong not only physically but emotionally. I pitched every fourth day for most of my career and I liked it. The night before a start, I tried to visualize how I would pitch to each hitter. They say a good manager stays two innings ahead. I pitched the whole game in my head.

"Because I was a New York kid, when I went into Yankee Stadium I was pitching against Johnny Mize and Hank Bauer and Mickey Mantle and Roger Maris, the people I grew up cheering for. Even though the faces on the hitters were different, that was what I envisioned when I came to the stadium. You have to be pumped up no matter where you pitch. That was one of my ways."

Palmer broke in with the Orioles in 1965, and his first roommate was one of the grand masters, Robin Roberts, at the end of his own career. "Roberts was very outgoing," said Jim, "and he was hanging on, trying to get 300 wins [he didn't quite make it]. He told me that the best pitch was the high fastball, and I had a good one, and I ought to be smart enough to throw it. Robin had a very simple theory: Just kind of rock back like you're in a rocking chair and just get your arm out in front and throw the fastball over the plate. He said a lot of pitchers have a fear of throwing strikes, of putting the ball where it might get hit.

"To succeed as a pitcher you can't be afraid to fail. You put yourself out there in the center of the diamond, and all the eyes are on you. You're supposed to be in control. You have to know what it takes to win; I'm a firm believer in that. A lot of pitchers never learn. I think the slider changed the game in the 1950s, and now the hot pitch is the split-finger.

To me, the jury is still out. You look at San Francisco, where Roger Craig has been teaching it, and they have a lot of arm injuries."

Palmer was no cutup, no flake. He was a serious observer of the game who sometimes clashed with his longtime manager, Earl Weaver, who, he says, "stirred up things to break the boredom." Once, when Weaver removed him from a game, the 6'–3" Palmer, who towered over the squatty manager, held the ball out in front of him.

"Don't shove that ball in my face," screamed Weaver.

"When it left my hand," said Palmer, "it was chest high."

That same competitive streak led him to question the judgment of other pitchers.

"Ross Grimley pitched for us and for Cincinnati," he says, "and one night I saw him give up back-to-back-to-back home runs to Bobby Bonds, Roy Jackson, and Don Baylor. He came into the dugout and I said, 'Ross, how can you do that? I'd never throw back-to-back-to-back home runs.' He said, 'How do you know?' And I said, 'Because I'd walk the third guy.'

"So the next night, I'm on the mound, and Bonds hit a 3–2 fastball for a home run and Baylor hits a high fly ball to center field that I think is going out. I'm already checking to see who's on deck because I'm going to walk him. Then, to my surprise, the ball came down for an out and all the guys sitting on the bench are laughing. They knew what I had said the night before was something I was going to have to do."

It was no surprise that Palmer, as did Sutton and Seaver, had opportunities in television. He is an articulate guy who looks good in front of the camera. He may have achieved his widest fame from the commercials and print ads he did for Jockey underwear. On occasion, he has to explain that there is no connection with that work and his baseball nickname, which happened to be "Cakes."

It was Jim's habit to eat pancakes every day he was due to start, no matter how late he slept. My feeling is, whatever makes you strong, stay with it.

You have to appreciate a fellow like Jim Kaat, who was cut in midseason by the Cardinals, in July, cleaned out his locker, and left with a smile. "I have no complaints," he said. "I had a twenty-five-year vacation."

He was forty-four when they let him go, and only one active pitcher was his senior, Gaylord Perry. The year was 1983 and the Cardinals dropped him because they had picked up Dave Rucker from Detroit. Rucker was born in 1957, the year Kaat began his professional career. He is one of the few players at any position to compete in the big leagues in four calendar decades.

I catch a glimpse of him now and then on the field or in the stands, doing interviews for the "Game of the Week" on CBS. He makes the rounds during spring training, too, so he's another one who didn't really snip the cord.

"Guys never seem to be as happy after they're out of baseball," he says. "It's a dream life, really. Being a pitcher gave me a license to be a kid."

His father pitched fifteen years in the Pacific Coast League, back when it wasn't all that uncommon for a player to spend an entire career in the minors. Jim Kaat spent most of his career pitching for bad teams in Washington and Minnesota, but he did sneak into one World Series with the Twins. He moved on to Chicago, Philadelphia, and the Yankees before his last stop in St. Louis. When he was done he had 283 victories and 16 Gold Gloves. At 6'–4", he was a chesty left-hander who helped himself with his fielding skill.

One recent spring, Kaat was wondering why so many of our generation had pitched into their forties. He had a theory that made sense to me. "When we were kids," he said, "we did a lot of work by hand. Mowed the lawn, washed the car, shoveled snow, and walked. I used to walk everywhere. Now you see kids who haven't logged the sandlot innings that I did, and when they come into baseball you don't know how big they're going to be. When I was eighteen, my body was developed."

Kaat grew up in Michigan, and I'm sure he shoveled a lot more snow than we see in Texas. But I agree with much of what he said. Today kids think working with your hands means putting a quarter in a video game at an arcade in the shopping mall.

There are pitchers who give you years and those who give you innings, and some do both. I often think that the most underrated, overlooked stat in baseball is innings pitched.

Phil Niekro was a workhorse who four times pitched more than 300 innings, with a high of 342 in 1979, an incredible year that saw him win 21 games and lose 20.

But as managers turn increasingly to the bullpen specialist and the five-man starting rotation, you are going to see the workhorse of old disappear from the game. Don Drysdale, Bob Gibson, Juan Marichal, and Tom Seaver, along with their other skills, had the ability to give a team a lot of innings. In 1973 Bert Blyleven gave the Twins 300 innings, started 40 games, and completed 25 of them.

I topped the 300 mark that year and the next for the Angels. Whitey Herzog, who was on the coaching staff that year, likes to tell people that in 1974 I averaged 157 pitches per nine innings. In one twelve-inning game I threw 255 pitches. I don't know if that would make any sense today, but I can't claim that it shortened my career.

I didn't realize how the totals were shrinking until I looked it up. The last pitcher to work 300 innings in a regular season was Steve Carlton in 1980. Orel Hershiser and Dave Stewart have accomplished it if you include their postseason totals.

The pitcher who best fits the description of a workhorse today is Jack Morris, Detroit's ace for so long, who helped pitch the Twins to the world championship in 1991. The standard is going to be 250 innings, and Morris has been good for that nearly every season. He got to finish a lot of games with the Tigers because Sparky Anderson trusted him even more than he did his bullpen. That's remarkable when you consider that Willie Hernandez, the Cy Young Award winner and the most valuable player in 1984, was their stopper. And they had a top setup man too in Aurelio Lopez. It wasn't as if Detroit suffered from a shabby bullpen.

But more and more I hear the complaint from starters that they are being turned into part-time workers, five-inning pitchers. Even Sparky, one of the managers I consider responsible for this trend, sounds nostalgic when he talks about the workhorses, the ones who got the ball every fourth day.

"I remember how Lefty Phillips used to talk about the benefits of a four-man rotation," said Anderson, referring to the manager the Angels fired just before I joined them. "He always said that your number one man is your number one— you can identify him pretty easily. And he said you usually can identify who your number two is and your number three and your number four. But he said that the *other* teams will identify your fifth man for you. And he said if you used him too much, you'd find out in a hurry why he was number five."

Morris, Roger Clemens, Bret Saberhagen, and Dave Stewart all have the stamina and size to work 300 innings in a season, but the trend is against them. I do detect a certain irony here: players are supposed to be bigger and stronger. They have more sophisticated training methods available to them.

And yet the innings pitched continue to go down, and the workhorse is giving way to the wagon train team.

1. Johnny Vander Meer's two straight no-hitters.

2. Cy Young's 511 career victories.

3. Jack Chesbro's 41 wins in 1904.

4. Most consecutive innings without relief: John W. Taylor, Chicago Cubs and St. Louis Cardinals, 203 games, June 20, 1901, through August 9, 1906.

5. Carl Hubbell's 24 consecutive wins, 1936–37.

6. Elroy Face's 22 consecutive wins by a relief pitcher, 1958–59.

7. Steve Carlton's 15 consecutive wins with a last-place team, the 1972 Phillies. (Carlton finished with 27 of his club's 59 victories.)

8. Most games started and lost in one day, two, by Wilbur Wood, White Sox, against the Yankees, on July 20, 1973 (modern era).

9. Fewest pitches in a complete game, 58, by Red

Barrett of the Boston Braves while shutting out the Reds, 2–0, in 1944.

10. Lowest batting average in a season, .000, by Bob Buhl, 1962, 0-for-70 with the Braves and Cubs (minimum to qualify, 50 at bats).

The
Rivals

The duel between the pitcher and batter in baseball is one of the most personal in all of sports. Only in boxing, where the opponents actually drip blood and sweat on each other, are the feelings of fear and loathing more directly expressed. So a book about pitchers would only be half a book without a chapter on their foes.

On every club I have been around, there is a kind of mental wall between the pitchers and the hitters. There really is a kind of fraternity among pitchers. It's not a faction or a clique, in the sense of Billy Martin's famous phrase: to succeed as a manager you have to keep the five guys who hate you away from the five who are neutral. A pitcher's survival depends on figuring out how a hitter thinks. And they don't want to be figured out.

I always divided the best hitters into two categories: the great hitters, like Henry Aaron, who hit for power and average, and the pure power hitters, like Reggie Jackson. It is a little early to say if Jose Canseco will fit into the first category. It is a sure bet that Cecil Fielder belongs in the second. The Detroit slugger is never going to bat .300 because he is never going to leg out an infield hit.

Sometimes a hitter will knock one so far, or achieve a distinction so rare, you feel almost a kinship with him, a sense of pride rather than rivalry. Once, Steve Blass of the Pirates threw a four-hitter against the Cubs, and Billy Williams collected all four hits. Said Blass: "Billy had two home runs and two doubles, but he hit one off all four of my pitches—fastball, curve, change-up, and slider. It was a very democratic day for him." As far as Blass was concerned, Williams hit for the cycle, but not in the traditional sense.

The real test of a hitter is how great a threat he represents with a runner on third and less than two out in the late innings of a tie game. That is a game-winning situation. The hitters I most hated to face were Pete Rose, Rusty Staub, Carl Yastrzemski, Matty Alou, Rico Carty, George Brett, and Steve Garvey.

I can anticipate a question from the gallery: you didn't mention Frank Robinson or Al Kaline. But I didn't face them that much; their careers were ending when I came to the American League. I missed Mickey Mantle completely.

The hitters who gave me difficulty were the left-handers who made contact and didn't strike out much, the type that wouldn't chase my curve ball, would never do much to help me. I kept running into Staub in both leagues because our careers ran almost the same course. At the start of a game, Rusty would have his arms on the dugout rail, studying every pitch I made. I just dreaded seeing him there. By the late innings, I knew he had a bead on what I had working, what I was trying to do.

To this day I hate to see Brett come to bat with a runner on third. He doesn't strike out often and he'll go with the pitch wherever I throw it. I preferred going up against the free swingers, with the exception—in my early years with the

Mets—of Willie McCovey and Willie Stargell. They were left-handed power hitters who were selective enough to wait on a good pitch, and they just didn't miss a fastball.

My rookie year with the Mets, we went into San Francisco and Dick Selma was going to start the opener. At our team meeting Gil Hodges went over the Giants' hitters, and he gave special attention to McCovey. He said, "We're going to put a shift on McCovey, but we're not going to throw him any fastballs inside. Keep the fastball up and *not* over the plate. We're going to try to get him to hit the ball in the air to the alleys, where we got a chance."

Anyway, that was our theory. That night Dick Selma gave up three straight home runs to Willie . . . boom, boom, boom. In the locker room, he told the press he had thrown him fastballs inside, and a writer said, "I thought you guys weren't going to do that."

Selma said, "I didn't think anybody could hit my fastball." I guess he thought Hodges was talking about the rest of us, not him. And he must have figured the first two homers were flukes. Dick was one of those pitchers with abundant ability who never made the most of it. He had an arm as good as I had ever seen. He could pitch eight innings one day and go out the next, pick up a ball, and from the mound throw it over the fence. He was strong for his size, 160 pounds or so, but he didn't have the mental makeup to carry him for a career.

The Mets let him go in the expansion draft to San Diego, and the Padres traded him to Chicago. He was with them in 1969 when we were chasing the Cubs down the stretch. It was Selma who said, "If the Mets catch us I'll jump off the John Hancock Bridge." The Hancock, someone pointed out to him, was a building, not a bridge.

The Angels had no way of knowing what was inside my head when they traded for me. But I remember Harry Dalton, the general manager, telling me that a lot of people "won't let themselves be successful." I put that remark in the category of a quiet truth that sneaks up on you. The longer I stayed in the game the more evidence I saw. Success bothers some people. They get nervous. They think it can't last. They look for things to go wrong. I'll tell you, if you look for things to go wrong, they will pop up everywhere.

The polar opposite of this type of personality was Pete Rose, with whom I had a career-long rivalry, one I enjoyed and respected. Pete was the ultimate challenge. He rarely struck out and I was a strikeout pitcher. He was a great breaking ball hitter. He couldn't hit my fastball, but he would foul it off, lay off the borderline pitches, try to get me in the hole. He was the complete hitter, whose objective was always to give himself the maximum opportunity to reach base.

It became an issue with Pete, my throwing him a curve ball over the plate, and he finally dared me. Before the fifth game of the league championship series in 1980, in the Astrodome, Rose was the first visiting player on the field. He always was. He would come out early and watch the home team take batting practice. I was standing around behind the cage because, as the starter, I was going to hit with the regular lineup.

This was the year before he would pass Stan Musial's record for the most hits in the National League, on his way to breaking Ty Cobb's all-time mark. He looked over at me, putting on his surly act, and said, "I wish you would get that bleeping curve ball of yours over just once."

All that season I had set him up for the curve and had either overthrown it or missed a corner. I never could break off that one curve ball in a situation where I needed it to put him away. The thought may have been in the back of my mind, but it wasn't as if I kept a chart.

So I said, "Yeah, why is that, Pete?"

He said, "Because when you do, I'm going to hit it right off your bleeping forehead." I looked at him, and I thought, "Well, the same to you."

I never sensed that he was trying to use psychology on me. Rose just kept himself pumped up, and he had the same effect on others.

Lo and behold, in his second at bat in that game, I got ahead of him in the count, a ball and two strikes. I thought, "Man, I have him set up for my curve ball." There was no grinning now. I was deadly serious, because this was the playoffs and he had lit the rage in me. "You just wait and see this curve, you son of a gun," I'm thinking.

I threw him what was probably the best curve ball I had thrown all year. He hit a line drive that would have struck me square in the head if I hadn't thrown up my glove in self-defense. Whap! It bounced off and rolled in front of the mound. I ran over, picked it up, and threw him out, and all the way across the field, as he trotted to the bench, he pointed at me, with a smirk that said, "Ah-hah, what did I tell you?" I had to give him credit. He made a believer out of me.

He just knew he could drive that pitch right up the middle. I was lucky to get my glove up. In a normal situation, I would have been relieved to have gotten an out, and grateful that my head was still connected to my neck. But in that case, the entire scene was elevated because Rose had done exactly what he said he would.

In Houston, we always tried to pitch him on his hands, looking for the inside strike. He couldn't turn on that pitch but he would foul it off and stay alive. All of which was part of the backdrop for the encounter that would come in the summer of 1981.

There have not been many moments in my life more intense than the afternoon in Philadelphia when Pete tried to break the National League record for career hits. Stan Musial was in the stands. To make the setting more interesting, months earlier Rose had projected when he would break the record, and against which pitcher—me.

I remember reading his prediction in the paper. He wasn't being frivolous. He had checked out the schedule, added up how many hits he should have by what date, and saw that the Phillies would be playing a series against the Houston Astros (he had left the Reds as a free agent after the 1978 season).

His first time up, I was trying to get a ground ball out of him. I tried to throw a fastball away and he hit a soft line over shortstop for the base hit that tied Musial. They stopped the game to throw out the ball, and I decided I was going to be the aggressor now. I wouldn't just try to get an out. I wanted to strike him out. If I was going into the record book, I'd go down with my best stuff.

Did it matter? It mattered because of the prediction. He may have paid me a fine compliment, as many pointed out, but he also drew me into his act. You felt like the sap in a theater audience who gets called onto the stage so the magician can pull handkerchiefs out of your ear.

So the game came down to a very personal matter, as one-on-one as baseball ever gets. When my career is over and I look back on the high spots, that confrontation will be near the top because Pete Rose was the greatest competitor of my time. And the later, painful, and disheartening events couldn't alter that fact. He took his limited physical gifts and made himself one of the historic players in the game, an all-star at five positions.

On his next three trips to the plate, he struck out twice swinging and the third time on a curve ball looking. After his last strikeout, in the eighth inning, he broke his bat on the ground and went into the dugout. Ironically, I felt my hamstring tightening as I pitched to the next hitter, and they took me out of the game.

As I left the mound in Veterans Stadium, Pete appeared on the top step of the dugout and tipped his cap to me. I think that showed the bigness of his character, of his personality. I can't count the number of people who told me later they got goosebumps when he—how do I put this?—saluted me for denying him the record.

There was one other twist to our duel that afternoon. The game was played on what turned out to be the last day before the players' strike that interrupted the 1981 season. Six weeks would pass before play would be resumed. The commissioner decided there would be a split season. To buy time for the players to return and shake off some of the rust, we started the second half by making up the All-Star game in Cleveland.

When I walked into the National League clubhouse, Mike Schmidt, the Phillies' third baseman, was standing by the door. When he saw me he turned and yelled across the room, "Hey, Pete, here's Nolan."

Rose was facing his locker. He turned around and said, "Screw you, Ryan." He blamed me for the six-week delay between his tying and record-breaking hits.

My duels with Rose enabled me to feel an odd kinship with hitters. You never knew how they might react. My 3,000th strikeout came against the Reds' Cesar Geronimo, who took it in stride. He had been Bob Gibson's 3,000th as well.

When I broke Walter Johnson's record, the batter was a pinch hitter, Brad Mills of Montreal. He didn't even know what was going on, wasn't aware that he was number 3,509, until the crowd in Olympic Stadium stood and cheered.

As I came closer to my 4,000th strikeout, I drew a start against the New York Mets. Running in the outfield before the game, I passed Danny Heep, a former teammate of mine with the Astros, who had been traded to the Mets for Mike Scott.

As he ran by me, he tossed off a warning: "You're not getting me for 4,000, not me, not tonight." I just laughed. "That's okay," I said. "I don't figure it will be you, either." And we continued our wind sprints.

I still needed twelve strikeouts and I didn't expect to get them in one game. But as the innings rolled along they began to pile up, and after I fanned number eleven, guess who walked up to the plate? Danny Heep just stared at me as he stepped in, and he was shaking his head. It was all over his face: He knew he had a shot at becoming number 4,000, and I could see him thinking, "Why didn't I just keep my mouth shut?"

I started him off with a fastball and he took it on the

outside corner for a strike. I threw him another over the plate and he fouled it back to the screen: 0-and-2. I threw him a curve, down and in, a tough pitch for a hitter to lay off. He swung and missed and was gone on three pitches.

In 1989, after I had moved to the Rangers and Danny Heep had joined the Red Sox, I bumped into him in a restaurant in Arlington. He said, "I wish you would hurry up and get your 5,000th strikeout, so people would quit talking about me being number 4,000." I didn't have the heart to tell him he was always going to be number 4,000. He just wasn't going to be talked about as much.

Rickey Henderson of Oakland turned out to be number 5,000, and I thought he handled it pretty well. He said, "If you haven't been struck out by Nolan Ryan, you're a nobody." He took what could have been an embarrassing situation and dealt with it in a modest way.

He didn't come off quite so favorably in 1991, when he broke Lou Brock's career record for stolen bases. They stopped the game to present him with the actual base, and Brock came out of the stands to congratulate him. "Lou Brock was a great base stealer," he said to a crowd of 36,000 over the public address system. "But today I'm the greatest of all time." I think Rickey wanted a line that had the ring of the dying Lou Gehrig's speech in Yankee Stadium, and he didn't quite make it.

Pete Rose could dazzle you with his total recall of scores, hits, records: "The most hits I got were off Phil Niekro, seventy." You wondered if there was a computer in his brain where he stored his stats. He didn't force his information on anyone. But if they asked, he had the answers.

When he was in the batting cage, the players on both teams stopped to watch, the stance so scrunched up it was almost comical. Head down, bat straight back, knees bent. Squeezed up so tight you could stuff him into a bat bag. But when the pitch came, he uncoiled. He exploded.

Once in Houston after his last swing he raced around the bases, carrying his black bat with him. A Reds coach was hitting ground balls to the infielders, but as Pete rounded second base he swung at one of the grounders and knocked it right back to the startled coach.

In his dedication to the game, in his obsession with what he could accomplish, I marveled at him. In September 1985 he broke Cobb's record, and he made the point repeatedly: He didn't replace Ty Cobb, nor establish himself as the better batsman. He was just the fellow with the most hits in a lifetime, 4,256.

He never seemed uptight, avoiding the kind of ordeal Roger Maris and Henry Aaron endured before him. When Maris was tracking Babe Ruth's single-season home run record, his hair gradually fell out and he wound up snarling at reporters.

Aaron was a slightly different case, his pace less frantic. Still, he was made miserable by the comparisons to Ruth and the suggestion that he was unworthy of owning the career home run record. He would hide from the press in the trainer's room.

No one seemed to resent Rose breaking Cobb's record. Part of the pleasure was simply in observing the pleasure of Pete Rose. It was easier then, as a fan, or an opponent, to focus on the joy the game gave him. He was as much a symbol of his times as Cobb was of his, a lone wolf and a mean one, filing his spikes in full view of the opposing team.

In his first 23 years, Rose was on the disabled list once. He averaged 155 games a season up to his forty-first birthday. He lived most of his life in Cincinnati, less than 100 miles from the scene of two of America's great sports pageants, the Kentucky Derby and the Indianapolis 500, and he never saw either one.

He frequently referred to himself as a winner. Under the circumstances, it was the most modest of claims. He played in more winning games than any athlete in history—more than 1,900. If a rookie came up to the big leagues today and his team won a hundred games for the next nineteen years, he still wouldn't catch Rose.

Other players envied his ability to play at his level, and to ignore the private pressures that at times complicated his life. Whereas some players can't cope with a request for a photograph, Pete had a talent for living with turmoil. The story is told of Rose sitting in the clubhouse at Shea Stadium, a few hours before a game, when a reporter handed him a story torn off a wire service machine. The story said that his first wife, Karolyn, had filed for divorce, accusing Pete of infidelity. A circle of writers waited.

His head bent over the copy paper, Rose read the story. Then he looked up and said, "Who's pitching for the Mets?"

His passion for baseball, and a few other things, broke up his first marriage. He was open about his vanity and his vices. I don't think people excused them, but there was a tendency to say, "That's Pete." Even his nickname, Charlie Hustle, would have seemed sarcastic if applied to anyone else.

He never stopped hustling. When he was managing the Reds and playing first base, if an opposing hitter singled late in the game he would ask him if his pitcher still had good stuff. Did he believe what they told him? "Some of them," he said.

All of his career, I guess he just soaked up the daily box scores. At the start of a series, he would seek me out and say, "Hey, last week when so-and-so hit that double off you, what was the count? What pitch did you throw him? Was it low and away?"

I would look at him blankly. "What double, Pete?" I have trouble recalling who got the hits after that night's game, much less one played a week or two earlier. I'd say, "Gosh, Pete, I don't remember."

"What do you mean?" he demanded. "How could you not remember?" He would actually get testy about it, he was so driven, such a competitor, so focused on the game.

Friend or foe, no one who saw him compete could feel anything but sadness when Pete was convicted on two counts of tax evasion. He went through large sums of money to cover the debts from his gambling losses. He spent five months in prison, six in a halfway house, did a thousand hours of community service, and was fined over $50,000. He was suspended from baseball for gambling and conduct "detrimental to the game." He can be reinstated at some point, but under conditions that were not made public. His election to the Hall of Fame became the subject of continuing, bitter debate, his prospects uncertain.

For Pete Rose, that was the real life sentence.

NOLAN RYAN'S
TEN TOUGHEST
OUTS

1. Pete Rose

2. George Brett

3. Rusty Staub

4. Mark Belanger

5. Tony Gwynn

6. Joe Morgan

7. Willie McCovey

8. Will Clark

9. Kirby Puckett

10. Cal Ripken, Jr.

EPILOGUE

I wanted to end this on a light and breezy note, but baseball isn't always a light and breezy place. Over a relatively short span of time, you can get up close to a lot of laughter and tears.

The 1991 season in many ways provided a large dose of hope for all the underdogs of sport. Minnesota and Atlanta both went from worst to first in one year, and then met in a close and exciting World Series. The Twins won, with the pitching of the veteran Jack Morris deciding the seventh game.

A fresh name in the National League joined the list of Cy Young Award winners, Tommy Glavine of the Braves. Roger Clemens collected his third in the American League, giving him a strong early claim to being the pitcher of the 1990s.

It was a good year for the Ryans. I had to work around a series of nagging injuries, but I finished with twelve wins, including my seventh no-hitter. In the preseason, I got to pitch against my son Reid, then eighteen and a freshman at the University of Texas. He did all right, too, although the Rangers scored four runs off him in the two innings he worked.

I don't remember ever being nervous before a game, but I was probably more distracted than Reid. A few days earlier, he had called to warn me that their mound was in rough shape. The Rangers sent a couple of our people over to Austin to rebuild it. Reid was looking after me.

As each season gets closer to being my last, I find there are more things to think about, among them the players who have dropped out along the way. I think about the bravery of Dave Dravecky and Jim Abbott.

Dravecky wasn't in uniform in 1991. He had made a dramatic and emotional comeback the year before, after the removal of a malignant tumor from his left arm, his pitching arm, in 1988. The surgeons said it would be a miracle if he pitched again.

I don't know if I actually believe in miracles, but I do believe in Dave Dravecky. He started throwing again in mid-1989, pitched three games in the minors, and rejoined the Giants in August. In his first start after his return, he gave the Reds one hit in seven innings, left the game in the eighth, and got the win, 4–3. It was a goose-bump performance. Roger Craig, his manager, had been with the Dodgers when Don Larsen pitched his perfect game for the Yankees in the 1956 World Series. Craig said this one had as much drama. People cried.

Then, five days later, in his next start at Montreal, Dravecky's arm snapped as he threw a fastball to Tim Raines in the sixth inning. "I thought I had been shot by a sniper," he said. The pain threw him to the ground.

Weeks earlier, Tom House had told me that this was the risk Dravecky was taking, that the surgery and the treatment had so reduced the muscle mass that his arm could break just from the force of his delivery.

I'm not sure if doctors understand the principles of

throwing a baseball, the acceleration and deceleration. This isn't meant to be a second guess; the decision to pitch again was Dave's. But throwing a baseball is an unnatural act. Something has to take the brunt of that stress, either the muscle or the bone.

When they ran out of other options in June 1991, the doctors amputated Dravecky's arm and shoulder. I saw him in a television interview with Barbara Walters, and film clips of Dave playing catch one-handed with his little girl in his backyard. There were scenes of him speaking to audiences, moving them to tears. He described looking in the bathroom mirror at the hospital with his shirt off for the first time: "I thought, 'Whoa, boy! They did take a lot.' Then I said, 'Okay, Lord, this is what you've allowed me to live with. Now let's make the best of them.' " That was the message: no matter how difficult the loss, or how great the pain, you have to go on. And Dave was doing just that.

Jim Abbott was born with no right hand, and it would be hard to figure the odds of his ever playing college ball, much less making the leap from college (Michigan) to the majors. He won eighteen games in his third season and established himself as a premier pitcher with the California Angels.

You could see right off that he had the pitches—fastball, curve, and slider. The tactical fear was that he couldn't field his position. The human fear was that he couldn't defend himself against a liner up the middle.

So hitters kept bunting on him and he kept throwing them out. He is so quick and smooth that after a while, if you don't look for it, you aren't really conscious of how he switches the glove. He keeps it on the stump of his right arm, and his follow-through brings his left hand within a few inches of it. He grabs it and slips his hand inside in one motion.

He knows that the line drive hit right through the box is the one that scares other people—for him. He gets asked about it a lot. He doesn't have an answer. He says when it comes, he'll do the best he can.

I think his reactions are so sharp, he'll be fine. I caught a line drive with my mouth one night. I had a bloody lip that needed stitches and a few loose teeth, and I didn't smile for a day or two. Having two hands didn't prevent it, but I was able to stay in the game.

I don't know if there is an adequate way to express my admiration for Dave Dravecky and Jim Abbott. But for one thing, I plan to be more careful when I use the words "courage" and "heart."

We get caught up so much in the competition that we tend to believe that life begins and ends with who won that day. There is much about baseball that seems unreal. You spend so many days and weeks, half the spring and summer, on the road. I feel as if I have been in more hotel rooms than the Gideon Bible.

The money, the publicity, the awards, the requests—all the things we call fame—can make it a difficult course to navigate. What you can't do is let it confuse you as a person. I'm surprised at how many ball players do manage to stay the same. In my experience, if a guy is a jerk when he gets to the majors, chances are he will be a jerk when he leaves.

But it was heartening to follow the examples of Dravecky and Abbott, to see how they coped, how they compensated. And then I thought of Donnie Moore.

I doubt that there were many people in baseball who were not stunned and saddened when Donnie shot his wife and killed himself in July of 1989. I knew him as a relief pitcher with the Cardinals and the Braves while I was with Houston. Everybody spoke well of him.

Then when he was one strike away from pitching the California Angels into their first World Series, he gave up a home run to Boston's Dave Henderson. Boston went on to win the American League playoffs and lose to the Mets in the Series.

I hesitate to try to analyze anything so tragic, or reach for connections that might not be there. But his teammates and closest friends said that Donnie Moore never recovered from giving up that home run. Of course, the fans got on him and the write-ups didn't make great reading. He was the goat, the pitcher who had cost the Angels the pennant. The fans booed him just about anytime he came into a game, and his wife, Tonya, said that some nights he would walk into the house and burst into tears.

I know what Brian Downing thought. He said it flat out, that the criticism "destroyed a man's life. Nobody was sympathetic . . . all you ever read about was one pitch."

I knew Moore as a scrapper, quiet and sensitive. You'd have to know a lot more about his emotional side, what else was going on in his life, to make an honest judgment. But if the boos and the stigma of being the Man Who Lost the Pennant drove him to such a desperate step, then the tragedy deepens.

Bobby Valentine's last year with the Angels was Donnie Moore's first. Now the manager of the Rangers, Bobby is married to the daughter of Ralph Branca, who threw the pitch that Bobby Thomson hit into the seats of the Polo Grounds in 1951. That three-run homer gave the Giants the win and the pennant over the Brooklyn Dodgers.

Ruth and I have talked with Mary Valentine about what her father had to endure. This isn't about irony or drama. It's about excesses, about the sometimes unbearable cost of losing. For over forty years, Ralph Branca has been known for that defeat, that home run, and what is generally considered the most famous moment in baseball history.

Mary Valentine told Ruth how her father felt the wrath of an entire city, and even after time softened the sting of it, there were still the jokes and arguments and an occasional crank call. "Even a guy who commits murder can get pardoned after 20 years," said Branca. "I never got pardoned."

It would be a bitter injustice if the fans rated him a loser. They just don't know Ralph Branca. He won twenty-one games for the Dodgers in 1947. He was twenty-one years old. He was never the same after he hurt his back, but he hung on for twelve seasons. He came from an educated family, and worked in civil service most of his life after baseball. At sixty-five, he is active in the program funded by The Equitable Old Timers games that assists former players who are down on their luck.

He wrote the foreword to Bobby Thomson's autobiography, and they have appeared together at benefits and on TV shows. Ralph has handled his moment with humor and grace. Twenty-five years after Thomson's homer in the gloaming, a writer called and asked Branca if anyone had reminded him what day it was. "Yes," he said. "First thing this morning, my wife rolled over and said, 'Happy anniversary, dear.' "

Does baseball share a responsibility for what happens to a Donnie Moore or a Pete Rose or a Denny McLain? Absolutely. I don't climb on many soapboxes, but every year the teams get one visit from an FBI agent, or a representative of the league, and they lecture us on whatever problem was most recently in the news. For years it was the story of Art Schlichter, the football quarterback who was banned from the NFL for gambling. Next year it will probably be Len Dykstra and the dangers of driving under the influence.

The teams don't spend nearly enough time talking about—especially to the younger players—how to handle stress, or the media, or the temptations that will be tossed their way by people who cultivate them.

I won't press that point and I won't try to get any heavier. I'm not at ease in that role. It's only a game, people keep saying, and for the most part we all want to think so. I know that as a player, and a fan, I prefer the fun and the myths and the legends.

I want to believe that a young boy actually cried out to Shoeless Joe Jackson, "Say it ain't so, Joe," as he left the courthouse where the Black Sox were being tried for fixing the 1919 World Series.

I never get tired of hearing how Babe Ruth pointed to the fence, calling his shot, but I wonder why the Cubs' Charlie Root didn't just plug him with his next pitch. I would have. I like to imagine the consternation of Detroit's Bob Cain as he faced Eddie Gaedel, the midget Bill Veeck once sent up as a pinch hitter for the St. Louis Browns. With his catcher, Bob Swift, on his knees trying to provide a target, Cain walked Gaedel—all three feet, seven inches of him—on four pitches. Baseball quickly closed whatever loophole Veeck had found that enabled him to pull that stunt. But he got away with it once, and if you work it right, once is enough.

A month or two before 1991 spring training began, I was interviewed for a *Sports Illustrated* cover story. Leigh Montville, the writer and a fine one, watched me pitch to Harry Spilman, my neighbor and a former teammate with the Astros. We were at my ranch in Alvin, where years ago I had marked off a field in what had been a cow pasture and built up a mound, mainly so my son's Little League team would have a place to practice.

I leveled the field, put up a twelve-foot fence behind home plate, seeded the grass, and kept it watered. Reid and his friends practiced there for a few years. When they outgrew it, I let the land go back to what it was. The cows and horses had the run of it, except when I needed to use the mound to get ready for the next season. You have to watch where you step and the grass is real patchy; otherwise, it suits me fine.

There are woods beyond the outfield, and Leigh remarked on the similarity to the baseball movie *Field of Dreams*. We joked about the line, intended in the fantasy to bring back Shoeless Joe Jackson: "If you build it, he will come."

I laughed and said, "I built it. He never came. Maybe I should have put in lights."

That was how the story ends—I mean *Sports Illustrated*'s story, not mine. This is not yet the time to get sentimental. I have another year or two, at least, ahead of me and I know that something new is out there waiting to happen. I don't intend to pitch forever. When I retire, I just want to be able to say, as Satchel Paige once did: "I never threw an illegal pitch. The trouble is, once in a while I tossed one that ain't never been seen by this generation."

APPENDIX

LYNN NOLAN RYAN, JR.

Born: January 31, 1947   Ht. 6'2"   Wt. 212

YEAR	CLUB	W-L	ERA	G	GS
1965	Marion-1	3–6	4.38	13	12
1966	Greenville	*17–2	2.51	*29	28
	Williamsport	0–2	0.95	3	3
	New York (NL)	0–1	15.00	2	1
1967	Winter Haven-2	0–0	2.25	1	1
	Jacksonville	1–0	0.00	3	0
1968	New York (NL)	6–9	3.09	21	18
1969	New York (NL)	6–3	3.54	25	10
1970	New York (NL)	7–11	3.41	27	19
1971	New York (NL)-3	10–14	3.97	30	26
1972	California	19–16	2.28	39	39
1973	California	21–16	2.87	41	39
1974	California	22–16	2.89	42	41
1975	California	14–12	3.45	28	28
1976	California	17–*18	3.36	39	39
1977	California	19–16	2.77	37	37
1978	California	10–13	3.71	31	31
1979	California-4	16–14	3.59	34	34
1980	Houston	11–10	3.35	35	35
1981	Houston	11–5	*1.69	21	21
1982	Houston	16–12	3.16	35	35
1983	Houston	14–9	2.98	29	29
1984	Houston	12–11	3.04	30	30
1985	Houston	10–12	3.80	35	35
1986	Houston	12–8	3.34	30	30
1987	Houston	8–16	*2.76	34	34
1988	Houston-5	12–11	3.52	33	33
1989	Texas	16–10	3.20	32	32
1990	Texas	13–9	3.44	30	30
1991	Texas	12–6	2.91	27	27
American League Totals		179–146	3.10	380	377
National League Totals		135–132	3.23	387	356
Major League Totals		314–276	3.15	767	733

....

* LED LEAGUE

1—Selected by New York Mets organization in June '65 free agent draft (10th round, regular phase) . . . Signed by Red Murff on 6/62/65.

2—On military list, Jan. 3–May 13, '67.

3—Acquired by California from New York Mets with pitcher Don Rose, catcher Francisco

B-R   T-R

CG	SHO	SV	IP	H	R	ER	BB	SO
2	1	0	78.0	61	47	38	56	115
9	5	0	183.0	109	59	51	*127	*272
0	0	0	19.0	9	6	2	12	35
0	0	0	3.0	5	5	5	3	6
0	0	0	4.0	1	1	1	2	5
0	0	0	7.0	3	1	0	3	18
3	0	0	134.0	93	50	46	75	133
2	0	1	89.0	60	38	35	53	92
5	2	1	132.0	86	59	50	97	125
3	0	0	152.0	125	78	67	116	137
20	*9	0	284.0	166	80	72	*157	*329
26	4	1	326.0	238	113	104	*162	*383
26	3	0	*333.0	221	127	107	*202	*367
10	5	0	198.0	152	90	76	132	186
21	*7	0	284.0	193	117	106	*183	*327
#22	4	0	299.0	198	110	92	*204	*341
14	3	0	235.0	183	106	97	*148	*260
17	#5	0	223.0	169	104	89	114	*223
4	2	0	234.0	205	100	87	*98	200
5	3	0	149.0	99	34	28	68	140
10	3	0	250.1	196	100	88	*109	245
5	2	0	196.1	134	74	65	101	183
5	2	0	183.2	143	78	62	69	197
4	0	0	232.0	205	108	98	95	209
1	0	0	178.0	119	72	66	82	194
0	0	0	211.2	154	75	65	87	*270
4	1	0	220.0	186	98	86	87	*228
6	2	0	239.1	162	96	85	98	*301
5	2	0	204.0	137	86	78	74	*232
2	2	0	173	102	58	56	72	203
169	46	1	2798.1	1921	1087	962	1546	3152
51	15	2	2365.0	1810	969	848	1140	2359
220	61	3	5163.1	3731	2056	1800	2696	5511

#TIED FOR LEAGUE LEAD

Estrada, and outfielder Leroy Stanton in deal for infielder Jim Fregosi on 12/10/71.
   4—Granted free agency on 11/1/79 . . . Signed by Houston as a free agent on 11/19/79.
   5—Granted free agency on 11/1/88 . . . Signed by Texas as a free agent on 12/7/88.

RYAN AS A RELIEVER							
W-L	**G**	**SV**	**IP**	**H**	**W**	**K**	**ERA**
6–1	34	3	60.0	43	47	60	4.05

MAJOR LEAGUE HITTING TOTALS

AVG	**AB**	**H**	**HR**	**RBI**
.110	852	94	2	33

BASEBALL CAREER PITCHING RECORDS

(Through 1991)

STRIKEOUTS		
1	Nolan Ryan	5511
2	Steve Carlton	4136
3	Tom Seaver	3640
4	Bert Blyleven	3631
5	Don Sutton	3574
6	Gaylord Perry	3534
7	Walter Johnson	3508
8	Phil Niekro	3342
9	Ferguson Jenkins	3192
10	Bob Gibson	3117

INNINGS PITCHED		
1	Cy Young	7356
2	Pud Galvin	5941
3	Walter Johnson	5923
4	Phil Niekro	5404
5	Gaylord Perry	5352
6	Don Sutton	5281
7	Warren Spahn	5244
8	Steve Carlton	5216
9	Grove Alexander	5189
10	Nolan Ryan	5163
11	Kid Nichols	5084
12	Tim Keefe	5061

GAMES STARTED		
1	Cy Young	815
2	Don Sutton	756
3	Nolan Ryan	733
4	Phil Niekro	716
5	Steve Carlton	709
6	Tommy John	700
7	Gaylord Perry	690
8	Pud Galvin	682
9	Walter Johnson	666
10	Warren Spahn	665

EARNED RUN AVERAGE		
(3000 or more ip)		
1	Mordecai Brown	2.06
2	Christy Mathewson	2.13
3	Walter Johnson	2.17
4	Will White	2.28
5	Eddie Plank	2.34
6	Ed Cicotte	2.37
7	Doc White	2.38
8	Jim McCormick	2.43
9	Chief Bender	2.46
10	Grover Alexander	2.56
11	Whitey Ford	2.75
12	Tom Seaver	2.86
13	Jim Palmer	2.86
14	Stan Covaleski	2.88
15	Juan Marichal	2.89
16	Wilbur Cooper	2.89
17	Bob Gibson	2.91
18	Carl Mays	2.92
19	Kid Nichols	2.94
20	Don Drysdale	2.95
21	Carl Hubbell	2.97
22	Lefty Grove	3.06
23	Warren Spahn	3.09
24	Gaylord Perry	3.10
25	Urban Faber	3.1475
26	Eppa Rixey	3.1497
27	Nolan Ryan	3.15

SHUTOUTS		
1	Walter Johnson	110
2	Grover Alexander	90
3	Christy Mathewson	80
4	Cy Young	76
5	Eddie Plank	69
6	Warren Spahn	63
7	Nolan Ryan	61
8	Tom Seaver	61
9	Bert Blyleven	60
10	Don Sutton	58
11	Ed Walsh	57
12	Pud Galvin	57
13	Mordecai Brown	57

VICTORIES		
1	Cy Young	511
2	Walter Johnson	416
3	Christy Mathewson	373
4	Grover Alexander	373
5	Warren Spahn	363
6	Pud Galvin	361
7	Kid Nichols	361
8	Tim Keefe	342
9	Steve Carlton	329
10	Eddie Plank	327
11	John Clarkson	326
12	Don Sutton	324
13	Phil Niekro	318
14	Gaylord Perry	314
15	Nolan Ryan	314
16	Tom Seaver	311
17	Charles Radbourn	311
18	Mickey Welch	308
19	Lefty Grove	327
20	Early Wynn	300

RYAN'S MILESTONE VICTORIES

NO.	DATE	OPPONENT	SCORE	OPPOSING PITCHER	NOTES
1	April 14, 1968	Houston	4–0	Larry Dierker	6.2 sho ip
50	April 11, 1973	Minnesota	4–1	Bill Hands	cg
100	June 1, 1975	Baltimore	1–0	Ross Grimsley	4th no-hitter
150	September 24, 1978	Chicago (AL)	7–3	Francisco Barrios	—
200	July 27, 1982	Cincinnati	3–2	Charlie Leibrandt	cg
250	August 27, 1986	Chicago (NL)	7–1	Jamie Moyer	6 sho ip
300	July 31, 1990	Milwaukee	11–3	Chris Bosio	7.2 ip

CY YOUNG AWARD WINNERS

American League

1958	Bob Turley, Yankees
1959	Early Wynn, White Sox
1961	Whitey Ford, Yankees
1964	Dean Chance, Angels
1967	Jim Lonborg, Red Sox
1968	Denny McLain, Tigers
1969	(tie) Mike Cuellar, Orioles, and Denny McLain, Tigers
1970	Jim Perry, Twins
1971	Vida Blue, Athletics
1972	Gaylord Perry, Indians
1973	Jim Palmer, Orioles
1974	Catfish Hunter, Athletics
1975	Jim Palmer, Orioles
1976	Jim Palmer, Orioles
1977	Sparky Lyle, Yankees
1978	Ron Guidry, Yankees
1979	Mike Flanagan, Orioles
1980	Steve Stone, Orioles
1981	Rollie Fingers, Brewers
1982	Pete Vuckovich, Brewers
1983	LaMarr Hoyt, White Sox
1984	Willie Hernandez, Tigers
1985	Bret Saberhagen, Royals
1986	Roger Clemens, Red Sox
1987	Roger Clemens, Red Sox
1988	Frank Viola, Twins
1989	Bret Saberhagen, Royals
1990	Bob Welch, Athletics
1991	Roger Clemens, Red Sox

Note: From 1956–66, there was one selection from both leagues.

CY YOUNG AWARD WINNERS

National League

1956	Don Newcombe, Dodgers
1957	Warren Spahn, Braves
1960	Vernon Law, Pirates
1962	Don Drysdale, Dodgers
1963	Sandy Koufax, Dodgers
1965	Sandy Koufax, Dodgers
1966	Sandy Koufax, Dodgers
1967	Mike McCormick, Giants
1968	Bob Gibson, Cardinals
1969	Tom Seaver, Mets
1970	Bob Gibson, Cardinals
1971	Ferguson Jenkins, Cubs
1972	Steve Carlton, Phillies
1973	Tom Seaver, Mets
1974	Mike Marshall, Dodgers
1975	Tom Seaver, Mets
1976	Randy Jones, Padres
1977	Steve Carlton, Phillies
1978	Gaylord Perry, Padres
1979	Bruce Sutter, Cubs
1980	Steve Carlton, Phillies
1981	Fernando Valenzuela, Dodgers
1982	Steve Carlton, Phillies
1983	John Denny, Phillies
1984	Rick Sutcliffe, Cubs
1985	Dwight Gooden, Mets
1986	Mike Scott, Astros
1987	Steve Bedrosian, Phillies
1988	Orel Hershiser, Dodgers
1989	Mark Davis, Padres
1990	Doug Drabek, Pirates
1991	Tom Glavine, Braves

Note: From 1956–66, there was one selection for all of major-league baseball.

NO-HITTERS, 1965–1991 (by one pitcher)

YEAR	DATE	H/A	PITCHER	SCORE
1965	June 14	H	Jim Maloney (Cin) vs. NY(NL) no-hitter for 10 innings. Lost in 11th (2 hits)	0–1
	Aug. 19	A (1st game)	2 Jim Maloney (Cin) vs. Chi (NL)	1–0
	Sept. 9	H	4 Sandy Koufax (LA) vs. Chi (NL)	1–0
	Sept. 16	H	Dave Morehead (Bos) vs. Cle (AL)	2–0
1966	June 10	H	Sonny Siebert (Cle) vs. Was (AL)	2–0
1967	June 18	H	Don Wilson (Hou) vs. Atl (NL)	2–0
	Aug. 6	H	Dean Chance (Min) vs. Bos (AL) 5 innings	2–0
	Aug. 25	A (2nd game)	2 Dean Chance (Min) vs. Cle (AL)	2–1
	Sept. 10	H (1st game)	Joel Horlen (Chi) vs. Det (AL)	6–0
1968	Apr. 27	H	Tom Phoebus (Bal) vs. Bos (AL)	6–0
	May 8	H	Catfish Hunter (Oak) vs. Min (AL)	4–0
	July 29	A (2nd game)	George Culver (Cin) vs. Phi (NL)	6–1
	Sept. 17	H	Gaylord Perry (SF) vs. St.L (NL)	1–0
	Sept. 18	A	Ray Washburn (St.L) vs. SF (NL)	2–0
1969	Apr. 17	A	Bill Stoneman (Mon) vs. Phi (NL)	7–0
	Apr. 30	H	3 Jim Maloney (Cin) vs. Hou (NL)	10–0
	May 1	A	2 Don Wilson (Hou) vs. Cin (NL)	4–0
	Aug. 13	H	Jim Palmer (Bal) vs. Oak (AL)	8–0

	Aug. 19	H	Ken Holtzman (Chi) vs. Atl (NL)	3–0
	Sept. 20	A	Bob Moose (Pit) vs. NY (NL)	4–0
1970	June 12	A (1st game)	Dock Ellis (Pit) vs. SD (NL)	2–0
	July 3	H	Clyde Wright (Cal) vs. Oak (AL)	4–0
	July 20	H	Bill Singer (LA) vs. Phi (NL)	5–0
	Sept. 21	H	Vida Blue (Oak) vs. Min (AL)	6–0
1971	June 3	H	2 Ken Holtzman (Chi) vs. Cin (NL)	1–0
	June 23	A	Rick Wise (Phi) vs. Cin (NL)	4–0
	Aug. 14	A	Bob Gibson (St.L) vs. Pit (NL)	11–0
1972	Apr. 16	H	Burt Hooton (Chi) vs. Phi (NL)	1–0
	Sept. 2	H	Milt Pappas (Chi) vs. SD (NL)	8–0
	Oct. 2	H	2 Bill Stoneman (Mon) vs. NY (NL)	7–0
1973	Apr. 27	A	Steve Busby (KC) vs. Det (AL)	3–0
	May 15	A	Nolan Ryan (Cal) vs. KC (AL)	3–0
	July 15	A	2 Nolan Ryan (Cal) vs. Det (AL)	6–0
	July 30	A	Jim Bibby (Tex) vs. Oak (AL)	6–0
	Aug. 5	H	Phil Niekro (Atl) vs. SD (NL)	9–0
1974	June 19	A	2 Steve Busby (KC) vs. Mil (AL)	2–0
	July 19	H	Dick Bosman (Cle) vs. Oak (AL)	4–0
	Sept. 28	H	3 Nolan Ryan (Cal) vs. Min (AL)	4–0
1975	June 1	H	4 Nolan Ryan (Cal) vs. Bal (AL)	1–0
	Aug. 24	H	Ed Halicki (SF) vs. NY (NL)	6–0
1976	July 9	H	Larry Dierker (Hou) vs. Mon (NL)	6–0
	Aug. 9	H	John Candelaria (Pit) vs. LA (NL)	2–0
	Sept. 29	A	John Montefusco (SF) vs. Atl (NL)	9–0

1977	May 14	H		Jim Colborn (KC) vs. Tex (AL)	6–0
	May 30	H		Dennis Eckersley (Cle) vs. Cal (AL)	2–0
	Sept. 22	A		Bert Blyleven (Tex) vs. Cal (AL)	9–0
1978	Apr. 16	H		Bob Forsch (St.L) vs. Phi (NL)	5–0
	June 16	H		Tom Seaver (Cin) vs. St.L (NL)	4–0
1979	Apr. 7	H		Ken Forsch (Hou) vs. Atl (NL)	6–0
1980	June 27	A		Jerry Reuss (LA) vs. SF (NL)	8–0
1981	May 10	H		Charlie Lea (Mon) vs. SF (NL)	4–0
	May 15	H		Len Barker (Cle) vs. Tor (AL)	3–0
	Sept. 26	H	5	Nolan Ryan (Hou) vs. LA (NL)	5–0
1983	July 4	H		Dave Righetti (NY) vs. Bos (AL)	4–0
	Sept. 9	H		Mike Warren (Oak) vs. Chi (AL)	3–0
	Sept. 26	H	2	Bob Forsch (St.L) vs. Mon (NL)	3–0
1984	Apr. 7	A		Jack Morris (Det) vs. Chi (AL)	4–0
	Apr. 21	A (2nd game)		David Palmer (Mon) vs. St.L. (NL) 5 innings	4–0
	Sept. 30	A		Mike Witt (Cal) vs. Tex (AL)	1–0
1986	Sept. 19	A		Joe Cowley (Chi) vs. Cal (AL)	7–1
	Sept. 25	H		Mike Scott (Hou) vs. SF(NL)	2–0
1987	April 15	A		Juan Nieves (Mil) vs. Bal (AL)	7–0
1988	Sept. 16	H		Tom Browning (Cin) vs. LA (NL)	1–0
	Sept. 24	A		Pascual Perez (Mon) vs. Phi (NL) 5 innings	1–0

1990	June 2	H	Randy Johnson (Sea) vs. Det (AL)	2–0
	June 11	A	6 Nolan Ryan (Tex) vs. Oak (AL)	5–0
	June 29	H	Dave Stewart (Oak) vs. Tor (AL)	5–0
	June 29	H	Fernando Valenzuela (LA) vs. St.L (NL)	6–0
	July 1	A	Andy Hawkins (NY) vs. Chi (AL) (pitched 8 innings)	0–4
	July 12	A	Melido Perez (Chi) vs. NY (AL) 6 innings	8–0
	Aug. 15	H	Terry Mulholland (Phi) vs. SF (NL)	6–0
	Sept. 2	A	Dave Stieb (Tor) vs. Cle (AL)	3–0
1991	May 1	H	7 Nolan Ryan (Tex) vs. Tor (AL)	3–0
	May 23	A	Tommy Greene (Phil) vs. Mon (NL)	2–0
	July 13	A	Bob Milacki, Mike Flanagan, Mark Wiliamson, Gregg Olson (Bal), combined vs. Oak (AL)	2–0
	July 28	A	Dennis Martinez (Mon) vs. LA (NL) (Martinez pitched perfect game)	2–0
	Aug 11	A	Wilson Alverez (Chi) vs. Bal (AL)	7–0
	Aug 26	H	Bret Saberhagen (KC) vs. Chi (AL)	7–0
	Sept. 11	H	Kent Mercker, Mark Wohlers, Alejandro Pena (Atl), combined vs. SD (NL)	1–0

300-VICTORY CLUB

DATE/# 300	PITCHER/AGE	TEAM/ LEAGUE	OPP.	H/A	SCORE	TOTAL WINS
Sep. 29, 1888	Pud Galvin (31)	Pit. (NL)	Phi.	A	4–2	361
June 4, 1890	Tim Keefe (33)	N.Y. (PL)	Bos.	H	9–4	342
July 28, 1890	Mickey Welch (31)	N.Y. (NL)	Pit.	A	4–2	307
June 2, 1891	Charles Radbourn (36)	Cin. (NL)	Bos.	A	10–8	308
Sep. 21, 1892	John Clarkson (31)	Cle. (NL)	Pit.	A	3–2	327
June 13, 1900	Kid Nichols (30)	Bos. (NL)	Pit.	H	1–0	361
July 6, 1901	Cy Young (34)	Bos. (AL)	Was.	H	7–0	511
July 5, 1912	Christy Mathewson (33)	N.Y. (NL)	Brk.	H	6–1	373
Aug. 11, 1915	Eddie Plank (39)	St.L. (FL)	K.C.	H	3–2	305
May 29, 1920	Walter Johnson (32)	Was. (AL)	Phi.	A	11–5	416
Sep. 20, 1924	Grover Alexander (37)	Chi. (NL)	N.Y.	A	7–3	373
July 25, 1941	Lefty Grove (41)	Bos. (AL)	Cle.	H	10–6	300
Aug. 11, 1961	Warren Spahn (40)	Mil. (NL)	Chi.	H	2–1	363
July 13, 1963	Early Wynn (43)	Cle. (AL)	K.C.	A	7–4	300
May 6, 1982	Gaylord Perry (43)	Sea. (AL)	N.Y.	H	7–3	314
Sep. 23, 1983	Steve Carlton (38)	Phi. (NL)	St.L.	A	6–2	329
Aug. 4, 1985	Tom Seaver (40)	Chi. (AL)	N.Y.	A	4–1	311
Oct. 6, 1985	Phil Niekro (46)	N.Y. (AL)	Tor.	A	8–0	318
June 18, 1986	Don Sutton (41)	Cal. (AL)	Tex.	H	5–1	324
July 31, 1990	Nolan Ryan (43)	Tex. (AL)	Mil.	A	11–3	314*

* Still active

RYAN'S STRIKEOUT RECORDS
(Major Leagues)

1. Most strikeouts, major leagues—5511.
2. Most strikeouts, season—383, California, 1973.
3. Most years, 100 or more strikeouts—24.
4. Most consecutive years, 100 or more strikeouts—22.
5. Most years, 200 or more strikeouts—15.
6. Most years, 200 or more strikeouts, American League—10.
7. Most years, 300 or more strikeouts—6.
8. Most strikeouts, losing pitcher, extra inning game—19, California, August 20, 1974, 11 innings, 1–0.
9. Most times, 15 or more strikeouts—26.
10. Most times, 10 or more strikeouts—211.
11. Most times, 10 or more strikeouts, season—23.
12. Three strikeouts, inning, on nine pitched balls—2, New York Mets, April 19, 1968; California, July 9, 1972.
13. Most consecutive strikeouts, game, American League—8, California, July 9, 1972, and July 15, 1973.
14. Most strikeouts, two consecutive games—32, California, August 7th (13) and August 12th (19), 1974.
15. Most strikeouts, three consecutive games—47, California, August 12th (19), August 16th (9) and August 20th (19), 1974; total 27.1 innings.

RYAN'S MILESTONE STRIKEOUTS

NO.	RATE	OPPONENT	PLAYER
1	Sep. 11, 1966	Atlanta	Pat Jarvis
100	June 18, 1968	Houston	Denny LeMaster
500	April 18, 1972	Minnesota	Charlie Manuel
1000	July 3, 1973	Oakland	Sal Bando
1500	August 25, 1974	New York (AL)	Sandy Alomar
2000	August 31, 1976	Detroit	Ron LeFlore
2500	August 12, 1978	Cleveland	Buddy Bell
3000	July 4, 1980	Cincinnati	Cesar Geronimo
3500	April 17, 1983	Montreal	Andre Dawson
3509*	April 27, 1983	Montreal	Brad Mills
4000	July 11, 1985	New York (NL)	Danny Heep
4500	Sep. 9, 1987	San Francisco	Mike Aldrete
5000	Aug. 22, 1989	Oakland	Rickey Henderson

* BREAKS WALTER JOHNSON'S ALL-TIME STRIKEOUT RECORD

MAY 15, 1973, AT KANSAS CITY
CALIFORNIA 3, KANSAS CITY 0

NOLAN RYAN chalked up the first of his major-league record seven no-hitters for the California Angels as he stopped the Kansas City Royals for the first hitless game by an Angels right-hander in the club's history. Ryan finished with 12 strikeouts as he recorded at least one whiff in every inning except the fifth. The only close call of the game came in the eighth inning when Royals pinch hitter Gail Hopkins hit a looping liner into left field which shortstop Rudy Meoli came up with on a running over-the-shoulder catch with his back to the plate. The Angels and Ryan got all the offensive support they needed from right fielder Bob Oliver, two of the three RBIs with a solo home run and a single.

| California | 200 | 001 | 000 | — | 3 | 11 | 0 |
| Kansas City | 000 | 000 | 000 | — | 0 | 0 | 0 |

Ryan and Torborg. Dal Canton, Garber (6) and Taylor, Kirkpatrick, WP-Ryan (5–3) LP-Dal Canton (2–2).

Ryan Pitching Line: 9 IP 0 H 0 R 0 ER 3 BB 12 SO

JULY 15, 1973, AT DETROIT
CALIFORNIA 6, DETROIT 0

THE "EASIEST" NO-HITTER for Ryan in terms of scores as he turned in his second no-hitter of the 1973 campaign, again on the road, by stopping the Detroit Tigers 6–0. Ryan had 17 strikeouts for the game with 16 of them coming in the first seven innings. However, his arm stiffened up somewhat in the top of the eighth as the Angels batted around while scoring five runs to break open a close game. Ryan had to rely on no special defensive accomplishments to preserve the no-hitter as he became the fifth man in history to throw two no-hitters in a season.

| California | 001 | 000 | 050 | — | 6 | 9 | 0 |
| Detroit | 000 | 000 | 000 | — | 0 | 0 | 0 |

Ryan and Kusnyer. J. Perry, Scherman (8), Farmer (8) and Sims. WP-Ryan (11–11). LP-J. Perry (9–9).

Ryan Pitching Line: 9 IP 0 H 0 R 0 ER 4 BB 17 SO

SEPTEMBER 28, 1974, AT ANAHEIM
CALIFORNIA 4, MINNESOTA 0

NOLAN RYAN makes the most of his final start of the 1974 campaign by ringing up his third career no-hitter to raise his final record to 22–16 at the expense of the Minnesota Twins, 4–0. Ryan started in splendid fashion as his first seven pitches were strikes, but he also had to contend with no less than eight walks—seven of them in the first five innings. The Angels won it with two runs in both the third and fourth innings with center fielder Morris Nettles driving home three of them.

Minnesota	000	000	000	—	0	0	2
California	002	200	00x	—	4	7	0

Decker, Butler (3) and Borgmann. Ryan and Egan. WP-Ryan (22–16). LP-Decker (16–14).

Ryan Pitching Line: 9 IP   0 H   0 R   0 ER   8 BB   15 SO

JUNE 1, 1975, AT ANAHEIM
CALIFORNIA 1, BALTIMORE 0

NOLAN RYAN moved into a tie with Dodgers great Sandy Koufax as he fired the fourth no-hitter of his career in nipping the Baltimore Orioles 1–0. Making his 12th start of the season, Ryan polished off the Orioles with nine strikeouts as he came up with his fourth no-hit effort in a period of 109 starts. The only offensive output in the game came in the bottom of the third when Angels third baseman Dave Chalk singled home Mickey Rivers.

Baltimore	000	000	000	—	0	0	0
California	001	000	000	—	1	9	1

Grimsley, Garland (4) and Hendricks. Ryan and Rodriguez. WP-Ryan (9–3). LP-Grimsley (1–7).

Ryan Pitching Line: 9 IP   0 H   0 R   0 ER   4 BB   9 SO

SEPTEMBER 26, 1981, AT HOUSTON
HOUSTON 5, LOS ANGELES 0

HISTORY WAS MADE when Nolan Ryan became the first man in the history of baseball to pitch five no-hitters in his career as he notched a crucial 5–0 win over the Los Angeles Dodgers. In winning, Ryan wound up with 11 strikeouts (the 135th time in his career that he fanned 10 or more men in a game) while walking only three. He threw a total of 129 pitches (52 balls, 77 strikes). Ryan stood at 10 strikeouts through the opening six innings, but set down only one more the rest of the way as he retired the final 19 batters in a row. Catcher Alan Ashby gave the Astros a 2–0 lead with a two-run single in the third and then Houston wrapped up the win with three more tallies in the eighth.

| Los Angeles | 000 | 000 | 000 | — | 0 | 0 | 1 |
| Houston | 002 | 000 | 03x | — | 5 | 11 | 0 |

Power, Goltz (4), Forster (5), Stewart (8), Howe (8), and Scioscia. Ryan and Ashby. WP-Ryan (10–5), LP-Power (1–3).

Ryan Pitching Line: 9 IP 0 H 0 R 0 ER 3 BB 11 SO

JUNE 11, 1990, AT OAKLAND
TEXAS 5, OAKLAND 0

NOLAN RYAN accomplished several milestones with the sixth no-hitter of his major-league career. At the age of 43 years, 4 months, 12 days, he became the oldest pitcher to ever throw a no-hitter while also becoming the first to reach that achievement in three different decades and with three different teams. Ryan was making just his second start since coming off the disabled list and was still bothered by the lower back trouble that had benched him for nearly three weeks. He allowed only two base runners, walks to Walt Weiss in the third and Mike Gallego in the sixth, while fanning 14 and throwing 132 pitches. The Rangers offense was provided by a pair of 2-run homers by Julio Franco and a solo blast by John Russell, who was catching Ryan for the first time.

| Texas | 210 | 020 | 000 | — | 5 | 9 | 0 |
| Oakland | 000 | 000 | 000 | — | 0 | 0 | 0 |

Ryan and Russell. Sanderson, Norris (7), Nelson (9), and Quirk, Steinbach (9). WP-Ryan (5–3), LP-Sanderson (7–3).

Ryan Pitching Line: 9 IP 0 H 0 R 0 ER 2 BB 14 SO

MAY 1, 1991, AT ARLINGTON
TEXAS 3, TORONTO 0

NOLAN RYAN pitched after only four days rest to allow him the opportunity to pitch in front of the home crowd on Arlington Appreciation Night. Ryan started out strong, striking out 13 of the first 21 batters, and finished the game with 16 strikeouts. Ryan allowed only two base runners on walks. All three Rangers runs were scored in the bottom of the third, with Ruben Sierra providing the offensive output on a two-run homer. It is interesting to note that Roberto Alomar was the final out of the game; his father, Sandy Alomar, was Ryan's second baseman in his first two no-hitters.

Toronto	000	000	000	—	0	0	0
Texas	003	000	00x	—	3	8	1

Ryan and Stanley. Key, MacDonald (7) and Fraser (8). WP-Ryan (3–2), LP-Key (4–1).

Ryan Pitching Line:	9 IP	0 H	0 R	0 ER	2 BB	16 SO

NOLAN'S SELECTIVE READING LIST

(A collection of works and sources having to do with baseball in general and pitching in particular)

Allen, Maury. *Baseball's 100*. New York: A&W Publishers, 1981.

Angell, Roger. *Season Ticket*. Boston: Houghton Mifflin, 1988.

Boswell, Thomas. *The Heart of the Order*. New York: Doubleday, 1989.

Koppett, Leonard. *The New York Mets*. New York: Collier Books, 1974.

Lyle, Sparky, with Peter Golenbock. *The Bronx Zoo*. New York: Crown, 1979.

Nash, Bruce, and Zullo, Allan. *The Baseball Hall of Shame's Warped Record Book*. New York: Collier Books, 1991.

Nemec, David. *Great Baseball Feats, Facts & Firsts*. New York: Plume, 1987.

Peary, Danny, editor. *Cult Baseball Players*. New York: Fireside, 1990.

Ryan, Nolan, and Frommer, Harvey. *Throwing Heat*. New York: Doubleday, 1988.

Thorn, John. *The Armchair Book of Baseball II*. New York: Charles Scribner's Sons, 1987.

Uecker, Bob, and Herskowitz, Mickey. *Catcher in the Wry*. New York: G. P. Putnam's Sons, 1982.

Newspapers and News Services

Associated Press
Dallas Morning News
Dallas Times Herald
Houston Chronicle
Houston Post
Los Angeles Herald-Examiner
Los Angeles Times
New York Daily News
New York Post
New York Times
Scripps-Howard News Service

INDEX

D

Dalkowski, Steve, 96–99
Dalton, Harry, 192
Dark, Alvin, 49, 51
Darling, Ron, 103
Dascenzo, Doug, 59, 72
Davidson, Donald, 179
Davis, Willie, 35, 65
Dawley, Bill, 59
Deal, Ellis (Cot), 57
Dean brothers, 175
Dean, Dizzy, 14, 111–12, 164, 175
Dedeaux, Rod, 33
DeMars, Billy, 97
Dempsey, Jack, 34
Denny, John, 151
Designated hitter rule, 75
Detroit Tigers, xii, 146; 1968
    World Series, 66–67; and
    Fidrych, 112–117; and McLain,
    164–67; and Morris, 186–87
Devine, Bing, 36
Dibble, Rob, 67, 78, 95; fastball
    speed, 74–75; hitting batters,
    and personality, 70–73
Dierker, Larry, 140–41; career
    and personality, 55–58
Dierker, Rick, 57
DiMaggio, Joe, 34, 36, 116, 142
Doran, Billy, 71–73
Downing, Brian, 207
Dr. K, 106
Drabosky, Moe, 142
Dravecky, Dave, 204–5, 206
Driessen, Danny, 171
Drysdale, Don, 5, 18–19, 28, 41,
    42, 44, 73, 78, 93; on batters
    compared to motorists, 64;
    consecutive scoreless innings,
    53; and fastball, 94–95; hair
    tonic used on ball charge, 86;
    innings pitched, 186; as intimi-
    dator, 60–63, 70; salary hold-
    out, 19–20; on Sandy Koufax,
    16, 18; and Sutton, 47–48

Dubious distinction awards,
    170–71
Duncan, Dave, 38
Duren, Ryne, 95, 96, 133, 153–
    55
Durocher, Leo, 2, 3, 85, 86; and
    inside pitches, 69
Dykstra, Len, 208

E

Eckersley, Dennis, 137
Elliott, Jumbo, 133
Ellis, Dale, 103
Ellis, Dock, 170, 171
Ellsworth, Dick, 170
Elston, Don, 170
Ewell, Jim, xviii

F

Face, Elroy, 137, 150; consecutive
    wins as reliever, 188
Fairly, Ron, 32–33, 70
Fame, xxiii, 16–17, 206
Fans, 92; booing of Dibble, 72;
    and Fidrych, 113–14, 116–17;
    and Gooden, 106–7, 108; and
    Hrabosky, 131; and idolization,
    17; Kansas City, and Ryan's
    seventh no-hitter, xii; and Tug
    McGraw, 143–44; and Mets
    1969 Series win, 12; and Mets
    trade of Seaver, 36; and nick-
    names, 50; and Don Sutton,
    41–42
Farrell, Turk, 62–63, 64
Fastball, 26, 53, 57, 176; and bow
    tie pitch, 77; and Roger Clem-
    ens, 104–5; Dalkowski and,
    96–99; Drysdale's, 64–65; Bob
    Feller and J.R. Richard, 95;
    high/inside and hitting of bat-
    ters, 74–75; Koufax and, 19;
    Tug McGraw's "Peggy Lee,"
    145; and moving up before
    pitch, 80–81; and power hit-

Hawkins, Andy, 53, 170
Heep, Danny, 196–97
Henderson, Dave, 206
Henderson, Rickey, 112, 197
Henke, Tom, 139
Hernandez, Willie, 15, 138, 187
Herring, Art, 170
Hershisher, Orel, 28; career and personality, 52–55; computer record on hitters, 53; consecutive scoreless innings record, 53–54, 172; innings pitched, 186
Herzog, Whitey, 119, 120, 138, 140; on innings pitched by Ryan, 186
Hiller, Chuck, 7
Hitters. *See* Batsmen
Hodges, Gil, 10, 12, 33, 69–70, 141, 143; on pitching to McGovey, 192; and Tug McGraw, 142
Holyfield, Evander, 182
Honeycutt, Rick, 93
Hooten, Burt, xxiv
Horseplay in baseball, xxiii. See *also* Flakes and jokers
Horton, Willie, 67
Hot dogs, 112
Hough, Charlie, 172, 176
Houk, Ralph, 85, 113
House, Tom, xxi–xxii, 204
Houston Astros, xvi, xvii, xxiii, 3, 14, 24, 40, 54–55, 72, 141, 173, 194, 196, 209; 1985–86 seasons, 83; 1980 playoffs, 45–46, 145; 1986 playoffs, 153; and Andersen, 125; Andujar with, 118–19; and Belinsky, 158; Belinsky suspension, 162; Corked Bat Case, 89; and Dierker, 55–58; and Kerfeld, 153–57; Perry's breaking of Fox's bat, 82; pitchers' home run contests,

89–91; Sutton with, 42–44, 46–47
Houston Colt .45s, 14, 63, 140
Howard, Elston, 148
Howard, Frank, 56
Howe, Art, 46
Howe, Steve, 15, 45
Howser, Dick, 122, 140
Hoyt, LaMarr, 151
Hrabosky, Al (Mad Hungarian), 78, 135, 146; career and personality, 130–32
Hubbell, Carl, 25–26, 188
Hunt, Ron, 2
Hunter, Billy, 170
Hunter, James "Catfish," 44, 104; arguments with Martin, 148; career and personality, 48–52; origin of nickname, 50–51
Hurst, Bruce, 59, 122
Hutchings, Johnny, 133

I
Innings pitched statistic, 186–87, 215; Ryan (1973), 186, 215
Inside pitching, 49, 60–77
Intimidators, xxiii, 60–78; current brand of, 76; fines and suspensions, 65; reasons for throwing at a batter, 64
Ivins, Molly, xvii

J
Jackson, Reggie, xvii, 81, 191; clashes with Martin and teammates, 148–49
Jackson, Roy, 184
Jackson, Shoeless Joe, 209
Jenkins, Ferguson, xvii, xxiv, 110
John, Tommy, 30, 179; career, injury, and humor, 172–75
Johnson, Davey, 105, 109
Johnson, Walter, 50, 53, 95;

Ruhle, Vern, 32, 46
Russell, Bill, 143
Russell, Jeff, 13
Ruth, Babe, xvii, 34, 142, 198; calling his shot, 208
Ryan, Connie, 170
Ryan, Nolan, 34, 204; 1966 record, 3; 1968 record, 9; 1991 record, xiv; 1977 salary, 36–37; 3000-4000th strikeouts, 196–97; 1969 World Series, 10–12; career and personality, xi-xvii; and Clemens, 99–100; football throwing exercise, xxi-xxii; innings worked, xiii, 213; and Jim Palmer, 180–81; longevity and pitching after forty, 6–8, 172; milestone victories, 216; no-hitters detailed, 226–29; pitching records, 8, 212–16, 220–25; and Pete Rose, xxiii, 193–96; seventh no-hitter, xii-xiv, 8–9, 229; strikeout records, xiv, 21, 216, 224–25; 5000th strikeout, xiv, 197; tolerance for aggravation, 100
Ryan, Reese, xv
Ryan, Reid, xii-xiii, 204
Ryan, Ruth Holdorf, xiii, xvi, 9, 11, 207

S
Saberhagen, Bret, 156, 187
St. Louis Browns, 208
St. Louis Cardinals, 14, 28, 57, 188; 1973 pennant race, 143–44; 1968 World Series, 66–67; and Andujar, 118, 119–20; and Carlton, 20–21; Herzog and bullpen, 138; and Hrabosky, 131; and Jim Kaat, 185
Salaries, 64
Sambito, Joe, 43, 99
San Diego Padres, xii, 192
San Francisco Giants, 19, 23, 55,

57, 64, 83, 170, 184, 192, 204; 1951 pennant, 207; and Roger Craig, 140; and intimidator pitchers, 65; and Perry, 82
Sanders, Ricky, 103
Santo, Ron, 69–70
Schatzeder, Dan, 15
Schlichter, Art, 208
Schmidt, Mike, 178, 196
Schott, Marge, 71
Schurr, Wayne, 170
Scioscia, Mike, 74
Score, Herb, 95–96
Scott, Dick, 170
Scott, Mike, 6, 83, 93, 156, 196; and split-finger fastball, 86
Scott, Rodney, 128
Screwball, 25–26, 143, 145; and Tug McGraw, 143, 145
Scuffball, 83, 92
Scurry, Rod, 13
Seattle Mariners, 81–82, 104
Seaver, Nancy, 37
Seaver, Tom, xvii, xxiv, 3, 44, 99, 106, 110, 180; 1969 championship season, 10–12, 35, 36; career and personality, 33–39; and fastball, 95; innings pitched, 186; as intimidator, and retribution, 69–70; with Mets, 9, 143; nickname and, 50; as thinking pitcher, 32–33
Seerey, Pat, 123–24
Selma, Dick, 2, 192
Setup men, 139
Shamsky, Art, 10
Shantz, Bobby, 63, 133
Shaw, Bob, 2
Shea Stadium, 12, 42
Shelton, Ron, 99
Short, Bob, 167
Sign stealing, 74, 75
Singer, Bill, 48, 93; and toothpaste, 86
Sinker pitch, 32, 53, 174

xxiv, 28, 30, 45, 46, 106, 145;
career and personality, 24–26;
with Los Angeles Dodgers, 153
Van Doren, Mamie, 157, 159
Vander Meer, Johnny, 188
Vargo, Ed, 171
Veeck, Bill, xix, 208–9
Virdon, Bill, 42, 119
Visualization technique, 183
Vuckovich, Pete, 151

W

Waddell, Rube, 112
Wagner, Dick, 141
Walk, Bob, 76
Walker, Dewayne, xxiv
Walker, Rube, xxi
Walling, Denny, 45
Walters, Barbara, 205
Warmups, 140
Washington Senators, 167, 171
Watson, Bob, 72
Weaver, Earl, 97, 184
Weiss, Al, 12
Weiss, George, 36
Westrum, Wes, 2–3
White, Bill, 66, 72
Wilhelm, Hoyt, 133, 150, 176
Williams, Billy, 191
Williams, Charlie, 170
Williams, Dick, 139
Williams, Stan, 70, 78
Williams, Ted, 36, 97

Wilson, John, 55
Wilson, Willie, 145
Winchell, Walter, 157, 159
Winfield, Dave, 81, 103
Winkles, Bobby, 170
Witt, Mike, 104
Wood, Wilbur: and knucklers,
176; two games started and
lost in one day (1973), 188
Woodeshick, Hal, 57, 137
World Series: 1919, 209; 1956,
171, 172; 1965, 18–19; 1967, 95;
1968, 66–67; 1969, 10–12, 141;
1973, 143–44; 1974, 48–49, 146;
1977, 146; 1980, 144–45; 1981,
24; 1982, 47, 119; 1986, 100,
138; 1987, 179; 1988, 54; 1990,
91; 1991, 203; Red Sox versus
Mets, 206; and relief pitching,
138, 146
Worrell, Todd, 138, 140
Worthy, James, 103–4
Wynn, Early, 5, 65, 83

Y

Yastrzemski, Carl, xvii, 66, 166,
191
Yeager, Chuck, 96
Year of the Pitcher (1968), 66
Yelding, Eric, 71–72
Young, Cy, xvii; 511 career wins,
188. *See also* Cy Young Awards
Young, Dick, 37, 108